THE WOK BIBLE

THE COMPLETE BOOK OF STIR-FRY COOKING

THE WOK BIBLE

THE COMPLETE BOOK OF STIR-FRY COOKING

Over 180 sensational classic and modern stir-fry dishes from east and west for pan and wok, shown step by step in more than 700 stunning photographs

SUNIL VIJAYAKAR
BECKY JOHNSON
JENNI FLEETWOOD

H·H
HERMES
HOUSE

This edition is published by Hermes House,
an imprint of Anness Publishing Ltd, Blaby Road, Wigston,
Leicestershire LE18 4SE; info@anness.com

www.hermeshouse.com; www.annesspublishing.com

If you like the images in this book and would like to investigate using
them for publishing, promotions or advertising, please visit our
website www.practicalpictures.com for more information.

Publisher: Joanna Lorenz
Editorial Director: Helen Sudell
Executive Editor: Joanne Rippin
Photographs: Nicki Dowey, Gus Filgate, Craig Robertson
Additional Recipes: Yasuko Fukuoka, Deh-Ta Hsiung
Designer: Adelle Morris
Production Controller: Wendy Lawson
Editorial Reader: Alison Bolus
The Publisher would like to thank Travel Ink for use of their images
on pages 8–9

© Anness Publishing Ltd 2012

A CIP catalogue record for this book is available from
the British Library.

PUBLISHER'S NOTE
Although the advice and information in this book are believed to be
accurate and true at the time of going to press, neither the authors
nor the publisher can accept any legal responsibility or liability for
any errors or omissions that may have been made nor for any
inaccuracies nor for any loss, harm or injury that comes about
from following instructions or advice in this book.

NOTES
Bracketed terms are intended for American readers.

For all recipes, quantities are given in both metric and imperial
measures and, where appropriate, in standard cups and spoons.
Follow one set of measures, but not a mixture, because they are
not interchangeable.

Standard spoon and cup measures are level.
1 tsp = 5ml, 1 tbsp = 15ml, 1 cup = 250ml/8fl oz.

Australian standard tablespoons are 20ml.
Australian readers should use 3 tsp in place of 1 tbsp for
measuring small quantities.

American pints are 16fl oz/2 cups.
American readers should use 20fl oz/2.5 cups in place of
1 pint when measuring liquids.

Electric oven temperatures in this book are for conventional ovens.
When using a fan oven, the temperature will probably need to be
reduced by about 10–20°C/20–40°F. Since ovens vary, you should
check with your manufacturer's instruction book for guidance.

The nutritional analysis given for each recipe is calculated per
portion (i.e. serving or item), unless otherwise stated. If the recipe
gives a range, such as Serves 4–6, then the nutritional analysis
will be for the smaller portion size, i.e. 6 servings. The analysis
does not include optional ingredients, such as salt added to taste.

Medium (US large) eggs are used unless otherwise stated.

Main front cover image shows Sweet Rice Vermicelli –
for recipe, see page 249.

CONTENTS

INTRODUCTION

The wok is a wonderful invention, as suited to contemporary cooking as it is to recreating classic recipes from its country of origin. There should be one in every kitchen, as it proves its worth over and over again. In a wok you can stir-fry, deep-fry, sauté, steam and simmer. It makes short work of soups and sauces, and is as handy for poaching pears as it is for braising beef.

When it comes to design, the wok is a hugely effective cooking vessel. Heat radiates up the sides to produce a pan that cooks fast and efficiently. Its depth gives plenty of room for tossing and turning without fallout, and the sloping sides ensure that the food always returns to the narrow base, where the heat is most intense.

Wok sales have rocketed in recent years. In the 1960s and 70s, a wok was something of a novelty, often bought in a burst of enthusiasm after a visit to a Chinese restaurant, then left to rust at the back of a kitchen cupboard. And rust they did, largely because people didn't know how to look after them. Part of the problem was the fact that most of the woks on sale were constructed of carbon steel. This was – and still is – an excellent material, but it needs an initial treatment to develop a non-stick, rust-resistant surface.

Fortunately, there were enough fans of this excellent pan to spread the word, and the wok gradually gained ground. It was still used mainly for Chinese food

Left: The wok is a great tool for frying small pieces, or portions, of meat.

only, however, and filled the same sort of specialist slot as the fondue pot or waffle iron. Fusion food changed all that. When chefs no longer viewed each nation's cuisine as sacrosanct, and started inventing new dishes that combined ingredients from several sources, they did us all a favour. The wok stopped being used solely for sweet and sour pork, and came to be seen as a practical pan for all sorts of dishes.

Around the same time, the pattern of everyday life was changing. People weren't just eating out more: they were adopting more flexible eating habits. Often there wasn't enough time to cook an elaborate meal, so something that could be whizzed up in a wok was absolutely ideal. When it became apparent that this utensil was a fixture, rather than a short-lived culinary craze, manufacturers started producing woks in different materials, including non-stick ones that needed very little aftercare or special treatment. Flat-based versions were developed for use on modern electric stoves, the first electric appliances appeared, and more and more cookbooks catered for the quick and convenient style of cooking the wok promised.

Throughout all this, the wok delivered, and is still delivering. Today, it is its role in promoting healthy eating that is catching the public imagination. What the wok does extremely well is to cook a sizeable quantity of vegetables with a small amount of protein and the minimum of fat. When carbohydrate is added, in the form of noodles or rice, you have a well-balanced dish that any nutritionist would approve of. Deep-frying doesn't score a lot of brownie points in the health stakes, but if the oil is hot enough, the outer surface will be sealed immediately after the food is immersed, and the amount of oil absorbed will be limited. Steaming, however, gets a gold star. This is one of the healthiest ways to cook, since no additional fat is needed, the natural flavour of the food is preserved, and colours remain bright and true.

When you own a wok, you will find yourself discovering new uses for it, whether cooking spaghetti sauce, braising chicken portions, simmering fruit in syrup, making risotto, steaming asparagus or smoking salmon. It may not be the only pot you'll ever need, but it will be the one you use most often.

Below: Squash and pumpkin benefit from slow simmering in the wok to develop their sweet flavour.

Below: Tofu is a staple ingredient in China and Japan, and is used in many different types of wok recipes.

Right: The use of the wok has developed from its origins in Asia and the Far East, into a pan used all over the world for many different dishes.

THE UNIVERSAL WOK

Left: Ready-cooked meals are laid out in a dazzling variety in a market stall in Bangkok. The food will be taken home and quickly heated up in a wok.

The wok has been the utensil of choice throughout Asia for thousands of years. It was originally developed in China as a fast and efficient way of cooking over wood or charcoal. Fuel was scarce and expensive, so it made sense to cook food fast in just one pan. The first woks were made of hammered iron. They had rounded bases and looked like inverted straw hats of the type worn by peasant farmers. The conical shape wasn't a drawback when the wok was wedged among logs on an open fire or seated on the well of a primitive stove. In fact, it was a positive advantage, since oil in the narrow base heated rapidly and the pan became extremely hot as flames licked up the thin slanted sides. Small pieces of food cooked very quickly and evenly, provided they were kept on the move. If a liquid was heated in the wok, and a bamboo steamer set on top, the basket could be used for steaming. This was another way of making the most of available fuel, especially when steamers were stacked on top of each other.

Right: Men cook chapattis in a huge bubbling wok, ready for a family celebration in New Delhi.

WOKS BECOME WIDESPREAD

Use of the wok started to spread. In Japan it became known as the *chukanabe*, in Thailand it was dubbed the *kata* and in India, a long-handled version was the forerunner of the *karahi*. When introduced to Indonesia, the wok was christened the *wadjang*. Filipinos liked the wok so much they developed two versions: the large *kawa* and the smaller *kawali*.

Wherever the wok is used, the basic design is the same, but what is cooked in it is not. Mongolian cooks use their woks for heating milk and making yak butter tea; the Japanese make tempura in theirs and Indians use a karahi for braising foods. In Malaysia, where a wok is called a *kuali*, the pan plays a significant role in the Kadazan wedding ceremony. The bridal pair are seated facing each other and a *kuali*, brimming with rice, is placed before them to signify that they will never go hungry.

THE TRAVELLING WOK

Asians who emigrated to Europe, America and elsewhere took their woks with them. Often these became family heirlooms, and as they passed from one generation to the next, so too did favourite family recipes. There's a lovely theory that the metal in a wok holds the memory of everything that has ever been cooked in it, so these grand old woks, blackened and battered but still efficient, are imprinted with decades of delicious meals.

Left: A large quantity of soy sauce simmers away in a huge, mechanically stirred wok, in Chengdu, China.

others are flat-based so that they sit safely on electric stoves. They come in a variety of materials and sizes, from 25cm/10in to supersized 90cm/36in commercial models. You can even buy a wok that fits on a kettle barbecue, so you can stir-fry outside as the sun sets.

For the average family of three or four, the standard 36cm/14in pan wok is ideal. Even the Aga, the classic cooking range, now incorporates a twin-flamed wok burner in many of its models. This is proof, perhaps, that the wok is here to stay, and not just for stir-fries and other Asian dishes.

HOW THE WOK WORKS

For a wok to work efficiently, it must be capable of becoming very hot very quickly, but should cool down rapidly when removed from the heat so that the food does not continue to cook, and go past the point of perfection. The original cast-iron woks did both these jobs well but were very heavy, so when thin carbon steel came along, it was widely welcomed as an alternative.

Carbon steel is light but durable, and conducts heat quickly and evenly. Despite the fact that there are now many more types of wok on the market, carbon steel is still reckoned to give the best results. If it is properly "seasoned", a carbon steel wok will quickly develop its own natural non-stick surface that will last if cared for. However, for easy care, some people prefer a wok made of stainless steel or a modern alloy such as spun aluminium and titanium, with a non-stick coating.

A WORLDWIDE SUCCESS

Today the wok is an essential utensil in kitchens all over the globe, and there are dozens of variations on the theme, including electric versions. Some woks have the traditional rounded base;

Right: Thailand is famous for its street food. Here a man cooks pad thai noodles in Bangkok.

WOKS, TOOLS AND ACCESSORIES

Left: Woks come in many different shapes and sizes and can be used to cook meals for one or for many.

using a steel wok over time, but you will gain by having an easy-care utensil that will give you very satisfactory results. It is essential to use a non-stick pan if you are cooking acidic foods such as fruits, which would discolour in a steel wok.

SIZE AND SHAPE

An average 36cm/14in wok is ideal for most kitchens, and will sit comfortably on the average burner. If you have a large family, or intend to cook whole fish on a regular basis, choose a 40cm/16in model. Whether you buy a round-based wok or a flat-based one depends on the type of stove you have, as well as your personal preference. Purists plump for round-based woks, claiming the shape gives perfect results, as the area of intense heat is very small and the upward slope uninterrupted. However, a round-based wok will wobble if placed on an electric stove. To stabilize it, you would have to use a wok stand or ring, but the round base could still reflect heat back and damage the electric

Choosing a wok isn't difficult. There are dozens of versions on the market, from conventional carbon steel and stainless steel models to modern non-stick woks that are sold solo or in gift packs with tools and even serving bowls. If you're a serious cook who likes the classical approach, begin your search at a large Asian food store, where you can examine traditional carbon steel woks in a range of shapes and sizes, hefting them in your hands to find the weight and size that suits. If you buy a good quality pan and season it properly, it will give you years of excellent service, and will actually improve with age. A cheaper wok may well have to be replaced after a year or so. Avoid very cheap woks, as they may rust despite your best efforts, or develop hot spots.

NON-STICK WOKS

If you prefer a non-stick wok, look for one made from reinforced titanium, which is guaranteed against scratching and can safely be washed in the dishwasher. You won't get the patina and flavour build-up that comes with

Below: A double-handled wok is ideal for using as a serving dish as well as a cooking vessel.

element. So, for electric stoves, or any stove with a level cooking surface, flat-based woks are best. If you have a gas stove, you can use either style of wok. You probably won't need a wok ring, but if you do, make sure that the wok sits down snugly, so that it is close to the heat source.

Both single-handled woks and twin-handled Cantonese woks are available. The single-handed wok is reckoned to be best for stir-frying, while the twin is more stable and is recommended for deep-frying, steaming and braising. Some woks offer you both features by giving you a 30cm/12in long handle matched with a short, round "helper" handle on the opposite side so that the wok can easily be moved from stove to table. Whichever type you buy, get a domed lid, so that you can use your wok for steaming or braising.

ELECTRIC WOK

The electric wok doesn't get quite as hot as a carbon steel wok over high heat, but is efficient, convenient and very good for cooking braised dishes and risotto. It can make a meal in moments, busy cooks like it because it leaves the stove free for other items, and others value its stability and the fact that the heat is thermostatically

Below: An electric wok is ideal for braising and slow cooking.

controlled. Electric woks come in various sizes but all are similar in design, with a heat element recessed in the stay-cool base. The wok that sits securely on the base will inevitably have a non-stick coating, but may need to be given a token seasoning before being used for the first time. The handbook will give instructions on how this is to be done – usually it merely means coating the wok with oil and heating it for 5 minutes, then wiping it clean and letting it cool down.

TOOLS AND ACCESSORIES

It isn't necessary to buy special tools for wok cookery, but there are a few items that will prove useful.

Cleavers and Knives

Cutting meat and vegetables for stir-frying so that the maximum surface area is exposed to the heat is quite an art, and Chinese cooks swear that the best tool for the job is a cleaver. This short-handled implement has a large, flat blade that can be used to cut everything from paper-thin vegetable slices to meat on the bone. When the blade is held flat, it can be used like a spatula, to transport the prepared food to the wok. Cleavers come in several sizes and weights. Number one is the heaviest and resembles a chopper more than a knife. Its 23cm/9in long blade is 10cm/4in wide, and is mainly used for

*Above:
A Chinese
cleaver is finely
balanced.*

slicing. The medium weight number two cleaver is the most popular choice for general kitchen use. It is used for both slicing and chopping. The back of the blade is ideal for pounding meat to tenderize it, and the flat surface can be used to crush garlic or ginger. Good quality kitchen knives can be used instead of a cleaver. A 10cm/4in paring knife and a 20cm/8in cook's knife will be the most useful sizes. It is vital to keep blades sharp, either by using a steel or a stone.

Mortar and Pestle

South-east Asian cooks like to use their woks for making quick curries. These depend for their flavour on curry pastes that are freshly made using ingredients like galangal, garlic and lemon grass. A granite mortar is best for this purpose, since the rough surface amplifies the pounding action of the pestle and also helps to grip the ingredients so they do not escape from the bowl. Buy a mortar that measures at least 18cm/7in across. This is sufficient for mixtures of up to 450ml/³⁄₄ pint/scant 2 cups.

Draining or Steaming Rack

Most woks, whether standard or electric, come with a rainbow-shaped metal rack that clips on to the rim. This item, sometimes called a tempura rack, is useful when deep-frying. As items cook, they can be set to drain on the rack. Surplus oil will drip back into the pan, and the drained foods can be moved to a piece of kitchen paper when the rack is full. The rack can also be used for steaming, and is particularly useful in an electric wok.

Spatulas and Scoops

It is useful to have at least two wooden spatulas for stir-frying, preferably with a rounded side that follows the contours of the wok. Another useful implement is the *charn*, a long-handled spatula shaped like a shovel, which makes it easy to scoop and toss foods that are being stir-fried. If you use a charn in a non-stick pan, take care not to scratch the surface.

Ladle

You will need a ladle for spooning soups or other liquids out of the wok. Choose one with a deep bowl. Although black nylon ladles are recommended for non-stick woks, they do scorch easily, so stainless steel ladles are a better bet. Some ladles have graduated markings inside that indicate how much liquid they contain. This is useful when you need to spoon out a specific quantity of stock. If your ladle is not marked in this

Below: You may need a wok ring on your stove top to keep the wok steady.

Above: Essential wok tools include a dome-shaped lid, wooden or bamboo chopsticks, a long-handled spatula and a large ladle.

way, measure the liquid it holds by filling it with water and spooning this into a measuring jug (cup). Making a note of the amount for future reference will help you when you are following a recipe that specifies a particular amount of liquid to be removed from the wok.

Chopsticks

If you wander through an Asian street market you will sometimes see food being stirred in giant woks with extra-long chopsticks. These are ideal for the dextrous, but tongs or two spatulas can be used instead.

Skimmers

These are long handled utensils with wire or bamboo scoops at one end. These can be cup- or saucer-shaped and are used to fish food out of hot oil or stock. Saucer-shaped skimmers are also called spiders, since they resemble circular webs.

Wok Ring

This circular metal stand gives stability to a round-based wok when used on an electric or gas stove. The rings come in several sizes and designs. The most common ones look like crumpet rings or cookie cutters, and consist of solid metal that may be punched with ventilation holes. Thick wire stands are also available, and these are recommended for gas stoves. It is important to buy a ring that supports your wok securely while allowing it to be as close to the heat source as possible without putting out the flame. If your wok has a flat base you won't need a ring. If you intend using a wok ring on an electric stove, check with the manufacturer, as this practice can damage the element.

Steamers

Steaming is one of the healthiest ways of cooking, since no fat is required and the natural flavour of the food is preserved. A wok is ideal for this purpose, since its shape gives you a large surface area of water to turn into steam. There are several ways of steaming in a wok. For just a few items, you can use the semicircular rack that clips on to the side of the pan.

Left: A perforated metal scoop and a traditional wire skimmer.

Above: Racks can be clipped to the side of a wok to drain deep-fried food on.

Alternatively, you can place items to be steamed on a heatproof plate, provided you raise the plate above the surface of the water or stock by means of a trivet or upturned cup. You can also steam items by the Chinese method, using stackable bamboo baskets. An expanding metal steamer will also work well, but take care that the feet do not scratch the surface of the wok if it has a non-stick coating. Whichever means you use, you will need to trap the steam somehow, either by fitting a domed lid over the wok, or making sure the steamer itself is tightly covered.

Preparing a Steamer
Before you use a bamboo steamer for the first time, scrub it well, using a mild soap if you like, then rinse it thoroughly, Place the wet steamer over boiling water in a wok. Steam it empty for at least 10 minutes, then leave to air dry. Store in a well-ventilated place.

Bamboo Steamers

Although stainless-steel steamers are regarded as being more hygienic, natural bamboo steamers do an excellent job, since the material allows steam to circulate freely with only minimal condensation. The steamer baskets can be bought singly or in sets and come in various sizes. Standard steamers have a diameter of 25cm/10in and are about 15cm/6in tall. This is the ideal size for a 36cm/14in wok. When the basket is in use, there should be at least 5cm/2in space between it and the side of the wok. Steamers can be stacked.

Left: A stack of steamers increases the amount of food you can cook at one time.

Seasoning a Wok
First wash the wok thoroughly in warm, soapy water to remove any preservative coating. Rinse it well, shake off the excess water, then place the wok over low heat to dry. Add a little cooking oil (not olive oil) and, using kitchen paper, wipe the pan to coat it evenly. Take care not to burn yourself. Heat gently for 10–12 minutes, then wipe off the oil with clean kitchen paper. Don't be alarmed when it blackens – this is perfectly natural. Repeat the process for as long as it takes for the paper to come away clean, by which time the wok itself will have darkened. The more it is used, the better the wok's natural non-stick coating will become and the easier it will be to clean. If a wok should rust – perhaps because it has been put away wet or abandoned in a cupboard for months – it should be rubbed down with wire wool or fine sandpaper and then seasoned again. A cast iron or carbon steel wok is less likely to rust if it is oiled lightly before being stored.

Cleaning a Wok
A properly seasoned wok should never be washed with soap. Remove any food that sticks to the surface, then wash the wok in hot water. Dry thoroughly by placing the wok over the heat for a few minutes. Leave to cool, then rub a little oil into the surface.

FISH AND SEAFOOD

Given the versatility of the wok, there's literally no end to the ingredients that can be cooked in it. However, there are some items that lend themselves particularly well to stir-frying, steaming and braising. Inevitably, these are ingredients that cook quickly, a prime example of which is fish and seafood. Fish can be cooked in a wok in various ways. The more robust types, such as cod, haddock and halibut, can be cut into bitesize portions and stir-fried. Stir-frying is also an excellent way of cooking prawns (shrimp) and scallops.

COD AND HADDOCK

White fish such as cod is a great choice for soups and fish curries. Add the pearly white cubes to the liquid in the wok towards the end of cooking so that they keep their shape. They will be ready to eat in a couple of minutes. Cod and haddock can also be steamed. Haddock has a more delicate flavour and softer texture. This fish is a good choice for deep-frying. Dip pieces in batter before adding them to hot oil.

HALIBUT

A delicious flatfish, halibut has a fine, meaty texture. For steaming whole, choose the small variety, often called chicken halibut, or opt for steaks cut

Below: Firm-fleshed, white fish, such as cod and haddock, are ideal for cooking as steaks or in bite-sized pieces.

Right: Fish, such as sea bass, are perfect for cooking whole in the wok.

from the middle. Halibut is robust enough to hold its own against spicy flavours and tastes great with tomatoes in a curry.

PRAWNS

The most common shellfish ingredient in Asian cooking, prawns – or shrimp, as they are known in the US – are one of the finest ingredients for stir-frying, steaming or deep-frying, since they require very little time to cook. Larger varieties such as tiger prawns are particularly good. When buying prawns in the shell, allow about 300g/11oz per serving, as there is a lot of wastage.

SALMON

Although salmon can be cooked in a variety of ways, it is particularly good steamed in a bamboo basket. Flaked salmon makes great fish cakes.

Above: Scallops should be flash fried or steamed to retain their soft texture.

SCALLOPS

These tender molluscs are delectable but very delicate, so take care not to overcook them. Scallops are delicious steamed with ginger and spring onions (scallions), or try them seared and served on wilted pak choi (boy choy).

SEA BASS

Fish such as sea bass can be steamed whole in the wok. Choose a fish that weighs about 450g/1lb for two people. Strong flavours such as ginger, garlic, soy sauce and lemon grass work well with sea bass.

SQUID

For stir-frying, slit the body of the squid from top to bottom and turn it inside out. Flatten it, then score the flesh with a knife to make a criss-cross pattern. Cut lengthwise into ribbons. These will curl when stir-fried.

MEAT AND POULTRY

Only the tenderest cuts of meat are suitable for wok cookery, especially if they are to be stir-fried. Traditional Asian recipes favour chicken, duck and pork, but there is no reason to limit yourself to these choices. Beef, lamb and even ostrich taste great when cooked in the wok.

BEEF

Steak is ideal for stir-frying, whether you choose fillet (tenderloin), rump (round) or sirloin. Look for deep red meat with a light marbling of fat. If a recipe requires beef to be very thinly sliced, place it in the freezer for about half an hour beforehand. For stir-fries, strips of beef are often marinated in a mixture that includes soy sauce and oil. When cooking, have the wok very hot, add a few strips at a time, and move them to the sides of the wok before adding more. If too much meat is added to the wok at the same time, the temperature will drop and the strips of beef will simply stew in the liquid that accumulates during cooking.

CHICKEN

Tender breast portions or fillets are perfect for stir-frying. If thin strips of chicken are required, flatten the breast fillets by placing them between two sheets of clear film (plastic wrap) and beating them lightly but firmly with a rolling pin.

Below: Chicken, when flattened and cut into thin strips, is ideal for stir fries.

Left: Pork is a great favourite in Chinese and Asian dishes.

DUCK

In China and Thailand, duck is sometimes cooked whole, but is more often thinly sliced and stir-fried, or cubed and used to make a spicy curry. Most of the meat on a duck is concentrated in the breast, so, despite

Below: Lamb is not used in the Far East but makes a great wok ingredient.

Below: Duck is tender and full of flavour, and ideal for fast wok cooking.

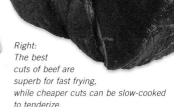

Right: The best cuts of beef are superb for fast frying, while cheaper cuts can be slow-cooked to tenderize.

the cost, it can be more practical to buy breast portions instead of whole birds. Duck breasts can be steamed in a wok, then sliced, moistened with a little of the stock from the steamer and served in a salad.

LAMB

Choose lean leg of lamb for stir-frying, or lamb fillet (tenderloin), which is cut from the middle of the neck. The meat should be firm and pink. The paler the meat, the younger the lamb. To make medallions of lamb, cut the fillet into thin, even slices. These can be stir-fried or braised in the wok. Alternatively, cut the lamb into strips. Soy sauce and lamb go well together and marinating lamb in it for 2–3 hours before frying imparts the most wonderful flavour.

PORK

Fillet (tenderloin) is the most tender cut and is relatively inexpensive, given the fact that it consists of solid meat with very little wastage. Choose fillets that are pale pink all over, with no areas of discoloration. The flesh should be fairly firm, never flaccid, and slightly moist to the touch.

To prepare pork fillet, first pull away the membrane that surrounds the meat and remove any fat. Using a sharp knife, slice away the tendon and sinew, which looks like a tougher strip of membrane. For stir-frying, slice pork fillet in neat, even strips; for braising, opt for medallions, cut on the diagonal.

VEGETABLES AND AROMATICS

When you cook vegetables and aromatics in a wok, the aim is to retain maximum flavour and texture. The flavour must be there in the first place, so shopping carefully is the first step towards good cooking. Buy vegetables at the peak of condition, preferably from a farmer's market or greengrocer that sources produce locally, rather than buying shrink-wrapped items that have travelled great distances between soil and superstore. The best vegetables for wok cookery are those that stay crisp after stir-frying.

*Above:
Baby corn.*

Above: Beansprouts.

Banana Leaves
Not strictly an ingredient, these large, pliable leaves are used in Thai cooking in particular, to wrap food for steaming in the wok. The leaves impart a mild smoky flavour to the food.

BABY CORN

These miniature corn cobs are good for stir-frying, either whole or sliced in half through their length. The shape and colour create interest and they keep their crunch when cooked.

BEANSPROUTS

Highly nutritious, beansprouts are delicious in stir-fries. They are highly perishable, so make sure they are absolutely fresh and use them as soon as possible after you purchase them.

CHINESE LEAVES

This sweet-tasting green vegetable is often mistaken for a type of lettuce but is actually a brassica, which accounts for its American name, "Chinese cabbage". An excellent salad ingredient, when stir-fried, the white stalk stays crisp and provides a contrast to the softer texture of the leaves. To prepare, remove any discoloured or damaged leaves, trim the root, then slice the head across into thin shreds. Chinese leaves are sometimes used to make a bed in a bamboo steamer for cooking pieces of fish or meat.

MANGETOUT PEAS

Americans call these "snow peas" but the French word, which means "eat all", describes them better, since the entire pod is consumed.

PEPPERS

Sweet "bell" peppers are ideal ingredients for the wok, contributing colour as well as flavour. When cooked quickly they retain some crunch and are delightfully juicy. To prepare a pepper, make an incision all the way around the stem-end. Pull off the lid and, with any luck, the core and seeds will come away too. Cut the pepper in half, remove any remaining seeds and

Left: Chinese leaves.

hard ribs, then dice the flesh or cut it into neat slices. Slice the flesh off the lid too.

PAK CHOI

Known by various names, including "bok choy" and "Chinese chard", this member of the cabbage family is distinguished by its fat white stems. Many people think the stalks taste even better than the glossy green leaves, but both are great steamed or in a stir-fry. The stems take slightly longer to cook than the leaves, so start them first.

Below: Pak choi.

MOOLI

A long white root also known as "daikon" used as a crisp, sharp, cool addition to a salad – or cooked. Whether steamed or fried, it retains its crisp texture, but develops a sweeter flavour.

MUSHROOMS

All mushrooms cook quickly and are great for the wok. Fresh shiitake and oyster mushrooms are readily available and are excellent in stir-fries, but button (white) mushrooms can be used instead. Dried mushrooms add an intense flavour. Soak them in warm

Above: Mooli.

Above: Mushrooms.

water for 30 minutes, then lift them out of the soaking water, remove the stems and slice or chop the caps. Strain the soaking water and add it to stocks or soups when needed.

SPRING ONIONS

Many wok recipes call for spring onions (scallions) to be stir-fried at the start of cooking. Regular onions or shallots can be used instead. The purpose of using these aromatic vegetables is to give overall depth of flavour, so they should be finely diced or sliced so that they blend with other ingredients and do not physically dominate the dish.

SEAWEED

There are several types of edible seaweed, including kombu, nori, wakame and hijiki. Their main function in wok cookery is to flavour stocks, soups and simmered dishes.

WATER CHESTNUTS

Much more readily available canned than fresh, water chestnuts, and the similar bamboo shoots are both very good in stir-fries, so keep some in the storecupboard at all times. Water chestnuts add a wonderful crisp texture and nutty flavour.

CHILLIES

These fiery peppers are often used in curries and spicy stir-fries. There are many varieties in different strengths, and even chillies from the same plant can vary in intensity, so treat them with caution. When preparing chillies, protect yourself from the capsaicin they contain by wearing gloves, or wash your hands thoroughly with soap afterwards to prevent chilli-burn. To prepare chillies, slit them and scrape out the seeds and pith. Most of the heat is in the seeds, so add them only if you want a very spicy result. If you grind chillies to make a curry paste, avoid standing with your face directly over the mortar.

GALANGAL

This looks like ginger but can be distinguished by its finger-like sprouts. When young, these are pale pink in colour and taste almost lemony. As the plant matures, the skin thickens and the creamy skin turns pale gold. The flavour is now quite peppery. Galangal is used in the same way as ginger and is often incorporated in pastes.

GARLIC

The universal aromatic, garlic is great for stir-frying but burns easily at the very high temperatures achieved in the wok. It is best to cook it briefly or add with other vegetables. Garlic can be crushed easily with a cleaver.

Left: Galangal.

Above: Seaweed.

Below: Ginger.

GINGER

A favourite ingredient in Asian and Eastern cooking traditions, ginger adds a wonderful warmth and flavour to savoury and sweet foods. Peel off the skin and either chop or grate the flesh.

LEMON GRASS

The distinctive citrus flavour of this plant makes it a favourite ingredient in stir-fries or curry pastes. Lemon grass stalks are sold in bundles. To prepare, peel away and discard the fibrous layers surrounding each stalk. Only the tenderest part of the stalk – the bottom 10-15cm/4-6in – is suitable for stir-frying. It can either be sliced or pounded into a paste. Don't discard offcuts: add them to water used for steaming fish or chicken in the wok. Lemon grass can be bought dried and preserved in jars, but these make poor substitutes.

Left: Lemon grass.

RICE

Many of the savoury dishes cooked in a wok either incorporate rice or are served with rice. Fried rice is a wok standard, but the pan can also be used to make a pilaff or a risotto.

THAI JASMINE RICE

This delicately scented long grain rice is the ideal accompaniment for stir-fries and similar dishes and is also a good choice for making fried rice. The uncooked grains are translucent and become fluffy and white when boiled. The flavour is slightly nutty. Fried rice often includes vegetables such as shredded pak choi (bok choy) or spring greens (collards), together with aromatic flavourings such as garlic and chilli. In vegetarian versions, coconut or cashew nuts are favourite additions. Protein can be added in the form of strips of omelette, chicken, beef or pork or prawns (shrimp).

BASMATI RICE

For Indian cooking and fusion food, basmati is the obvious choice. This long grain rice lives up to its Hindi name, which translates as "the fragrant one". The grains are long and slender and have very good texture. Basmati is the best type of rice to use for a pilaff, and a wok with a tight-fitting lid is an ideal pan for the task.

RISOTTO RICE

Italians recommend using a heavy pan for making risotto, but maybe that's because they didn't invent the wok. The latter works extremely well, the only

Below: Thai jasmine rice.

Above: Risotto rice.

drawback being that the large surface area makes for more rapid evaporation of the liquid added to the rice, so it is particularly important to stir the mixture constantly and check the rice frequently to prevent it from becoming overcooked. You may also need to add slightly more liquid than the amount listed in a recipe, so make sure you have some

Below: Basmati rice.

spare. When the rice is creamy, but the grains retain a hint of firmness at the centre, the risotto is ready.

Long grain rice isn't suitable for making risotto. What is needed is a comparatively large, plump short grain with a high proportion of starch. As the rice cooks, the rice dissolves in the stock that is constantly added to give the finished dish a creamy texture. There are several varieties of risotto rice. Carnaroli and Vialone Nano give excellent results. The starchy outer layer of the grain dissolves, but the centre retains enough "bite" to provide the perfect contrast. Arborio also works well but contains more amylopectin than the other two varieties, so has a tendency to become pappy if overcooked. Removing the risotto from the heat before it is fully cooked, and leaving it to stand, covered, for 4–5 minutes, overcomes this drawback.

Serving Rice Safely
Serve rice as soon as it is cooked, if possible. Never keep it warm for long periods or food poisoning might result. The danger comes from *bacillus cereus*, which is often present in uncooked rice. If the rice is boiled and served straight away there is little risk, but if cooked rice is left to stand at room temperature, or kept warm for a long period, any toxic spores present may multiply. If you intend using cooked rice in a salad, it is important to cool it quickly and keep it covered in the refrigerator until required. If you reheat rice, don't just warm it; it must be piping hot right through.

NOODLES AND WRAPPERS

In Asia, where the wok originated, noodles are an integral part of the diet, served in soups, salads, stir-fries and sweet dishes. They are a symbol of longevity in China and are often on the menu at birthday parties, weddings and wakes. Although noodles are traditionally used with wok dishes, there's nothing to stop you substituting pasta if you prefer.

Above: Fine rice noodles.

Noodles suitable for wok cookery are usually made from wheat flour or rice flour, but can also be based on mung beans, buckwheat, seaweed or more exotic ingredients. They generally come in bundles, bound by slips of paper or formed into nests, and can be fresh, semi-cooked or dried. Most noodles taste fairly bland, which makes them a

Above: Rice stick noodles.

good vehicle for spicy food. Children love to slurp them in soup, workers value them as fast food and their digestibility makes them a good choice for anyone. They can be served on their own, with a simple sauce, or form part of an elaborate dish. Noodle paste is also used to make wrappers for spring rolls and other deep-fried treats.

Below: Egg noodles are available in both fresh and dried form.

EGG NOODLES

Like Italian pasta, Asian wheat noodles can be plain or enriched with egg. In China, both types are available, but egg noodles (easy to spot at the supermarket because they are usually labelled as such) are those with which people in the West are most familiar. Japanese egg noodles are called *ramen*.

WHEAT FLOUR NOODLES

Plain wheat noodles go by various names. In Japan they are called *udon*. They come in several widths; *somen* being a slim type similar to the Korean *somyen*. Wheat noodles need to be boiled briefly before use. Fresh ones will often be ready in less than 1 minute; dried noodles take 3–5 minutes. Exact timing depends on the type, the thickness and whether the noodles will be mixed with other ingredients and cooked for a while longer. Some types can be added straight to the wok. See individual recipes for more information.

RICE FLOUR NOODLES

Pre-cooking is part of the process of making rice noodles, so they need even less preparation than wheat noodles. Before use, just soak them in hot water for 5–10 minutes or for as long as it takes for the strands to become soft. If you intend to fry them, this step can be skipped, but use the very thin noodles rather than the thicker rice sticks.

BUCKWHEAT AND CELLOPHANE NOODLES

Soba are Japanese noodles made from buckwheat with wheat flour to give elasticity. They have an earthy flavour. *Soba* are often served cold, with enough sauce to coat the strands but not swamp the taste. Cook them in boiling water until tender. Made from mung beans,

cellophane noodles (also sold as glass, jelly or bean thread noodles) are transparent when cooked and look pretty in a salad or stir-fry.

WRAPPERS

Simple snacks such as spring rolls, wontons, tung tong and rice paper parcels are easy to deep-fry in the wok, and because of the shape of the pan, you need less oil than in a conventional deep-fat fryer. Square, rectangular and round wrappers are available in packets from Asian food stores. Like noodles, wrappers are made from either rice or from wheat, or wheat mixed with egg.

Below: Square wonton wrappers.

Below: Japanese somen noodles are wheat-based.

OILS AND FATS

Although the design of a wok means that oil is the ingredient you need least of – unless you are deep-frying – the type you use is important because of the high temperatures involved.

CORN OIL

Extracted from the germ of the corn kernel, this polyunsaturated oil is almost tasteless, although it can have a discernible odour. It is very good for both stir-frying and deep-fat frying since it can withstand high heat without reaching smoking point.

GROUNDNUT OIL

Also known as peanut oil, this is ideal for use in the wok, as it reaches a high temperature without smoking and has a neutral flavour that won't mask the taste of the food. Like olive oil, groundnut oil is monounsaturated, although it does contain a slightly higher percentage of saturated fat than corn or sunflower oil. Some people are allergic to groundnut oil, so inform guests if you have used it for cooking.

Below: sunflower oil (left); groundnut oil (middle); olive oil (right).

LARD

Although this animal fat is no longer widely used for frying in the West, because of the health implications, it remains a common cooking medium in parts of China. The disadvantage of using lard, other than the fact that it is a saturated fat, is that it is often strongly flavoured.

OLIVE OIL

This type of oil is never used for Asian cooking. The flavour simply doesn't go with Asian ingredients. You can still use it in a wok, however, for Mediterranean-type dishes with tomato-based sauces, olives, and herbs such as oregano.

RAPESEED (CANOLA) OIL

This monounsaturated oil is particularly popular in North America. It is pale gold in colour and has a mild flavour and aroma. The smoking point is not quite as high as for corn oil, but the refined oil is regarded as a good choice for stir-frying and deep-frying.

SESAME OIL

Light sesame oil can be used for frying, but the dark type made from roasted sesame seeds is largely used for flavouring. It has a nutty taste, which becomes more pronounced if the oil is warmed. It mustn't be allowed to get too hot, though, or it will burn. A few drops of sesame oil are often added to soup, noodles or a stir-fry before serving.

SUNFLOWER OIL

Another much-used polyunsaturated oil, this has a mild flavour. With a smoking point that rivals that of corn oil and groundnut oil, it is a very good choice for wok cookery.

Above: Sesame oil (top); chilli oil (bottom). These oils are used to flavour dishes rather than as a frying medium.

WOK OIL

This product, specially developed for the wok, combines soya and sesame oils and is flavoured with ginger, garlic and pepper. It's an expensive way to start a stir-fry, but gives good results and is convenient if you have little time.

Butter

When making a typical Asian stir-fry in your wok, you need the fat to be very hot so that the food is instantly seared. Butter won't work for this as it burns at high temperatures, becoming blackened and unpleasant tasting. However, if you are using your wok as a saute pan, perhaps for a risotto or similar dish, there's no reason why you can't benefit from the delicious flavour of butter. Using half butter and half oil is a good compromise, since the oil enables the butter to withstand higher temperatures.

TOFU AND SOYA PRODUCTS

This inexpensive protein food is made from soya beans, and was invented by the Chinese. It is now widely used throughout the world as an alternative to fish and meat. When it comes to wok cookery, tofu and similar soya products score on several fronts. They are highly nutritious, easy to use and need little or no cooking. Although most forms are virtually tasteless, they take on surrounding flavours, so are useful for adding bulk while boosting food values. Tofu is low in fat and cholesterol-free.

SILKEN TOFU

This white product is the softest, most delicate form of tofu. A creamy version comes in tubs and can be used for dips or desserts, including a non-dairy ice cream. The slightly firmer type of silken tofu comes in cubes, which break down very easily, so must be handled gently. If you use silken tofu cubes in a stir-fry, add them right at the end and don't toss the mixture too vigorously.

FIRM TOFU

This lightly pressed product is sold in cakes or blocks, either submerged in water or vacuum-packed, and can be cubed or sliced. It makes a good addition to a stir-fry, especially if it is marinated in soy sauce or tamari with strong flavours such as

Right: Deep-fried tofu. Below: Fresh firm tofu.

ginger, garlic or fermented black beans. Firm tofu also tastes good in a Thai-style curry.

FRIED TOFU

At first glance, this doesn't look much like tofu. Slice the nut-brown block, however, and the white interior is exposed. The outer colour is the result of deep-frying in vegetable oil, a process than not only adds flavour, but also makes the bean curd more robust. Fried tofu won't break down when cooked, whether you stir-fry it or braise the chunks in a sauce.

GLUTEN

This is precisely what it says it is – gluten derived from wheat flour – which can be treated to masquerade as meat, poultry or fish. Flavoured, pre-cooked gluten comes in cans. The contents only need to be heated before being served.

TEMPEH

To make this Indonesian speciality, whole soya beans are

Left: Pressed fried tofu.

fermented with a cultured starter, which gives the product a nutty, savoury flavour and causes it to solidify so that it can be cut into blocks. The beans remain visible under a velvety coating that resembles the rind you find on Brie. Their presence makes for a product that is firmer and more chewy than most other forms of tofu. In the wok, tempeh can be steamed, stir-fried, deep-fried or braised.

TVP/TEXTURED VEGETABLE PROTEIN

This meat substitute is made from soya flour from which the fat has been removed. It can be flavoured and shaped to mimic minced beef and is also sold in cubes or slices. The very low fat content means that it keeps well without refrigeration.

Below: Tempeh.

Above: Silken tofu.

SAUCES AND FLAVOURINGS

When you own a wok, being a spontaneous cook becomes second nature. It is fun to raid the pantry and refrigerator and rustle up a stir-fry. As long as you start with oil and aromatics, you can add almost any variety of vegetable, plus meat, poultry, tofu or whatever else takes your fancy. A good sauce, or a stock made from a paste, will bring all the flavours together.

CURRY PASTE BLOCKS

If you can find the imported curry pastes formed in blocks in specialist food stores, then do use them, as they impart a wonderful authentic flavour to the food. There are, however, also bottled curry sauces that make good substitutes. Shrimp paste has a very powerful flavour. It is made from salted, dried and pulverized shrimp, and is then compressed and sold in blocks or small cans or tubs. It must always be cooked, and used sparingly.

CHILLI SAUCE

Mainly used as a dipping sauce, this tastes great with crisp fried prawns (shrimp) or spiced noodle pancakes.

Below: There are several kinds of soy sauce from dark and thick to lighter, less rich types.

Above: Sweet chilli sauce.

It comes in various strengths and the sweetness also varies. The sweeter varieties go well with chicken.

FISH SAUCE

Read the list of ingredients for this Thai sauce, and you might be disinclined to try it. Opening the bottle could confirm your suspicions as it has a very pungent odour, but add it to a soup, stir-fry or braised dish and you will be amazed at the depth of flavour it imparts.

HOISIN SAUCE

Thick and sweet, this Chinese sauce is made from fermented beans, sugar, vinegar, salt, chillies, garlic and sesame oil, combined in varying proportions. It makes a good marinade, but you may need to thin it.

MISO PASTE

This Japanese fermented soy bean and grain paste is produced in various strengths. White miso is the lightest and sweetest. The most widely used form is the medium strength mugi miso, and there is also a very strong dark brown variety, hacho miso. Miso's principal use is for making different kinds of soup, but it can also be used in sauces, marinades and dressings.

OYSTER SAUCE

Popular in China and Thailand, this is based on soy sauce and oyster extract. It has a distinctive flavour and is great in soups and stir-fries.

PLUM SAUCE

Fruity, sweet and spicy, this is made from plums, ginger, garlic and chilli. It makes a good dip.

SOY SAUCE

Made from fermented soya beans, soy sauce is an essential ingredient throughout the Far East, and each country has its own version. There are three basic types, the colour governed by the stage at which the sauce is bottled, and the presence of other ingredients. The lightest soy sauce is Japanese. Then comes the Chinese light soy sauce. China also has a dark soy sauce that is good with red meats. Tamari is a Japanese dark sauce that is full of flavour but isn't too salty. Thailand has a sweet soy sauce.

TERIYAKI SAUCE

This Japanese sauce is sold commercially but you can make your own by mixing equal proportions of shoyu and mirin in a pan. Add a little sugar to sweeten the mixture. Stir over gentle heat until the sugar has dissolved, then cool. If not using immediately, store in the refrigerator.

Left: Dark hoisin sauce.

Ready-made Stir-fry Sauces

Dozens of different stir-fry sauces are on sale in the supermarket. The quality varies, but some are very good indeed, and are a boon when you've only got a few minutes to throw a meal together. Apart from the obvious sweet and sour, and black bean sauce, other examples include lemon and sesame seed, black bean with garlic, hoisin and spring onion (scallions) and spicy tomato Szechuan. Some sauces are more fusion food than authentic Asian, but why not? Owning a wok means opening your eyes to the wider possibilities it offers.

HERBS AND SPICES

Above: Kaffir lime leaves.

In view of the speed of wok cookery, any added flavourings need to deliver pretty smartly. Most herbs do the job well, but spices need to be chosen with care, as many of them have an impact only after lengthy cooking.

BASIL

Thai basil is a popular ingredient in South-east Asian cooking. It has a typical sweet basil aroma, overlaid with hints of aniseed or liquorice. The leaves are often added whole to stir-fries and curries. Another strain of basil, with a much more assertive flavour, is holy basil. This herb has a peppery taste, which only develops fully when heated. It is often used in soups and stir-fries, but isn't suitable for salads.

CORIANDER

Although you can use a wide range of herbs in wok cookery, coriander (cilantro) is probably the most useful. Its fresh green leaves have a distinctive, spicy flavour. Coriander roots and stems are often used in curry pastes.

Above: Shiso.

Add chopped coriander to stir-fries at the last minute or the flavour will be lost. Dried coriander is used in curry.

FIVE-SPICE POWDER

A classic spice mix widely used in Chinese cooking, particularly in braised dishes. It contains star anise, Szechuan peppercorns, fennel seeds, cloves and cinnamon and has a pungent, slightly sweet flavour.

KAFFIR LIME LEAVES

Although difficult to find fresh, lime leaves are easily obtained dried. They give a lovely authentic, warm, spicy citrus flavour to a dish.

MINT

Often used with fresh coriander in fillings for spring rolls and similar deep-fried snacks, mint is also good in a noodle salad.

PANDANUS LEAVES

These fragrant leaves are principally used as a wrapper, or as a liner for ramekins for poaching. The leaves look very attractive when wrapped around pieces of chicken, threaded on skewers and deep-fried in a hot wok.

SHISO

A herb with a distinctive aroma, this is an important ingredient in Japanese cooking. Despite being a form of mint, the flavour is redolent of basil.

STAR ANISE

This distinctive-looking spice has a warm flavour that puts it in the same category as cinnamon and nutmeg. It is used in savoury and sweet dishes.

Above: Star anise.

TAMARIND

Imagine a very intense lemon taste with no bitterness. That's tamarind, a popular product in South-east Asia. It is sold in blocks that need soaking, but can also be bought pre-prepared in jars.

Above: Pandanus leaves.

WASABI

This is often referred to as Japanese horseradish, even though it is no relation. Like watercress, it grows wild in mountain streams, but is also cultivated. Like mustard, it is mainly sold either as a paste or as a powder which must be mixed with warm water. Treat wasabi with caution – the pale green colour may look pretty but it packs a terrific punch, and too much could ruin a dish.

WINE FOR THE WOK

Rice wine seems to be far better suited to wok cookery than anything the grape can offer, and is used both as a marinade and in sauces. It is important to differentiate between sake, which is a dry rice wine used for drinking and cooking, and the much sweeter mirin, which is used only for cooking. These are Japanese products. The Chinese also make rice wine. Theirs tends to be dry, like sake, but with a distinctly different flavour. The best Chinese rice wine comes from Shaoxing, in eastern China. Mirin can be used as a marinade, often combined with soy sauce.

Right: Rice wine.

PREPARATION TECHNIQUES

Successful wok cooking is all about preparation, especially when you are stir-frying, which is so fast it is essential to have everything ready before you begin. That means slicing vegetables, meat or fish to the size required, having sauces handy and making sure that implements needed are within reach.

CUTTING AND SLICING VEGETABLES

Asian cooks take great care over the preparation of ingredients. There's an aesthetic reason for this – food must look as well as taste good – but careful cutting also serves a practical purpose. Cutting all the pieces to a similar size means they cook quickly and evenly.

Root Vegetables

Firm root vegetables, such as carrots, parsnips and mooli (daikon) can be diced, sliced or cut into matchsticks. Use a cook's knife or a cleaver. Trim the vegetable, then take a thin slice off each side to square it up. Slice lengthways. Pile the slices on top of each other and cut them into sticks.

Onions

Used for their flavour, all members of the onion family are used in stir-fries and other dishes. Shallots have a mild flavour but are fiddly to prepare. Spring onions (scallions) are often used cooked, raw and as a garnish in many Asian and Eastern cooking traditions. They make a perfect stir-fry ingredient, as their flavour is retained. If shreds are called for, cut off the dark green top, then slice the portions of stem lengthways in half, then into strips.

Above: Use a mixture of peppers for maximum colour impact.

Above: Cut meat into small pieces or strips so that it cooks quickly.

Other Vegetables

Aubergines (eggplants), courgettes (zucchini), sweet (bell) peppers green beans, mushrooms and corn are common stir-fry ingredients.

Less robust than root vegetables, courgettes shouldn't be cut too small. Ovals, sliced at an angle, work best. Aubergines are thinly sliced for tempura, cubed for slow-cooked dishes, or cut into strips for frying. If peppers

Below: Aubergine, sliced for tempura.

are called for in a dish, cut them in thin slices, as they can take longer to cook than other ingredients.

Mushrooms of all kinds are favourite ingredients. Shitake mushrooms are a particular favourite of Chinese and Thai cooks, and are often used dried for a more intense flavour.

If fresh corn is in season, and a recipe calls for it as an ingredient, use this instead of tinned or frozen. To free the corn from the cob, hold the top with one hand, and slice the kernels away.

Green beans for stir-fries should be the very freshest available; if they are slightly woody, trim the sides as well as the tops and bottoms, and slice thinly. Broccoli and cauliflower should be cut into small florets for stir-fries.

PREPARING MEAT, FISH AND POULTRY

How you prepare meat and fish depends on the type and dish, but for stir-fries you should always use the best and freshest cuts. The cheaper cuts, such as stewing beef or belly pork. are ideal for slow cooked dishes that have time to tenderize. When you are using chicken or pork in a stir-fry, you need to make sure it is cooked right through, and shows no sign of pinkness.

For stir-fries cut meat and fish across the grain. This not only helps the food to cook evenly, but also prevents it from disintegrating. Prawns (shrimp) and scallops can be left whole, and need only minutes to cook. They are usually the last ingredient to be added to a stir-fry, to prevent them going rubbery.

Below: Prawns can be left in their shells or peeled.

STIR-FRYING TECHNIQUES

Most of the cooking you are likely to do in your wok will be stir-frying, so it makes sense to get to grips with the technique from the start. Have all the ingredients close at hand, including measured items such as sauces.

PREHEATING THE WOK

The most important thing to remember is that the wok must be preheated. If the wok is hot when you add the oil, it will coat the surface with a thin film, preventing food from sticking. The best way to do this is to add a trickle of oil, necklace-fashion, around the inner rim so that it runs down evenly. You don't need much – 15–30ml/1–2 tbsp will be ample. Tilt the pan, if necessary, to spread the oil evenly.

Have the heat as high as possible if you are stir-frying meat, so that it is seared the moment it touches the wok. For fish or vegetables, the heat can be slightly lower. A simple test to ensure the wok is hot enough for stir-frying is to flick a few drops of water on to the surface after oiling. If this results in a loud sizzling sound, and the water immediately boils off, add your meat. If the water sizzles but remains visible for a few seconds before vanishing, the heat is right for fish or vegetables. Use oil with a high smoking point, such as groundnut (peanut) or corn oil.

COOKING AROMATICS

Individual recipes vary, but it is usual to start a stir-fry by adding aromatics such as garlic, ginger, chillies and spring onion (scallions) to the oil, then to fry meat, if used, and finish with the

Below: Make sure the oil in the wok is hot before adding any ingredients.

vegetables. Cooking aromatics flavours the oil. If this is their only function, they are fished out before anything else is added to the wok.

STIR-FRYING MEAT

When stir-frying meat, don't overload the wok or you will bring down the temperature. Add a few pieces at a time, sear them for a few seconds, flip them over and sear the other side, then push them away from the centre, where the heat is concentrated, and add more meat to the well. When the meat has been sealed, either push the pieces on to the sloping sides of the wok, so they will stay warm without continuing to fry, or remove them to a dish.

STIR-FRYING VEGETABLES

Add the vegetables to the wok, starting with varieties that take the longest to cook, such as carrots, broccoli and

Below: When cooking aromatics, be careful not to let them burn.

Above: Sauces are added at the end of the cooking process.

sweet (bell) peppers. Vegetables that need very little cooking, such as mooli (daikon) and mushrooms should be added next, with leafy vegetables tossed in right at the end. Keep the food on the move all the time, flipping and turning it with a spatula. Although the technique is called stir-frying, use a tossing and turning action, rather than stirring.

ADDING A SAUCE

When the vegetables are lightly cooked but still crisp, mix in the meat or other ingredients and then add any suggested sauces. A cornflour (cornstarch) mixture will thicken as well as flavour the mixture. If you are using a cornflour-based sauce, make a well in the stir-fry so you can stir it on its own for a minute or so before mixing it in.

Below: The wok is ideal for frying meat because of its high and even heat.

DEEP-FRYING TECHNIQUES

Provided a few safety precautions are taken, a wok is a useful pan for shallow and deep-frying. The shape means that you need less oil than in a conventional deep-fryer, yet still have a large surface area for cooking the food.

HEATING THE OIL

Start by making sure that the wok is stable. A flat-based wok is safest for deep-frying. If you use a round-based wok, make sure it will not wobble. Use a stand if necessary. The wok must be cold when the oil is added. This is the opposite advice to that given for stir-frying, when oil is added to a hot wok. Use an oil with a low smoking point and never fill the wok more than one-third full. This is more than adequate for most foods, and there will be less risk of the cook being splashed with hot fat or, worse, of the fat catching fire.

THE RIGHT TEMPERATURE

For deep-frying, oil needs to be at just the right temperature, so that the outside of the food becomes beautifully crisp while the centre cooks through to tender perfection. The precise temperature required will depend upon the density of what is being cooked and whether it has a coating of some kind, but around 180–190°C/350–375°F is suitable for most foods. A deep-fat thermometer, which can be clipped safely to the side of the wok before the oil is heated, is the safest and surest way of checking the temperature, but you can also test it by adding a cube of bread to the hot oil. The bread should brown in 45 seconds, if it sinks or fries

Below: Make sure there is enough oil for the volume of food being fried.

Above: Wrappers create a delicious crispy coating and keep food moist.

more slowly any food cooked in the wok would be greasy; if it burns, the same fate lies in wait for the food; if it sizzles on contact and bobs up to float on the surface, the temperature is just right.

COATING

Food can be coated in batter or a simple egg-and-breadcrumb mixture before being deep-fried. This protects, adds a contrasting texture and locks in the flavour. Dip the item to be coated in to the batter and gently shake off any excess before adding it to the hot oil. Flour or cornflour (cornstarch), egg and breadcrumbs can also be used for coating. Another method of protecting delicate food is to enclose it in a dough wrapper before deep-frying. This method is used for wontons and spring rolls, and the crispy result is delicious.

DEEP-FRYING TIPS

Don't overcrowd the wok. Add a few pieces at a time, lowering them gently into the oil to avoid splashing. Lift out carefully and either drain on a rack that

Above: Coating food before frying helps retain its moisture and flavour.

Hot Tips for Safe Deep-frying

- Don't fill the wok more than one-third full.
- Make sure it is stable.
- Be extra careful when adding food to the oil or retrieving it.
- Never leave a hot wok unattended.
- If the oil does catch fire, turn off the heat if you can and cover the wok with a heavy cloth or mat to exclude the air. This will put out the fire. Never throw water on an oil fire and don't try to move the wok.

---

has been clipped on to the side of the wok, or drain on kitchen paper and keep hot. Wait a minute or two before cooking successive batches, so that the oil gets the chance to return to its optimum temperature.

Below: Lift deep-fried food in and out of the hot wok with a long-handled tool.

STEAMING TECHNIQUES

This is a supremely healthy method, since the food is cooked without added fat and most of the nutrients are preserved. It is also simple, fast and efficient, whether you use a steamer specifically made for the wok or improvise with a trivet and a plate.

SUITABLE FOR STEAMING

All sorts of foods can be steamed, from fish to vegetables, poultry and even pancakes, custards and breads. Tender cuts of chicken cook well in the steamer but this is not the ideal cooking method for red meat. Check your chosen recipe for any advance preparation required. If you are cooking fish, is it whole or in portions? If whole, you may be advised to slit the skin and insert flavourings, such as fresh herbs, citrus slices or even a spicy rub. Delicate foods may need to be wrapped before being steamed. Banana leaves and lettuce leaves are popular for this purpose, as wraps or to line the steamer.

SELECTING A STEAMER

A steamer is simply a device for cooking foods by means of moist heat. The food should never touch the water that generates the steam, and the moisture must be trapped. You can steam food by simply placing it on a raised plate inside your wok, but steaming is simpler in a utensil designed for the purpose. Bamboo steamers are efficient and easy to use. So are stainless-steel steamers, but they are much more expensive. It is also possible to steam foods on the rack supplied with your wok, but this will only accommodate small amounts.

Below: Whole chickens, when steamed, have a special flavour and tenderness.

Above: A bamboo steamer is best when steaming in a wok, as it fits perfectly.

ASSEMBLING THE STEAMER

Food can be placed directly in the steamer basket, but this method tends to be reserved for dim sum or breads. It is more usual for a recipe to recommend lining the steamer with baking parchment or leaves before adding the food. This stops the food sticking and prevents small pieces from slipping through the slats. If you use this technique, make sure steam can still circulate. Using leaves for lining won't pose problems as steam will find its way around them, but parchment should be pierced. Alternatively, the food can be put on a plate or bowl inside the steamer so long as the steam holes are not blocked. Custards and some fish dishes are cooked this way.

Before you use a steamer in your wok for the first time, check the fit. You may have to use a trivet or upturned cup to keep the base of the steamer above the water. If a steamer is large, the sloping sides of the wok may prevent it from descending to the water level.

Steamer baskets are stackable, so you can cook several items at once, with the most delicate foods on top. The steamer will probably have its own cover, but if it doesn't, you will need to cover the wok itself, preferably with a domed lid so that condensed water runs down the sides and drips back into the water, rather than on to the food.

GETTING UP STEAM

The liquid to generate the steam can be water or stock. Aromatic flavourings like lemon grass, ginger or seaweed can be used to scent the steam. Fill the wok to a depth of around 5cm/2in, bring the liquid to the boil, carefully insert the steamer and cover with the lid. During steaming, keep checking the water level and top up if necessary. Tip the lid away from you to avoid being scalded.

Below: Individual fish custards are steamed to retain flavour and texture.

SIMMERING AND SMOKING

Although the wok is most closely associated with stir-fries and steamed food, it is also great for soups and sauced dishes such as Thai curries, braised pork belly or Beef Rendang. The frying stage that is the starting point for many of these dishes is easily accomplished in a wok, and after more ingredients are added, simmering is a cinch.

RAPID REDUCTION

The shape of the wok, with a wide surface area tapering to a narrow heat base, makes for rapid reduction of sauces. Where the aim is to concentrate the liquid, this is ideal, but you need to keep an eye on what's cooking, and top up the stock or sauce if necessary. For this reason, a wok isn't the best pan for a stew or similar dish that needs to be cooked for a very long time. A heavy pan is better for that purpose, but if you do use a wok, make it a stainless steel or non-stick one. Extended slow cooking in a carbon steel wok may erode the seasoned surface.

BLANCHING AND BOILING

For stir-frying, vegetables are usually cooked in relays, as some are much denser than others. Blanching toughies such as carrots and broccoli in boiling water gives them a head start so they can be stir-fried alongside more tender

Below: The wok is ideal for boiling or blanching green leafy vegetables.

Above: Fast boiling reduces a sauce, and gives a more intense flavour.

Above: Slow, gentle simmering produces a rich creamy taste and texture.

vegetables. Bring a wok of water to the boil, add the vegetables and cook for the required length of time (usually about 2–3 minutes). Lift the vegetables out of the wok with a skimmer or spider, plunge them into cold water so that they stop cooking, then drain and pat dry.

A wok can also be used for poaching fruit and cooking rice or noodles.

Wok Smoking

You don't need elaborate equipment to smoke poultry or seafood. A carbon steel wok works well, especially if you follow the Chinese tradition and use a tea leaf mixture as the smoking medium. The only drawback is the obvious one – use an extractor fan or be prepared for your smoke alarm to go off.

1 Line a carbon steel wok (not any other type) with foil, allowing a generous overlap. Sprinkle in 30ml/2 tbsp each of raw long grain rice, sugar and tea leaves.

2 Fit a wire rack on top of the wok and place the food to be smoked in a single layer on top. Mackerel fillets, salmon and duck or chicken breast portions work well. Cover the wok with a lid or inverted pan and cook over a very high heat until you see smoke.

3 Lower the heat so that the smoke reduces to wisps that seep from under the lid, and cook until the food is done. A mackerel fillet takes around 8–10 minutes; large fresh prawns (shrimp) 5–7 minutes, duck or chicken breast portions 18–20 minutes.

COOKING RICE AND NOODLES

Many of the Chinese and Thai recipes in this book are based on rice or noodles, which may be used as an accompaniment rather than part of the main dish. If you are using your wok for the meat or vegetable accompaniment, you will probably be cooking your rice or noodles in a pan.

COOKING RICE

There are several ways of cooking rice, but the absorption method is best for jasmine rice, basmati, short grain rice and glutinous rice. The proportion of water to rice will depend on the type of rice used, but as a guide, you will need about 600ml/1 pint/2½ cups water for every 225g/8oz/generous 1 cup rice.

1 Rinse the rice thoroughly and put it in a pan. Pour in the water. Do not add salt. Bring to the boil, then reduce the heat to the lowest possible setting.

2 Cover tightly and cook for 20–25 minutes, or until the liquid is absorbed.

3 Without lifting the lid, remove the pan from the heat. Leave it to stand in a warm place for 5 minutes to rest, and complete the cooking process. If cooked rice is required for a fried rice dish, cool it quickly, then chill it before frying.

Steamed Sticky Rice

Thais like their accompanying rice to be sticky. To get the authentic texture steam it in a bamboo steamer. Make sure you buy the right rice, usually called sticky or glutinous rice.

Rinse the rice in several changes of water, then leave to soak overnight in a bowl of cold water. Line a large bamboo steamer with muslin (cheesecloth). Drain the rice and spread out evenly on the muslin. Cover the rice and steam for 25–30 minutes, until the rice is tender. (Check the water level and add more if necessary.)

Making a Risotto in the Wok

The wok is not only suitable for Asian dishes, it also makes great risotto. Have the hot stock ready in a pan.

Melt butter, oil or a mixture in a wok and fry an onion. Add risotto rice and stir to coat the grains. Add a dash of white wine, then when that is absorbed begin adding hot stock, a ladleful at a time. Stir constantly until the stock is absorbed, then add more. It will take about 20 minutes for the rice to become tender. Add a little butter and stir in. Remove the pan from the heat and cover. Leave for 2 minutes, then serve.

COOKING NOODLES

If you are cooking noodles, either to serve solo or as part of a composite dish, do not rely entirely on the recipe – check the packet, too. Par-cooked noodles only need to be soaked in hot water; others must be boiled. Ready-to-use noodles need no attention at all, and can simply be added to a stir-fry and tossed over the heat until hot.

Preparing Rice Noodles
Rice noodles have been par-cooked when you buy them, so they only need to be soaked in hot water before use.

Add the noodles to a large bowl of just-boiled water and leave for 5–10 minutes or until softened, stirring occasionally to separate.

Preparing Wheat Noodles
Wheat noodles have to be cooked in boiling water. They take very little time, however.

Bring a large pan of water to the boil, add the fresh egg noodles and cook for 2–4 minutes or until tender. Drain well. If the noodles are going to be mixed into a stir-fry and cooked further, give them just 2 minutes initially.

DIPS AND GARNISHES

With a wok, it takes next to no time to rustle up treats like spring rolls, potato puffs and crisp-fried crab claws. Try them with these delicious dips.

Thai Red Curry Dip

This tastes good with mini spring rolls, or can be tossed with rice noodles for a simple accompaniment.

SERVES 4

    200ml/7fl oz/scant 1 cup coconut cream
    10–15ml/2–3 tsp Thai red curry paste
    4 spring onions (scallions), plus extra, thinly sliced, to garnish
    30ml/2 tbsp chopped fresh coriander (cilantro)
    1 fresh red chilli, seeded and thinly sliced in rings
    5ml/1 tsp soy sauce
    juice of 1 lime
    sugar, to taste
    25g/1oz/3 tbsp dry-roasted peanuts, finely chopped
    salt and ground black pepper

Pour the coconut cream into a small bowl and stir in the curry paste. Trim the spring onions, slice them diagonally, then stir into the coconut cream with the coriander, chilli, soy sauce and lime juice. Add enough sugar to give a sweet-sour flavour and season with salt and pepper. Spoon into a serving bowl and top with the peanuts and thinly sliced spring onion.

Wasabi and Soy Dip

Try this with crab cakes or fish cakes. The combination works extremely well, especially if you add a squeeze of lime just before dipping.

SERVES 4

    175ml/6fl oz/³⁄4 cup soy sauce or shoyu
    10ml/2 tsp wasabi paste
    2 spring onions (scallions), diagonally sliced
    1 fresh red chilli, seeded and thinly sliced in rings (optional)

Mix the soy sauce or shoyu with the wasabi paste in a bowl. Float the spring onion slices on top. The chilli slices can be added or left out, depending on how spicy you want the dip to be. Top with just one or two rings for colour.

Sweet Chilli Sauce

This sweet, spicy sauce has a wonderfully aromatic flavour and lovely translucent red colour. It can be used both for flavouring and as a dipping sauce. Any remaining sauce can be stored in the refrigerator in an airtight container for 1–2 weeks.

SERVES 4

    6 large red chillies
    60ml/4 tbsp white vinegar
    250g/9oz caster (superfine) sugar
    5ml/1tsp salt
    4 garlic cloves, chopped

Place the chillies in a food processor. Add the vinegar, sugar, salt and garlic. Blend until smooth, transfer to a pan and cook over a medium heat until thickened. Leave to cool and then transfer to a bowl.

Tamarind Sauce

This sweet, tangy dipping sauce has a fruity flavour and is perfect served with spicy deep-fried snacks. The quantities here are suitable for one serving, but if there is any left over, transfer into an airtight container and store in the refrigerator for 1–2 weeks.

MAKES 1 SMALL JAR
  90ml/6 tbsp tamarind paste
  90ml/6 tbsp water
  45ml/3 tbsp caster (superfine) sugar

Place all the ingredients in a small pan and bring the mixture to the boil. Reduce the heat and cook gently for 3–4 minutes, stirring occasionally. Remove the pan from the heat and transfer to a small bowl. Leave to cool before serving.

Ginger and Hoisin Dip

Chunky and bursting with flavour, this dip is delicious with prawn (shrimp) crackers. The dip can be stored in the refrigerator for up to 1 week.

SERVES 4
  60ml/4 tbsp hoisin sauce
  120ml/4fl oz/$\frac{1}{2}$ cup passata (bottled strained tomatoes)
  4 spring onions (scallions), thinly sliced
  4cm/1$\frac{1}{2}$in piece fresh root ginger, peeled and finely chopped
  2 fresh red chillies, seeded and cut into fine strips
  2 garlic cloves, crushed
  few drops of roasted sesame oil

Mix the hoisin and passata in a bowl. Stir in the spring onions, ginger, chillies and crushed garlic. Add the sesame oil, mix well and serve.

GREAT GARNISHES

Thai cooks enjoy garnishing their dishes with beautifully cut vegetables. Here are some suggestions for easy finishing touches that look fabulous. A cucumber frill makes a lovely garnish for duck, steamed salmon, a stir-fry or salad.

Cut a cucumber in half lengthways. Scoop out the seeds from one half and place it cut side down. Using a knife held at an angle, thinly slice the cucumber, cutting almost through so the slices remain attached at the base. Fan the slices out. Turn in alternate slices to form loops, then bend into a semi-circle with the loops on the outside, so that they resemble petals.

1 Using a small pair of scissors or a slim-bladed knife, slit a fresh red chilli carefully lengthways from the tip to within 1cm/$\frac{1}{2}$in of the stem end. Repeat this at regular intervals around the chilli, keeping the stem end intact, until it resembles a tassel. Slit more chillies in the same way.

2 Rinse the chillies in cold water to wash away the seeds. Place in a bowl of iced water and chill for at least 4 hours. For very curly chilli flowers, leave the bowl in the refrigerator overnight.

Wasabi paste
This bright green paste packs a whopping punch. It is made from a Japanese herb and tastes like a cross between hot mustard and horseradish. A little goes a long way to flavour dips and sauces. Try mixing it with mayonnaise for a delicious dip to serve with steamed asparagus. The most convenient way to buy wasabi is in a tube. If you use powdered wasabi, mix it in an egg cup with the same volume of tepid water, then stand the egg cup upside down for 10 minutes to allow the flavour to develop without letting the wasabi dry out.

CRISPY SNACKS AND FINGER FOOD

A wok isn't just for wonderful main courses — it is a great accessory when it comes to the little treats that add spice to life. Spring rolls, samosas and puff pastry parcels can be cooked to crisp perfection in minutes, ready for dipping into scrumptious sauces. Spiced Noodle Pancakes and Pea and Potato Pakoras provide two more good reasons for heating the oil and starting to sizzle. For serving with drinks, try Roasted Coconut Cashew Nuts — piled in paper cones to save fingers from getting sticky — or choose one of the more substantial snacks that can double as an appetizer.

PRAWN AND SESAME TOASTS

THESE ATTRACTIVE LITTLE TOAST TRIANGLES ARE IDEAL FOR SERVING WITH PRE-DINNER DRINKS AND ARE ALWAYS A FAVOURITE HOT SNACK AT PARTIES. THEY ARE SURPRISINGLY EASY TO PREPARE AND YOU CAN COOK THEM IN YOUR WOK FOR JUST A FEW MINUTES. SERVE THEM WITH A SWEET CHILLI SAUCE.

SERVES FOUR

INGREDIENTS
  225g/8oz peeled raw prawns (shrimp)
  15ml/1 tbsp sherry
  15ml/1 tbsp soy sauce
  30ml/2 tbsp cornflour (cornstarch)
  2 egg whites
  4 slices white bread
  115g/4oz/½ cup sesame seeds
  oil, for deep-frying
  sweet chilli sauce,
    to serve

1 Process the prawns, sherry, soy sauce and cornflour in a food processor.

2 In a grease-free bowl, whisk the egg whites until stiff. Fold them into the prawn and cornflour mixture.

3 Cut each slice of bread into four triangular quarters. Spread out the sesame seeds on a large plate. Spread the prawn paste over one side of each bread triangle, then press the coated sides into the sesame seeds so that they stick and cover the prawn paste.

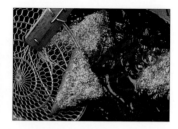

4 Heat the oil in a wok or deep-fryer, to 190°C/375°F or until a cube of bread, added to the oil, browns in about 45 seconds. Add the toasts, a few at a time, prawn side down, and deep-fry for 2–3 minutes, then turn and fry on the other side until golden.

5 Drain on kitchen paper and serve hot with sweet chilli sauce.

Energy 392Kcal/1634kJ; Protein 19.1g; Carbohydrate 21.1g, of which sugars 1.2g; Fat 25.8g, of which saturates 3.4g; Cholesterol 110mg; Calcium 270mg; Fibre 2.7g; Sodium 557mg.

ROASTED COCONUT CASHEW NUTS

SERVE THESE WOK-FRIED HOT AND SWEET CASHEW NUTS IN PAPER OR CELLOPHANE CONES AT PARTIES.
NOT ONLY DO THEY LOOK ENTICING AND TASTE TERRIFIC, BUT THE CONES HELP TO KEEP CLOTHES
AND HANDS CLEAN AND CAN SIMPLY BE CRUMPLED UP AND THROWN AWAY AFTERWARDS.

SERVES SIX TO EIGHT

INGREDIENTS
    15ml/1 tbsp groundnut (peanut) oil
    30ml/2 tbsp clear honey
    250g/9oz/2 cups cashew nuts
    115g/4oz/1⅓ cups desiccated (dry
      unsweetened shredded) coconut
    2 small fresh red chillies, seeded and
      finely chopped
    salt and ground black pepper

VARIATIONS
Almonds also work well, or choose
peanuts for a more economical snack.

1 Heat the oil in a wok or large frying
pan and then stir in the honey. After a
few seconds add the nuts and coconut
and stir-fry until both are golden brown.

2 Add the chillies, with salt and pepper
to taste. Toss until all the ingredients
are well mixed. Serve warm or cooled in
paper cones or on saucers.

Energy 301Kcal/1247kJ; Protein 7.2g; Carbohydrate 9.7g, of which sugars 5.5g; Fat 26.2g, of which saturates 11.1g; Cholesterol 0mg; Calcium 14mg; Fibre 3g; Sodium 95mg.

GOLDEN BEEF AND POTATO PUFFS

THESE CRISP, GOLDEN PILLOWS OF PASTRY FILLED WITH SPICED BEEF AND POTATOES ARE DELICIOUS SERVED PIPING HOT, STRAIGHT FROM THE WOK. THE LIGHT, FLAKY PASTRY PUFFS UP WONDERFULLY IN THE HOT OIL AND CONTRASTS ENTICINGLY WITH THE FRAGRANT SPICED BEEF FILLING WITHIN.

SERVES FOUR

INGREDIENTS

15ml/1 tbsp sunflower oil
½ small onion, finely chopped
3 garlic cloves, crushed
5ml/1 tsp finely grated fresh root
  ginger
1 fresh red chilli, seeded and finely
  chopped
30ml/2 tbsp hot curry powder
75g/3oz minced (ground) beef
115g/4oz mashed potato
60ml/4 tbsp chopped fresh
  coriander (cilantro)
2 sheets ready-rolled, fresh
  puff pastry
1 egg, lightly beaten
vegetable oil, for frying
salt and ground black pepper
fresh coriander leaves, to garnish
tomato ketchup, to serve

1 Heat the oil in a wok, then add the onion, garlic, ginger and chilli. Stir-fry over a medium heat for 2–3 minutes. Add the curry powder and beef and stir-fry over a high heat for a further 4–5 minutes, or until the beef is browned and just cooked through, then remove from the heat.

2 Transfer the beef mixture to a large bowl and add the mashed potato and chopped fresh coriander. Stir well, then season and set aside.

COOK'S TIP

For a change in texture, you can use ready-made shortcrust pastry in place of the puff pastry. The puffs will be transformed into little golden crescents that have a firmer, crisper shell but the same succulent beef filling.

3 Lay the pastry sheets on a clean, dry surface and cut out 8 rounds, using a 7.5cm/3in pastry (cookie) cutter.

4 Place a large spoonful of the beef mixture in the centre of each pastry round. Brush the edges of the pastry with the beaten egg and fold each round in half to enclose the filling. Press and crimp the edges with the tines of a fork to seal.

5 Fill a wok one-third full of oil and heat to 180°C/350°F or until a cube of bread, dropped into the oil, browns in 40 seconds.

6 Deep-fry the puffs, in batches, for 2–3 minutes until puffed up and golden brown. Drain on kitchen paper and serve garnished with fresh coriander leaves. Offer a small bowl of tomato ketchup for dipping.

VARIATION

Try equal quantities of tomato ketchup and brown sauce as an alternative dip.

Energy 408Kcal/1695kJ; Protein 9g; Carbohydrate 24.2g, of which sugars 1.8g; Fat 31.8g, of which saturates 4.2g; Cholesterol 67mg; Calcium 46mg; Fibre 0.5g; Sodium 202mg.

TUNG TONG

POPULARLY CALLED "GOLD BAGS", THESE CRISP PASTRY PURSES HAVE A CORIANDER-FLAVOURED FILLING BASED ON WATER CHESTNUTS AND CORN. THEY ARE THE PERFECT VEGETARIAN SNACK, CRISP AND CRUNCHY ON THE OUTSIDE, WITH A SUCCULENT CORN AND WATER CHESTNUT FILLING.

MAKES EIGHTEEN

INGREDIENTS
18 spring roll wrappers, about
    8cm/3¼in square, thawed
    if frozen
oil, for deep-frying
plum sauce, to serve
For the filling
4 baby corn cobs
130g/4½oz can water chestnuts,
    drained and chopped
1 shallot, coarsely chopped
1 egg, separated
30ml/2 tbsp cornflour (cornstarch)
60ml/4 tbsp water
small bunch fresh coriander
    (cilantro), chopped
salt and ground black pepper

1 Make the filling. Place the baby corn, water chestnuts, shallot and egg yolk in a food processor or blender. Process to a coarse paste. Place the egg white in a cup and whisk it lightly with a fork.

2 Put the cornflour in a small pan and stir in the water until smooth. Add the corn mixture and chopped coriander and season with salt and pepper to taste. Cook over a low heat, stirring constantly, until thickened.

3 Leave the filling to cool slightly, then place 5ml/1 tsp in the centre of a spring roll wrapper. Brush the edges with the beaten egg white, then gather up the points and press them firmly together to make a pouch or bag.

4 Repeat with the remaining wrappers and filling. Heat the oil in a wok to 190°C/375°F or until a cube of bread, added to the oil, browns in about 45 seconds. Fry the bags, in batches, for about 5 minutes, until golden brown. Drain on kitchen paper and serve hot, with the plum sauce.

Energy 55Kcal/229kJ; Protein 1.2g; Carbohydrate 6.3g, of which sugars 0.4g; Fat 2.9g, of which saturates 0.4g; Cholesterol 12mg; Calcium 19mg; Fibre 0.5g; Sodium 42mg.

FIRECRACKERS

IT'S EASY TO SEE HOW THESE PASTRY-WRAPPED PRAWN SNACKS GOT THEIR NAME. NOT ONLY DO THEY WHIZ AROUND IN THE WOK LIKE ROCKETS, BUT WHEN YOU BITE INTO THEM THEIR CONTENTS EXPLODE WITH FLAVOUR. MARINATING THE PRAWNS IN CURRY PASTE MAKES ALL THE DIFFERENCE.

3 Place a wonton wrapper on the work surface at an angle so that it forms a diamond shape, then fold the top corner over so that the point is in the centre. Place a prawn, slits down, on the wrapper, with the tail projecting from the folded end, then fold the bottom corner over the other end of the prawn.

4 Fold each side of the wrapper over in turn to make a tightly folded roll. Tie a noodle in a bow around the roll and set it aside. Repeat with the remaining prawns and wrappers.

5 Heat the oil in a wok to 190°C/375°F or until a cube of bread, added to the oil, browns in 40 seconds. Fry the prawns, a few at a time, for 5–8 minutes, until golden brown and cooked through. Drain well on kitchen paper and keep hot while you cook the remaining batches.

COOK'S TIP
Soak the egg noodles to be used as ties for the rolls in a bowl of boiling water for 2–3 minutes, until soft, drain, refresh under cold running water and drain.

MAKES SIXTEEN

INGREDIENTS
  16 large, raw king prawns (jumbo shrimp), heads and shells removed but tails left on
  5ml/1 tsp red curry paste
  15ml/1 tbsp Thai fish sauce
  16 small wonton wrappers, about 8cm/3¼in square, thawed if frozen
  16 fine egg noodles, soaked (see Cook's Tip)
  oil, for deep-frying

1 Place the prawns on their sides and cut two slits through the underbelly of each, one about 1cm/½in from the head end and the other about 1cm/½in from the first cut, cutting across the prawn. This will prevent the prawns from curling when they are cooked.

2 Mix the curry paste with the fish sauce in a shallow dish. Add the prawns and turn them in the mixture until they are well coated. Cover and leave to marinate for 10 minutes.

Energy 71Kcal/298kJ; Protein 3.2g; Carbohydrate 7.1g, of which sugars 0.2g; Fat 3.5g, of which saturates 0.5g; Cholesterol 25mg; Calcium 20mg; Fibre 0.3g; Sodium 30mg.

CRISP-FRIED JAPANESE PANKO PRAWNS

WHEN BUTTERFLIED AND BATTERED TIGER PRAWNS ARE DEEP-FRIED IN THE WOK, THEY CURL UP BEAUTIFULLY, AND LOOK GORGEOUS ON DARK GREEN SEAWEED TOPPED WITH WHITE RICE. WASABI, SOY SAUCE, SWEET CHILLI SAUCE AND PICKLED GINGER ARE TRADITIONAL ACCOMPANIMENTS.

SERVES FOUR

INGREDIENTS

20 large raw tiger or king prawns
(jumbo shrimp), heads removed
30ml/2 tbsp cornflour (cornstarch)
3 large (US extra large) eggs,
lightly beaten
150g/5oz *panko* (Japanese-style
breadcrumbs)
sunflower oil, for frying
4 sheets of nori
400g/14oz cooked sushi rice
wasabi, soy sauce, sweet chilli sauce
and pickled ginger, to serve

1 Peel and devein the prawns, leaving the tails on. Using a small, sharp knife, cut down the back of each prawn, without cutting all the way through, and gently press the prawns out flat to butterfly them.

2 Place the cornflour, beaten eggs and *panko* in 3 separate bowls. Dip each prawn first in the cornflour mixture, next in the egg and then in the *panko*, to coat evenly. Fill a wok one-third full of sunflower oil and heat to 180°C/ 350°F (or until a cube of bread, added to the oil, browns in 45 seconds).

3 Working in batches, deep-fry the prawns for 1 minute, or until lightly golden and crisp. Remove with a slotted spoon and drain on kitchen paper.

4 Carefully cut each nori sheet into a 10cm/4in square. Place each square on a serving plate and divide the sushi rice among them, then spread out the rice using the back of a spoon. Top each serving with 5 deep-fried prawns and serve with wasabi, soy sauce, sweet chilli sauce and pickled ginger.

COOK'S TIP

Panko are Japanese-style breadcrumbs, which give a fabulously crunchy result when deep-fried. They make the perfect coating for these tender, juicy prawns, which remain unbelievably succulent when cooked. If you can't find panko, use coarse, dried breadcrumbs instead.

Energy 472Kcal/1989kJ; Protein 20.2g; Carbohydrate 63g, of which sugars 1g; Fat 17.4g, of which saturates 2.8g; Cholesterol 240mg; Calcium 127mg; Fibre 0.9g; Sodium 437mg.

SATAY PRAWNS

This delicious dish is inspired by the classic Indonesian satay. The combination of mild peanuts, aromatic spices, sweet coconut milk and zesty lemon juice in the spicy dip is perfect and is guaranteed to have guests coming back for more.

SERVES FOUR TO SIX

INGREDIENTS
450g/1lb king prawns (jumbo shrimp)
25ml/1½ tbsp vegetable oil
For the peanut sauce
25ml/1½ tbsp vegetable oil
15ml/1 tbsp chopped garlic
1 small onion, chopped
3–4 fresh red chillies, seeded
   and chopped
3 kaffir lime leaves, torn
1 lemon grass stalk, bruised
   and chopped
5ml/1 tsp medium curry paste
250ml/8fl oz/1 cup coconut milk
1cm/½in piece cinnamon stick
75g/3oz/⅓ cup crunchy
   peanut butter
45ml/3 tbsp tamarind juice, made
   by mixing tamarind paste with
   warm water
30ml/2 tbsp Thai fish sauce
30ml/2 tbsp palm sugar or light
   muscovado (brown) sugar
juice of ½ lemon
For the garnish
spring onions (scallions),
   cut diagonally
½ bunch fresh coriander
   (cilantro) leaves (optional)
4 fresh red chillies, finely sliced
   (optional)

1 Remove the heads from the prawns and peel, leaving the tail ends intact. Slit each prawn along the back with a small, sharp knife and remove the black vein. Rinse under cold running water, pat completely dry on kitchen paper and set the prawns aside.

2 Make the peanut sauce. Heat half the oil in a wok or large, heavy frying pan. Add the garlic and onion and cook over a medium heat, stirring occasionally, for 3–4 minutes, until the mixture has softened but not browned.

3 Add the chillies, kaffir lime leaves, lemon grass and curry paste. Stir well and cook for a further 2–3 minutes, then stir in the coconut milk, cinnamon stick, peanut butter, tamarind juice, fish sauce, sugar and lemon juice. Cook, stirring constantly, until well blended.

4 Bring to the boil, then reduce the heat to low and simmer gently for 15–20 minutes, until the sauce thickens. Stir occasionally with a wooden spoon to prevent the sauce from sticking to the base of the wok or frying pan.

5 Shallow fry the prawns until they turn pink. Alternatively, thread the prawns on to skewers and cook under a hot grill (broiler) for 2 minutes on each side.

6 Remove the cinnamon stick from the sauce and discard. Arrange the prawns on a warmed platter, garnish with spring onions and coriander leaves and sliced red chillies, if liked, and serve with skewers for using to dunk into the sauce.

VARIATIONS
• For a curry-style dish, heat the oil in a wok or large frying pan. Add the prawns (shrimp) and stir-fry for 3–4 minutes, or until pink. Mix the prawns with the sauce and serve with jasmine rice.
• You can use this basic sauce for satay pork or chicken, too. With a sharp knife, cut pork fillet (tenderloin) or skinless, boneless chicken breast portions into long thin strips and stir-fry in hot oil until golden brown all over and cooked through. Then stir into the sauce, instead of the king prawns (jumbo shrimp).
• You could use Thai red or green curry paste for this recipe. Make your own or buy a good-quality product from an Asian food store. Once opened, jars of curry paste should be kept in the refrigerator and used within 2 months.
• You can make the satay sauce in advance and leave it to cool. Transfer to a bowl, cover with clear film (plastic wrap) and store in the refrigerator. Reheat gently, stirring occasionally, before stir-frying the prawns (shrimp).

Energy 1042Kcal/4361kJ; Protein 59.7g; Carbohydrate 61.7g, of which sugars 53.1g; Fat 63.7g, of which saturates 13.1g; Cholesterol 472mg; Calcium 408mg; Fibre 7.5g; Sodium 3255mg.

CRISP-FRIED CRAB CLAWS

CRAB CLAWS ARE READILY AVAILABLE FROM THE FREEZER CABINET OF MANY ASIAN STORES AND SUPERMARKETS. THAW THEM THOROUGHLY AND DRY ON KITCHEN PAPER BEFORE COATING THEM.

SERVES FOUR

INGREDIENTS
    50g/2oz/⅓ cup rice flour
    15ml/1 tbsp cornflour (cornstarch)
    2.5ml/½ tsp granulated sugar
    1 egg
    60ml/4 tbsp cold water
    1 lemon grass stalk
    2 garlic cloves, finely chopped
    15ml/1 tbsp chopped fresh
      coriander (cilantro)
    1–2 fresh red chillies, seeded and
      finely chopped
    5ml/1 tsp Thai fish sauce
    vegetable oil, for deep-frying
    12 half-shelled crab claws, thawed
      if frozen
    ground black pepper
For the chilli vinegar dip
    45ml/3 tbsp granulated sugar
    120ml/4fl oz/½ cup water
    120ml/4fl oz/½ cup red
      wine vinegar
    15ml/1 tbsp Thai fish sauce
    2–4 fresh red chillies, seeded
      and chopped

1 First make the chilli vinegar dip. Mix the sugar and water in a pan. Heat gently, stirring until the sugar has dissolved, then bring to the boil. Lower the heat and simmer for 5–7 minutes. Stir in the rest of the ingredients, pour into a serving bowl and set aside.

2 Combine the rice flour, cornflour and sugar in a bowl. Beat the egg with the cold water, then stir the egg and water mixture into the flour mixture and beat well until it forms a light batter.

3 Cut off the lower 5cm/2in of the lemon grass stalk and chop it finely. Add the lemon grass to the batter, with the garlic, coriander, red chillies and fish sauce. Stir in pepper to taste.

4 Heat the oil in a wok or deep-fryer to 190°C/375°F or until a cube of bread browns in 40 seconds. Dip the crab claws into the batter, then fry, in batches, until golden. Serve with the dip.

Energy 222Kcal/926kJ; Protein 10.1g; Carbohydrate 16.9g, of which sugars 0g; Fat 12.8g, of which saturates 1.7g; Cholesterol 78mg; Calcium 62mg; Fibre 0.3g; Sodium 256mg.

DEEP-FRIED SMALL PRAWNS AND CORN

INSPIRED BY THE JAPANESE DISH CALLED TEMPURA, THIS SIMPLE SNACK FOOD IS A GOOD WAY OF USING UP SMALL QUANTITIES OF VEGETABLES AND PRAWNS. IT IS EASY TO COOK IN A WOK.

SERVES FOUR

INGREDIENTS

    200g/7oz small cooked, peeled
      prawns (shrimp)
    4–5 button (white) mushrooms
    4 spring onions (scallions)
    75g/3oz/½ cup canned, drained or
      frozen sweetcorn, thawed
    30ml/2 tbsp frozen peas, thawed
    vegetable oil, for deep-frying
    chives, to garnish
For the tempura batter
    300ml/½ pint/1¼ cups ice-cold water
    2 eggs, beaten
    150g/5oz/1¼ cups plain
      (all-purpose) flour
    1.5ml/¼ tsp baking powder
For the dipping sauce
    400ml/14fl oz/1⅔ cups second dashi
      stock, made with instant dashi
      powder and water
    100ml/3fl oz/scant ½ cup shoyu
    100ml/3fl oz/scant ½ cup mirin
    15ml/1 tbsp chopped chives

1 Roughly chop half the prawns. Cut the mushrooms into small cubes. Slice the white part from the spring onions and chop this roughly.

2 To make the tempura batter, in a medium mixing bowl, mix the cold water and eggs. Add the flour and baking powder, and very roughly fold in with a pair of chopsticks or a fork. Do not beat. The batter should still be quite lumpy. Heat plenty of oil in a wok to 170°C/338°F.

3 Mix the prawns and vegetables into the batter. Pour a quarter of the batter into a small bowl, then drop gently into the oil. Using wooden spoons, carefully gather the scattered batter to form a fist-size ball. Deep-fry until golden. Drain on kitchen paper.

4 In a small pan, mix all the liquid dipping-sauce ingredients together and bring to the boil, then immediately turn off the heat. Sprinkle with chives.

5 Garnish the fritters with chives, and serve with the dipping sauce.

Energy 246Kcal/1039kJ; Protein 17.6g; Carbohydrate 37.4g, of which sugars 4.7g; Fat 4g, of which saturates 1g; Cholesterol 193mg; Calcium 117mg; Fibre 2g; Sodium 1963mg.

Deep-fried layered Shiitake and Scallops

A WOK DOES DOUBLE DUTY FOR MAKING THESE MUSHROOM AND SEAFOOD TREATS. THE NAGA-IMO (A TYPE OF YAM) IS STEAMED IN A BAMBOO BASKET, AND LATER THE WOK IS USED FOR DEEP FRYING. THE SNACKS ARE DELICATE; USE A KNIFE AND FORK IF CHOPSTICKS PROVE TRICKY.

SERVES FOUR

INGREDIENTS
4 scallops
8 large fresh shiitake mushrooms
225g/8oz naga-imo, unpeeled
20ml/4 tsp miso
50g/2oz/1 cup fresh breadcrumbs
cornflour (cornstarch), for dusting
vegetable oil, for deep-frying
2 eggs, beaten
salt
4 lemon wedges, to serve

1 Slice the scallops in two horizontally, then sprinkle with salt. Remove the stalks from the shiitake by cutting them off with a knife. Discard the stalks.

2 Cut shallow slits on the top of the shiitake to form a "hash" symbol or cut slits to form a white cross. Sprinkle with a little salt.

3 Heat a steamer and steam the naga-imo for 10–15 minutes, or until soft. Test with a skewer. Leave to cool.

4 Wait until the naga-imo is cool enough to handle. Skin, then mash the flesh in a bowl with a masher, getting rid of any lumps. Add the miso and mix well. Take the breadcrumbs into your hands and break them down finely. Mix half into the mashed naga-imo, keeping the rest on a small plate.

5 Fill the underneath of the shiitake caps with a scoop of mashed naga-imo. Smooth down with the flat edge of a knife and dust the mash with cornflour.

6 Add a little mash to a slice of scallop and place on top.

7 Spread another 5ml/1 tsp mashed naga-imo on to the scallop and shape to completely cover. Make sure all the ingredients are clinging together. Repeat to make eight little mounds.

8 Heat the oil to 150°C/300°F. Place the beaten eggs in a shallow container. Dust the shiitake and scallop mounds with cornflour, then dip into the egg. Handle with care as the mash and scallop are quite soft. Coat well with the remaining breadcrumbs and deep-fry in the oil until golden. Drain well on kitchen paper. Serve hot on individual plates with a wedge of lemon.

VARIATION
For a vegetarian option, use 16 shiitake mushrooms. Sandwich the naga-imo mash between two shiitake to make 8 bundles. Deep-fry in the same way as the scallop version.

COOK'S TIPS
• Fresh naga-imo produces a slimy liquid when it's cut. Try not to touch this as some people may react and develop a mild rash. When it's cooked, it is perfectly safe to touch.
• If you can't find naga-imo, use yam or 115g/4oz each of potatoes and peeled Jerusalem artichokes instead. Steam the potatoes and boil the artichokes until both are tender.

Energy 247Kcal/1032kJ; Protein 14.1g; Carbohydrate 15.5g, of which sugars 4.5g; Fat 14.8g, of which saturates 2.3g; Cholesterol 113mg; Calcium 57mg; Fibre 1.9g; Sodium 213mg.

CRISPY SALT AND PEPPER SQUID

THESE DELICIOUS MORSELS OF SQUID LOOK STUNNING AND ARE PERFECT SERVED WITH DRINKS, OR AS AN APPETIZER. THE CRISP, GOLDEN COATING CONTRASTS BEAUTIFULLY WITH THE SUCCULENT SQUID INSIDE. SERVE THEM PIPING HOT STRAIGHT FROM THE WOK.

SERVES FOUR

INGREDIENTS
750g/1lb 10oz fresh squid, cleaned
juice of 4–5 lemons
15ml/1 tbsp freshly ground
  black pepper
15ml/1 tbsp sea salt
10ml/2 tsp caster (superfine) sugar
115g/4oz/1 cup cornflour
  (cornstarch)
3 egg whites, lightly beaten
vegetable oil, for deep-frying
chilli sauce or sweet-and-sour sauce,
  for dipping
skewers or toothpicks, to serve

1 Cut the squid into large bitesize pieces and score a diamond pattern on each piece, using a sharp knife or a cleaver.

2 Trim the tentacles. Place in a large mixing bowl and pour over the lemon juice. Cover and marinate for 10–15 minutes. Drain well and pat dry.

3 In a separate bowl mix together the pepper, salt, sugar and cornflour. Dip the squid pieces in the egg whites and then toss lightly in the seasoned flour, shaking off any excess.

4 Fill a wok one-third full of oil and heat to 180°C/350°F or until a cube of bread, dropped into the oil, browns in 40 seconds. Working in batches, deep-fry the squid for 1 minute. Drain on kitchen paper and serve threaded on to skewers with chilli or sweet-and-sour sauce.

COOK'S TIP
Keep egg whites in the freezer, ready to thaw for use in dishes such as this.

Energy 346Kcal/1462kJ; Protein 31.2g; Carbohydrate 31.3g, of which sugars 2.6g; Fat 11.6g, of which saturates 1.8g; Cholesterol 422mg; Calcium 32mg; Fibre 0g; Sodium 1741mg.

SPICED NOODLE PANCAKES

THE DELICATE RICE NOODLES PUFF UP IN THE HOT OIL TO GIVE A FABULOUS CRUNCHY BITE THAT MELTS IN THE MOUTH. FOR MAXIMUM ENJOYMENT, SERVE THE GOLDEN PANCAKES AS SOON AS THEY ARE COOKED AND SAVOUR THE SUBTLE BLEND OF SPICES AND WONDERFULLY CRISP TEXTURE.

SERVES FOUR

INGREDIENTS
  150g/5oz dried thin rice noodles
  1 fresh red chilli, finely diced
  10ml/2 tsp garlic salt
  5ml/1 tsp ground ginger
  1/4 small red onion, very finely diced
  5ml/1 tsp finely chopped lemon grass
  5ml/1 tsp ground cumin
  5ml/1 tsp ground coriander
  large pinch of ground turmeric
  salt
  vegetable oil, for frying
  sweet chilli sauce, for dipping

1 Roughly break up the noodles and place in a large bowl. Pour over enough boiling water to cover, and soak for 4–5 minutes. Drain and rinse under cold water. Dry on kitchen paper.

2 Transfer the noodles to a bowl and add the chilli, garlic salt, ground ginger, red onion, lemon grass, ground cumin, coriander and turmeric. Toss well to mix, and season with salt.

COOK'S TIP
For deep-frying, choose very thin rice noodles. These can be cooked dry, but here are soaked and seasoned first.

3 Heat 5–6cm/2–2$\frac{1}{2}$in oil in a wok. Working in batches, drop tablespoons of the noodle mixture into the oil. Flatten using the back of a skimmer and cook for 1–2 minutes on each side until crisp and golden. Lift out from the wok.

4 Drain the noodle pancakes on kitchen paper and serve immediately with the chilli sauce for dipping.

Energy 190Kcal/791kJ; Protein 2g; Carbohydrate 31.8g, of which sugars 0.9g; Fat 5.6g, of which saturates 0.7g; Cholesterol 0mg; Calcium 9mg; Fibre 0.2g; Sodium 496mg.

TEMPURA SEAFOOD

THIS QUINTESSENTIALLY JAPANESE DISH ACTUALLY HAS ITS ORIGINS IN THE WEST, AS TEMPURA WAS INTRODUCED TO JAPAN BY PORTUGUESE TRADERS IN THE 17TH CENTURY.

SERVES FOUR

INGREDIENTS
8 large raw prawns (shrimp), heads
   and shells removed, tails intact
130g/4½oz squid body, cleaned
   and skinned
115g/4oz whiting fillets
4 fresh shiitake mushrooms,
   stalks removed
8 okra
⅛ nori sheet, 5 × 4cm/2 × 1½in
20g/¾oz dried harusame (a packet is
   a 150–250g/5–9oz mass)
vegetable oil and sesame oil,
   for deep-frying
plain (all-purpose) flour, for dusting
salt
For the dipping sauce
400ml/14fl oz/1⅔ cups second dashi
   stock, made using water and instant
   dashi powder
200ml/7fl oz/scant 1 cup shoyu
200ml/7fl oz/scant 1 cup mirin
For the condiment
450g/1lb mooli (daikon), peeled
4cm/1½in fresh root ginger, peeled
   and finely grated
For the tempura batter
ice-cold water
1 large (US extra large) egg, beaten
200g/7oz/2 cups plain flour, sifted
2–3 ice cubes

1 Remove the vein from the prawns, then make 4 × 3mm/⅛in deep cuts across the belly to stop the prawns curling up. Snip the tips of the tails and gently squeeze out any liquid. Pat dry.

2 Cut open the squid body. Lay it flat, inside down, on a chopping board, and make shallow criss-cross slits on the outside. Cut into 2.5 × 6cm/1 × 2½in rectangular strips. Cut the whiting fillets into similar-size strips.

3 Make two notched slits on the shiitake caps, in the form of a cross. Sprinkle your hands with some salt and rub over the okra, then wash the okra under running water to clean the surface.

4 Cut the nori into four long strips lengthways. Loosen the harusame noodles from the block and cut both ends with scissors to get a few strips. Make four bunches and tie them in the middle by wrapping with a nori strip. Wet the end to fix it.

5 Make the dipping sauce. In a pan, mix all the dipping-sauce ingredients and bring to the boil, then immediately remove from the heat. Set aside and keep warm.

6 Prepare the condiment. Grate the daikon very finely. Drain in a sieve, then squeeze out any excess water by hand.

7 Lay clear film (plastic wrap) over an egg cup and press about 2.5ml/½ tsp grated ginger into the bottom. Add 30ml/2 tbsp grated daikon. Press and invert on to a small plate. Make three more ginger and daikon moulds in the same way.

8 Half-fill a wok with 3 parts vegetable oil to 1 part sesame oil. Bring to 175°C/347°F over a medium heat.

9 Meanwhile, make the tempura batter. Add enough ice-cold water to the egg to make 150ml/¼ pint/⅔ cup, then pour into a large bowl. Add the flour and mix roughly with chopsticks. Do not beat; leave the batter lumpy. Add some ice cubes later to keep the temperature cool.

10 Dip the okra into the batter and deep-fry until golden. Drain. Batter the underside of the shiitake, and deep-fry.

11 Increase the heat a little, then fry the harusame by holding the nori tie with chopsticks and dipping them into the oil for a few seconds. The noodles instantly turn crisp and white. Drain on kitchen paper and sprinkle with salt.

12 Hold the tail of a prawn, dust with flour, then dip into the batter. Do not put batter on the tail. Slide the prawn into the hot oil very slowly. Deep-fry one to two prawns at a time until crisp.

13 Dust the whiting strips, dip into the batter, then deep-fry until golden. Wipe the squid strips well with kitchen paper, dust with flour, then dip in batter. Deep-fry until the batter is crisp.

14 Drain excess oil from the tempura on a wire rack for a few minutes, then arrange them on individual plates. Set the condiment alongside the tempura. Reheat the dipping sauce to warm through, then pour into four small bowls.

15 Serve immediately, mixing the condiment into the dipping sauce and dunking the tempura as you eat.

Energy 401Kcal/1683kJ; Protein 27.3g; Carbohydrate 42.8g, of which sugars 4.1g; Fat 14.5g, of which saturates 2.2g; Cholesterol 231mg; Calcium 167mg; Fibre 3.2g; Sodium 1080mg.

THAI SPRING ROLLS

CRUNCHY SPRING ROLLS ARE AS POPULAR IN THAILAND AS THEY ARE IN CHINA. THAIS FILL THEIR
VERSION WITH A DELICIOUS GARLIC, PORK AND NOODLE MIXTURE.

MAKES TWENTY-FOUR

INGREDIENTS
  24 x 15cm/6in square spring roll
    wrappers, thawed if frozen
  30ml/2 tbsp plain (all-purpose) flour
  vegetable oil, for deep-frying
  sweet chilli dipping sauce,
    to serve
For the filling
  4–6 Chinese dried mushrooms,
    soaked for 30 minutes in warm
    water to cover
  50g/2oz cellophane noodles
  30ml/2 tbsp vegetable oil
  2 garlic cloves, chopped
  2 fresh red chillies, seeded
    and chopped
  225g/8oz minced (ground) pork
  50g/2oz peeled cooked prawns
    (shrimp), thawed if frozen
  30ml/2 tbsp Thai fish sauce
  5ml/1 tsp granulated sugar
  1 carrot, grated
  50g/2oz piece of canned bamboo
    shoot, drained and chopped
  50g/2oz/⅔ cup beansprouts
  2 spring onions (scallions),
    finely chopped
  15ml/1 tbsp chopped fresh
    coriander (cilantro)
  ground black pepper

1 Make the filling. Drain the soaked mushrooms. Cut off and discard the stems, then chop the caps finely.

2 Place the noodles in a large bowl, cover with boiling water and soak for 10 minutes. Drain the noodles and snip them into 5cm/2in lengths.

3 Heat the oil in a wok, add the garlic and chillies and stir-fry for 30 seconds. Transfer to a plate. Add the pork to the wok and stir-fry until it has browned.

4 Add the mushrooms, noodles and prawns. Stir in the fish sauce and sugar, then add pepper to taste.

5 Tip the mixture into a bowl. Stir in the grated carrot, chopped bamboo shoot, beansprouts, spring onions and chopped coriander. Add the reserved chilli mixture and mix well.

6 Unwrap the spring roll wrappers. Cover them with a dampened dish towel while you are making the rolls, so that they do not dry out, and work on them one at a time. Put the flour in a small bowl and stir in a little water to make a paste. Place a spoonful of the filling in the centre of a spring roll wrapper.

7 Turn the bottom edge over to cover the filling, then fold in the sides. Roll up the wrapper almost to the top, then brush the top edge with the flour paste and seal. Fill the remaining wrappers.

8 Heat the oil in a wok to 190°C/375°F or until a cube of bread browns in about 40 seconds. Fry the spring rolls, in batches, until crisp and golden. Drain on kitchen paper and serve hot with sweet chilli dipping sauce.

Energy 74Kcal/310kJ; Protein 3.1g; Carbohydrate 7.2g, of which sugars 0.7g; Fat 3.8g, of which saturates 0.7g; Cholesterol 10mg; Calcium 13mg; Fibre 0.4g; Sodium 12mg.

FIERY TUNA SPRING ROLLS

THIS MODERN TAKE ON THE CLASSIC SPRING ROLL IS SUBSTANTIAL ENOUGH TO SERVE AS A MAIN MEAL WITH NOODLES AND STIR-FRIED GREENS. THE TUNA AND WASABI FILLING IS FANTASTIC.

SERVES FOUR

INGREDIENTS
  1 large chunk of very fresh thick
    tuna steak
  45ml/3 tbsp light soy sauce
  30ml/2 tbsp wasabi
  16 mangetout (snow peas), trimmed
  8 spring roll wrappers
  sunflower oil, for deep-frying
  soft noodles and stir-fried Asian
    greens, to serve
  soy sauce and sweet chilli sauce,
    for dipping

5 Top the tuna with 2 mangetout and fold over the sides and roll up. Brush the edges of the wrappers to seal.

6 Repeat with the remaining tuna, mangetout and wrappers.

7 Fill a large wok one-third full with oil and heat to 180°C/350°F or until a cube of bread browns in 45 seconds. Working in batches, deep-fry the rolls for 1–2 minutes, until crisp and golden.

8 Drain the rolls on kitchen paper and serve immediately with soft noodles and Asian greens. Serve the spring rolls with side dishes of soy sauce and sweet chilli sauce for dipping.

1 Place the tuna on a board. Using a sharp knife cut it into eight slices, each measuring about 12 x 2.5cm/4½ x 1in.

2 Place the tuna in a large, non-metallic dish in a single layer. Mix together the soy sauce and the wasabi and spoon evenly over the fish. Cover and marinate for 10–15 minutes.

3 Meanwhile, blanch the mangetout in boiling water for about 1 minute, drain and refresh under cold water. Drain and pat dry with kitchen paper.

4 Place a spring roll wrapper on a clean work surface and place a piece of tuna on top, in the centre.

COOK'S TIP
It is important to cut the tuna into neat, even slices. Chilling it briefly in the freezer, and using a very sharp knife or cleaver, makes this easier to achieve.

Energy 171Kcal/717kJ; Protein 14g; Carbohydrate 11.4g, of which sugars 1.7g; Fat 8g, of which saturates 1.3g; Cholesterol 14mg; Calcium 36mg; Fibre 0.8g; Sodium 825mg.

THAI AUBERGINE AND PEPPER TEMPURA WITH SWEET CHILLI DIP

THESE CRUNCHY VEGETABLES IN A BEAUTIFULLY LIGHT BATTER ARE QUICK AND EASY TO MAKE AND TASTE VERY GOOD WITH THE PIQUANT DIP. ALTHOUGH TEMPURA IS A SIGNATURE DISH OF JAPANESE CUISINE, IT HAS NOW BECOME POPULAR THROUGHOUT ASIA, WITH EACH COUNTRY ADDING ITS OWN CHARACTERISTIC TOUCH — IN THE CASE OF THAILAND, THIS CHILLI-FLAVOURED SAUCE.

SERVES FOUR

INGREDIENTS
2 aubergines (eggplants)
2 red (bell) peppers
vegetable oil, for deep-frying
For the tempura batter
250g/9oz/2¼ cups plain
    (all-purpose) flour
2 egg yolks
500ml/17fl oz/2¼ cups iced water
5ml/1 tsp salt
For the dip
150ml/¼ pint/⅔ cup water
10ml/2 tsp granulated sugar
1 fresh red chilli, seeded and
    finely chopped
1 garlic clove, crushed
juice of ½ lime
5ml/1 tsp rice vinegar
35ml/2½ tbsp Thai fish sauce
½ small carrot, finely grated

3 Make the tempura batter. Set aside 30ml/2 tbsp of the flour. Put the egg yolks in a large bowl and beat in the iced water. Tip in the remaining flour with the salt and stir briefly together – the mixture should resemble thick pancake batter but be lumpy and not properly mixed. If it is too thick, add a little more iced water. Do not leave the batter to stand; use it immediately.

4 Pour the oil for deep-frying into a wok or deep-fryer and heat to 190°C/375°F or until a cube of bread, added to the oil, browns in about 40 seconds.

6 Cook the fritters for 3–4 minutes, until they are golden and crisp all over, then lift them out with a metal basket or slotted spoon. Drain thoroughly on kitchen paper and keep hot.

7 Repeat until all the vegetables have been coated in batter and cooked. Serve immediately, with the dip.

1 Using a sharp knife or a mandolin, slice the aubergines into thin batons. Halve, seed and slice the red peppers thinly.

2 Make the dip. Mix together all the ingredients in a bowl and stir until the sugar has dissolved. Cover with clear film (plastic wrap) and set aside.

VARIATIONS
Tempura batter is also good with pieces of fish or whole shellfish, such as large prawns (jumbo shrimp) or baby squid, as well as with a variety of vegetables.

5 Pick up a small, haphazard handful of aubergine batons and pepper slices, dust it with the reserved flour, then dip it into the batter. Immediately drop the batter-coated vegetables into the hot oil, taking care as the oil will froth up furiously. Repeat to make two or three more fritters, but do not cook any more than this at one time, or the oil may overflow.

Energy 404Kcal/1699kJ; Protein 9.4g; Carbohydrate 61g, of which sugars 12.5g; Fat 15.4g, of which saturates 2.4g; Cholesterol 101mg; Calcium 124mg; Fibre 5.8g; Sodium 15mg.

PEA AND POTATO PAKORAS WITH COCONUT AND MINT CHUTNEY

THESE DELICIOUS GOLDEN BITES ARE SOLD AS STREET FOOD THROUGHOUT INDIA. THEY MAKE A WONDERFUL SNACK DRIZZLED WITH THE FRAGRANT COCONUT AND MINT CHUTNEY.

MAKES TWENTY-FIVE

INGREDIENTS
15ml/1 tbsp sunflower oil
20ml/4 tsp cumin seeds
5ml/1 tsp black mustard seeds
1 small onion, finely chopped
10ml/2 tsp grated fresh root ginger
2 fresh green chillies, seeded and
  chopped
600g/1lb 6oz potatoes, peeled, diced
  and boiled until tender
200g/7oz fresh peas
juice of 1 lemon
90ml/6 tbsp chopped fresh coriander
  (cilantro) leaves
115g/4oz/1 cup gram flour
25g/1oz/¼ cup self-raising
  (self-rising) flour
40g/1½oz/⅓ cup rice flour
large pinch of ground turmeric
10ml/2 tsp crushed coriander seeds
350ml/12fl oz/1½ cups water
vegetable oil, for deep-frying
salt and ground black pepper
For the chutney
105ml/7 tbsp coconut cream
200ml/7fl oz/scant 1 cup natural
  (plain) yogurt
50g/2oz fresh mint leaves, finely
  chopped
5ml/1 tsp golden caster
  (superfine) sugar
juice of 1 lime

1 Heat a wok and add the sunflower oil. When hot, add the cumin and mustard seeds and stir-fry for 1–2 minutes.

2 Add the onion, ginger and chillies to the wok and cook for 3–4 minutes. Add the cooked potatoes, stir a few times, then add the peas and stir-fry for 3-4 minutes. Season, then stir in the lemon juice and coriander leaves.

COOK'S TIP
Gram flour is made from ground chickpeas and is widely used in Asian cooking. It is available in most large supermarkets and Asian stores.

3 To make the batter, put the gram flour, self-raising flour and rice flour in a bowl. Season and add the turmeric and coriander seeds. Gradually whisk in the water to make a smooth, thick batter.

4 To make the chutney, place all the ingredients in a blender and process until smooth. Season, then chill.

5 Leave the mixture to cool slightly, then divide into 25 portions. Shape each portion into a ball and chill. To cook the pakoras, fill a wok one-third full of oil and heat to 180°C/350°F. Working in batches, dip the balls in the batter, then drop into the oil and deep-fry for 1–2 minutes. Drain the pakoras on kitchen paper and serve with the chutney.

Energy 126Kcal/525kJ; Protein 4.1g; Carbohydrate 8.3g, of which sugars 2.6g; Fat 8.8g, of which saturates 5.2g; Cholesterol 0mg; Calcium 35mg; Fibre 1.3g; Sodium 16mg.

POTATO, SHALLOT AND GARLIC SAMOSAS WITH GREEN PEAS

MOST SAMOSAS ARE DEEP-FRIED. THESE ARE BAKED, ALTHOUGH THEIR FILLING IS MADE IN A WOK. THEY ARE PERFECT FOR PARTIES, SINCE THE PASTRIES NEED NO LAST-MINUTE ATTENTION.

MAKES TWENTY-FIVE

INGREDIENTS

1 large potato, about 250g/
   9oz, diced
15ml/1 tbsp groundnut
   (peanut) oil
2 shallots, finely chopped
1 garlic clove, finely chopped
60ml/4 tbsp coconut milk
5ml/1 tsp Thai red or green
   curry paste
75g/3oz/¾ cup peas
juice of ½ lime
25 samosa wrappers or 10 x 5cm/
   4 x 2in strips of filo pastry
salt and ground black pepper
oil, for brushing

1 Preheat the oven to 220°C/425°F/ Gas 7. Bring a small pan of water to the boil, add the diced potato, cover and cook for 10–15 minutes, until tender. Drain and set aside.

2 Meanwhile, heat the groundnut oil in a wok and cook the shallots and garlic over a medium heat, stirring occasionally, for 4–5 minutes, until softened and golden.

3 Add the drained diced potato, coconut milk, red or green curry paste, peas and lime juice to the wok. Mash together coarsely with a wooden spoon. Season to taste with salt and pepper and cook over a low heat for 2–3 minutes, then remove the pan from the heat and set aside until the mixture has cooled a little.

4 Lay a samosa wrapper or filo strip flat on the work surface. Brush with a little oil, then place a generous teaspoonful of the mixture in the middle of one end. Turn one corner diagonally over the filling to meet the long edge.

5 Continue folding over the filling, keeping the triangular shape as you work down the strip. Brush with a little more oil if necessary and place on a baking sheet. Prepare all the other samosas in the same way.

6 Bake for 15 minutes, or until the pastry is golden and crisp. Leave to cool slightly before serving.

COOK'S TIP
Many Asian food stores sell what is described as a samosa pad. This is a packet, usually frozen, containing about 50 oblong pieces of samosa pastry. Filo pastry, cut to size, can be used instead.

Energy 42Kcal/178kJ; Protein 1.2g; Carbohydrate 8.5g, of which sugars 0.6g; Fat 0.6g, of which saturates 0.1g; Cholesterol 0mg; Calcium 14mg; Fibre 0.5g; Sodium 4mg.

CORN FRITTERS

SOMETIMES IT IS THE SIMPLEST DISHES THAT TASTE THE BEST. THESE FRITTERS, PACKED WITH CRUNCHY CORN, ARE VERY EASY TO PREPARE AND COOK QUICKLY IN A HOT WOK.

MAKES TWELVE

INGREDIENTS
3 corn cobs, total weight about
    250g/9oz
1 garlic clove, crushed
small bunch fresh coriander
    (cilantro), chopped
1 small fresh red or green chilli,
    seeded and finely chopped
1 spring onion (scallion),
    finely chopped
15ml/1 tbsp soy sauce
75g/3oz/⅔ cup rice flour or plain
    (all-purpose) flour
2 eggs, lightly beaten
60ml/4 tbsp water
oil, for shallow-frying
salt and ground black pepper
sweet chilli sauce, to serve

1 Using a sharp knife, slice the kernels from the cobs and place them in a large bowl. Add the garlic, chopped coriander, red or green chilli, spring onion, soy sauce, flour, beaten eggs and water and mix well. Season with salt and pepper to taste and mix again. The mixture should be firm enough to hold its shape, but not stiff.

2 Heat the oil in a wok. Add spoonfuls of the corn mixture, gently spreading each one out with the back of the spoon to make a roundish fritter. Cook for 1–2 minutes on each side.

3 Drain on kitchen paper and keep hot while frying more fritters in the same way. Serve hot with sweet chilli sauce.

Energy 77Kcal/322kJ; Protein 2.3g; Carbohydrate 7.8g, of which sugars 0.6g; Fat 4.1g, of which saturates 0.6g; Cholesterol 32mg; Calcium 24mg; Fibre 0.8g; Sodium 104mg.

GREEN CURRY PUFFS

SHRIMP PASTE AND GREEN CURRY SAUCE, USED JUDICIOUSLY, GIVE THESE PUFFS THEIR DISTINCTIVE, SPICY, SAVOURY FLAVOUR, AND THE ADDITION OF CHILLI STEPS UP THE HEAT.

MAKES TWENTY-FOUR

INGREDIENTS
   24 small wonton wrappers, about
      8cm/3¼ in square, thawed if frozen
   15ml/1 tbsp cornflour (cornstarch),
      mixed to a paste with 30ml/
      2 tbsp water
   oil, for deep-frying
For the filling
   1 small potato, about 115g/4oz,
      boiled and mashed
   25g/1oz/3 tbsp cooked petits pois
      (baby peas)
   25g/1oz/3 tbsp cooked corn
   few sprigs fresh coriander
      (cilantro), chopped
   1 small fresh red chilli, seeded and
      finely chopped
   ½ lemon grass stalk, finely chopped
   15ml/1 tbsp soy sauce
   5ml/1 tsp shrimp paste or fish sauce
   5ml/1 tsp Thai green curry paste

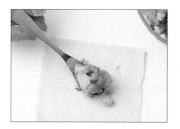

1 Combine the filling ingredients. Lay out one wonton wrapper and place a teaspoon of the filling in the centre.

2 Brush a little of the cornflour paste along two sides of the square. Fold the other two sides over to meet them, then press together to make a triangular pastry and seal in the filling. Make more pastries in the same way.

3 Heat the oil in a wok to 190°C/375°F or until a cube of bread, added to the oil, browns in about 40 seconds. Add the pastries to the oil, a few at a time, and fry them for about 5 minutes, until golden brown.

4 Remove from the wok and drain on kitchen paper. If you intend serving the puffs hot, place them in a low oven while cooking successive batches. The puffs also taste good cold.

COOK'S TIP
Wonton wrappers dry out quickly, so keep them covered, using clear film (plastic wrap), until you are ready to use them.

Energy 69Kcal/291kJ; Protein 1.4g; Carbohydrate 9.9g, of which sugars 0.4g; Fat 3g, of which saturates 0.4g; Cholesterol 1mg; Calcium 22mg; Fibre 0.5g; Sodium 58mg.

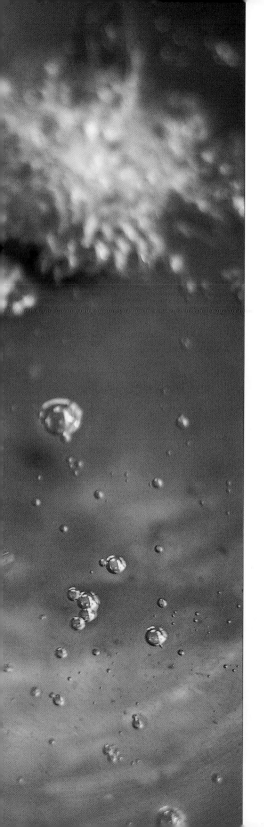

SOUPS AND APPETIZERS

For swift soups, such as those based on ready-made stock or canned bouillon, a wok is ideal. The large surface area makes for rapid evaporation, though, so you need to keep an eye on liquid levels and top up if necessary. This is an area where an electric wok can work wonders. Any preliminary cooking can be done at a high heat, and the thermostat can then be turned down so the soup simmers well. A wide variety of first courses can also be cooked in the wok, from Salmon, Sesame and Ginger Fish Cakes to Steamed Pork Buns with a spicy filling.

TOFU AND BEAN SPROUT SOUP

THIS LIGHT AND REFRESHING SOUP IS VERY QUICK AND EASY TO MAKE IN THE WOK. THE AROMATIC SPICY BROTH IS SIMMERED BRIEFLY AND THEN THE TOFU, BEAN SPROUTS AND NOODLES ARE QUICKLY COOKED. USE FIRM TOFU BECAUSE THE SOFTER VARIETY WILL DISINTEGRATE DURING COOKING.

SERVES FOUR

INGREDIENTS
  150g/5oz dried thick rice noodles
  1 litre/1¾ pints/4 cups
    vegetable stock
  1 fresh red chilli, seeded and finely
    sliced
  15ml/1 tbsp light soy sauce
  juice of 1 small lime
  10ml/2 tsp palm sugar
  5ml/1 tsp thinly sliced garlic
  5ml/1 tsp finely chopped
    fresh root ginger
  200g/7oz firm tofu
  90g/3½oz mung bean sprouts
  30ml/2 tbsp chopped fresh mint
  15ml/1 tbsp chopped fresh
    coriander (cilantro)
  15ml/1 tbsp chopped fresh
    sweet basil
  50g/2oz/½ cup roasted peanuts,
    roughly chopped
  spring onion (scallion) slivers and red
    (bell) pepper slivers, to garnish

1 Place the noodles in a bowl and pour over enough boiling water to cover. Soak for 10–15 minutes, until soft. Drain, rinse and set aside.

2 Place the stock, red chilli, soy sauce, lime juice, palm sugar, garlic and ginger in a wok over a high heat. Bring to the boil, cover, reduce to a low heat and simmer for 10–12 minutes.

3 Meanwhile, cut the firm tofu into neat cubes, using a sharp knife or cleaver. Add the tofu to the soup.

4 Add the drained noodles and bean sprouts to the soup and cook gently for just 2–3 minutes. Remove from the heat and stir in the herbs. Ladle the soup into bowls and scatter over the peanuts. Garnish with spring onion and red pepper slivers if liked.

COOK'S TIP
Palm sugar is dense and crumbly and needs to be grated or melted before use. Soft brown sugar can be substituted.

Energy 266Kcal/1108kJ; Protein 10.5g; Carbohydrate 35.1g, of which sugars 3g; Fat 8.8g, of which saturates 1.4g; Cholesterol 0mg; Calcium 321mg; Fibre 2.4g; Sodium 115mg.

HOT AND SOUR SOUP

ONE OF CHINA'S MOST POPULAR SOUPS, THIS IS FAMED FOR ITS CLEVER BALANCE OF FLAVOURS. THE "HOT" COMES FROM PEPPER; THE "SOUR" FROM VINEGAR. SIMILAR SOUPS ARE FOUND THROUGHOUT ASIA, SOME RELYING ON CHILLIES AND LIME JUICE TO PROVIDE THE ESSENTIAL FLAVOUR CONTRAST.

SERVES SIX

INGREDIENTS
- 4–6 Chinese dried mushrooms
- 2–3 small pieces of cloud ear (wood ear) mushrooms and a few golden needles (lily buds) (optional)
- 115g/4oz pork fillet (tenderloin), cut into fine strips
- 45ml/3 tbsp cornflour (cornstarch)
- 150ml/1/4 pint/2/3 cup water
- 15–30ml/1–2 tbsp sunflower oil
- 1 small onion, finely chopped
- 1.5 litres/2 1/2 pints/6 1/4 cups good quality beef or chicken stock, or 2 × 300g/11oz cans consommé made up to the full quantity with water
- 150g/5oz fresh firm tofu, diced
- 60ml/4 tbsp rice vinegar
- 15ml/1 tbsp light soy sauce
- 1 egg, beaten
- 5 ml/1 tsp sesame oil
- salt and ground white or black pepper
- 2–3 spring onions (scallions), shredded, to garnish

1 Place the dried mushrooms in a bowl, with the pieces of cloud ear and the golden needles, if using. Add sufficient warm water to cover and leave to soak for about 30 minutes.

2 Drain the mushrooms, reserving the soaking water. Cut off and discard the mushroom stems and slice the caps finely. Trim away any tough stem from the wood ears, then chop them finely. Using kitchen string, tie the golden needles into a bundle.

3 Lightly dust the strips of pork fillet with some of the cornflour; mix the remaining cornflour to a smooth paste with the measured water.

4 Heat the oil in a wok and fry the onion until soft. Increase the heat and fry the pork until it changes colour. Add the stock or consommé, mushrooms, soaking water, and cloud ears and golden needles, if using. Bring to the boil, then simmer for 15 minutes.

5 Discard the golden needles, lower the heat and stir in the cornflour paste to thicken. Add the tofu, vinegar, soy sauce, and salt and pepper.

6 Bring the soup to just below boiling point, then drizzle in the beaten egg by letting it drop from a whisk (or to be authentic, the fingertips) so that it forms threads in the soup. Stir in the sesame oil and serve at once, garnished with spring onion shreds.

Energy 103Kcal/429kJ; Protein 7.3g; Carbohydrate 7.3g, of which sugars 0.3g; Fat 5.1g, of which saturates 1g; Cholesterol 44mg; Calcium 135mg; Fibre 0g; Sodium 208mg.

BALINESE VEGETABLE SOUP

THE BALINESE BASE THIS POPULAR SOUP ON BEANS, BUT ANY SEASONAL VEGETABLES CAN BE ADDED OR SUBSTITUTED. THE RECIPE ALSO INCLUDES SHRIMP PASTE, WHICH IS KNOWN LOCALLY AS TERASI.

2 Finely grind the chopped garlic, macadamia nuts or almonds, shrimp paste and the coriander seeds to a paste using a pestle and mortar or in a food processor.

3 Heat a wok, add the oil, and when it is hot, fry the onion until transparent. Remove with a slotted spoon. Add the nut paste to the wok and fry it for 2 minutes without allowing it to brown.

4 Pour in the reserved vegetable water. Spoon off 45–60ml/3–4 tbsp of the cream from the top of the coconut milk and set it aside. Add the remaining coconut milk to the wok, bring to the boil and add the bay leaves. Cook, uncovered, for 15–20 minutes.

SERVES EIGHT

INGREDIENTS

   225g/8oz green beans
   1.2 litres/2 pints/5 cups lightly
     salted water
   1 garlic clove, roughly chopped
   2 macadamia nuts or 4 almonds,
     finely chopped
   1cm/$\frac{1}{2}$in cube shrimp paste
   10–15ml/2–3 tsp coriander seeds,
     dry-fried
   30ml/2 tbsp vegetable oil
   1 onion, finely sliced
   400ml/14fl oz can coconut milk
   2 bay leaves
   225g/8oz/4 cups beansprouts
   8 thin lemon wedges
   30ml/2 tbsp lemon juice
   salt and ground black pepper

1 Trim the beans and cut into small pieces. Bring the lightly salted water to the boil, add the beans to the pan and cook for 3–4 minutes. Drain, reserving the cooking water. Set the beans aside.

COOK'S TIP
Dry-fry the coriander seeds for about 2 minutes until the aroma is released.

5 Just before serving, reserve a few beans, fried onions and beansprouts for garnish and stir the rest into the soup. Add the lemon wedges, reserved coconut cream, lemon juice and seasoning; warm through, stirring well.

6 Pour into individual soup bowls and serve, garnished with the reserved beans, onion and beansprouts.

Energy 63Kcal/263kJ; Protein 2.2g; Carbohydrate 5.2g, of which sugars 4.2g; Fat 3.9g, of which saturates 0.5g; Cholesterol 3mg; Calcium 43mg; Fibre 1.2g; Sodium 84mg.

CRISPY WONTON SOUP

THE FRESHLY COOKED CRISPY WONTONS ARE SUPPOSED TO SIZZLE AND "SING" AS THE HOT FAT HITS THE SOUP, SO ADD THEM JUST BEFORE YOU TAKE THE BOWLS TO THE TABLE.

SERVES SIX

INGREDIENTS

2 cloud ear (wood ear) mushrooms, soaked for 30 minutes in warm water to cover
1.2 litres/2 pints/5 cups home-made chicken stock
2.5cm/1in piece fresh root ginger, peeled and grated
4 spring onions (scallions), chopped
2 rich-green inner spring greens leaves, finely shredded
50g/2oz drained canned bamboo shoots, sliced
25ml/1½ tbsp dark soy sauce
2.5ml/½ tsp sesame oil
salt and ground black pepper
For the filled wontons
5ml/1 tsp sesame oil
½ small onion, finely chopped
10 drained canned water chestnuts, finely chopped
115g/4oz finely minced (ground) pork
24 wonton wrappers
groundnut (peanut) oil, for frying

2 Place the wonton wrappers under a slightly dampened dish towel so that they do not dry out. Next, dampen the edges of a wonton wrapper. Place about 5ml/1 tsp of the filling in the centre of the wrapper. Gather it up like a purse and twist the top or roll up as you would a baby spring roll. Fill the remaining wontons in the same way.

3 To make the soup, drain the cloud ears, discarding the soaking liquid. Trim away any rough stems, then slice thinly.

4 Bring the stock to the boil, add the ginger and the spring onions and simmer for 3 minutes. Add the cloud ears, spring greens, bamboo shoots and soy sauce. Simmer for 10 minutes, then stir in the sesame oil. Season with salt and pepper, cover and keep hot.

5 Heat the oil in a wok to 190°C/375°F and fry the wontons for 3–4 minutes or until they are crisp and golden. Ladle the soup into warmed bowls, share the wontons among them, and serve.

1 Make the filled wontons. Heat the sesame oil in a small pan, add the onion, water chestnuts and pork and fry, stirring occasionally, until the meat is no longer pink. Tip into a bowl, season to taste and leave to cool.

COOK'S TIP
The wontons can be filled up to two hours ahead. Place them in a single layer on a baking sheet dusted with cornflour, to prevent them from sticking, and leave in a cool place.

Energy 108Kcal/456kJ; Protein 6.3g; Carbohydrate 14.4g, of which sugars 1.4g; Fat 3.3g, of which saturates 0.9g; Cholesterol 13mg; Calcium 69mg; Fibre 1.4g; Sodium 249mg.

TOKYO-STYLE RAMEN NOODLES IN SOUP

A WOK IS ALL YOU NEED TO MAKE THIS MULTI-LAYERED JAPANESE SOUP. THERE ARE MANY REGIONAL AND LOCAL VARIATIONS OF RAMEN, THIS IS A LEGENDARY TOKYO VERSION.

SERVES FOUR

INGREDIENTS
  250g/9oz dried ramen noodles
For the soup stock
  4 spring onions (scallions)
  7.5cm/3in fresh root ginger, quartered
  raw bones from 2 chickens, washed
  1 large onion, quartered
  4 garlic cloves, peeled
  1 large carrot, roughly chopped
  1 egg shell
  120ml/4fl oz/½ cup sake
  about 60ml/4 tbsp shoyu
  2.5ml/½ tsp salt
For the cha-shu (pot-roast pork)
  500g/1¼lb pork shoulder, boned
  30ml/2 tbsp vegetable oil
  2 spring onions (scallions), chopped
  2.5cm/1in fresh root ginger, peeled
    and sliced
  15ml/1 tbsp sake
  45ml/3 tbsp shoyu
  15ml/1 tbsp caster (superfine) sugar
For the toppings
  2 hard-boiled eggs
  150g/5oz pickled bamboo shoots,
    soaked for 30 minutes and drained
  ½ nori sheet, broken into pieces
  2 spring onions (scallions), chopped
  ground white pepper
  sesame oil or chilli oil

1 To make the soup stock, bruise the spring onions and ginger by hitting with the side of a large knife or a rolling pin. Pour 1.5 litres/2½ pints/6¼ cups water into a wok and bring to the boil. Add the chicken bones and boil until the colour of the meat changes. Discard the water and wash the bones under water.

2 Wash the wok, bring another 2 litres/3½ pints/9 cups water to the boil and add the bones and the other soup stock ingredients, except for the shoyu and salt. Reduce the heat to low, and simmer for up to 2 hours until the water has reduced by half, skimming off any scum. Strain into a bowl through a sieve lined with muslin (cheesecloth).

3 Make the *cha-shu*. Roll the meat up tightly, to 8cm/3½in in diameter, and tie it with kitchen string.

4 Wash the wok and dry over a high heat. Heat the oil to smoking point in the wok and add the chopped spring onions and ginger. Cook briefly, then add the meat. Turn often to brown the outside evenly.

5 Sprinkle with sake and add 400ml/14fl oz/1⅔ cups water, the shoyu and sugar. Boil, then reduce the heat to low and cover. Cook for 25–30 minutes, turning every 5 minutes. Remove from the heat.

6 Slice the pork into 12 fine slices. Use any leftover pork for another recipe.

7 Shell and halve the boiled eggs, and sprinkle some salt on to the yolks.

8 Pour 1 litre/1¾ pints/4 cups soup stock from the bowl into a large pan. Boil and add the shoyu and salt. Check the seasoning; add more shoyu if required.

9 Wash the wok again and bring 2 litres/3½ pints/9 cups water to the boil. Cook the ramen noodles according to the packet instructions until just soft. Stir constantly to prevent sticking. If the water bubbles up, pour in 50ml/2fl oz/¼ cup cold water. Drain well and divide among four bowls.

10 Pour the soup over the noodles to cover. Arrange half a boiled egg, pork slices, pickled bamboo shoots, and nori on top, and sprinkle with spring onions. Serve with pepper and sesame or chilli oil. Season to taste with a little salt, if you like.

COOK'S TIP
The cooked pork could be finely chopped and minced and used as part of the filling for spring rolls.

Energy 521Kcal/2193kJ; Protein 38.9g; Carbohydrate 55.6g, of which sugars 8.7g; Fat 17.5g, of which saturates 3.2g; Cholesterol 174mg; Calcium 57mg; Fibre 3g; Sodium 843mg.

Chinese Leaf, Meatball and Noodle Broth

This wonderfully fragrant combination of spiced meatballs, noodles and vegetables cooked slowly in a richly flavoured broth makes for a very hearty, warming soup. Serve it as a main course on a cold winter evening, drizzled with chilli oil for a little extra heat. Savoy cabbage can be substituted for Chinese leaves.

SERVES FOUR

INGREDIENTS

10 dried shiitake mushrooms
90g/3½oz bean thread noodles
675g/1½lb minced (ground) beef
10ml/2 tsp finely grated garlic
10ml/2 tsp finely grated fresh
 root ginger
1 fresh red chilli, seeded and
 chopped
6 spring onions (scallions),
 finely sliced
1 egg white
15ml/1 tbsp cornflour (cornstarch)
15ml/1 tbsp Chinese rice wine
30ml/2 tbsp sunflower oil
1.5 litres/2½ pints/6¼ cups chicken
 or beef stock
50ml/2fl oz/¼ cup light soy sauce
5ml/1 tsp sugar
150g/5oz enoki mushrooms, trimmed
200g/7oz Chinese leaves (Chinese
 cabbage) very thinly sliced
salt and ground black pepper
sesame oil and chilli oil,
 to drizzle (optional)

1 Place the dried mushrooms in a bowl and pour over 250ml/8fl oz/1 cup boiling water. Leave to soak for 30 minutes and then squeeze dry, reserving the soaking liquid.

2 Cut the stems from the mushrooms and discard, then thickly slice the caps and set aside.

3 Put the noodles in a large bowl and pour over boiling water to cover. Leave to soak for 3–4 minutes, then drain, rinse and set aside.

4 Place the beef, garlic, ginger, chilli, spring onions, egg white, cornflour, rice wine and seasoning in a food processor. Process to combine well.

5 Transfer the mixture to a bowl and divide into 30 portions, then shape each one into a ball.

6 Heat a wok over a high heat and add the oil. Fry the meatballs, in batches, for 2–3 minutes on each side until lightly browned. Remove with a slotted spoon and drain on kitchen paper.

7 Wipe out the wok and place over a high heat. Add the stock, soy sauce, sugar and shiitake mushrooms with the reserved soaking liquid and bring to the boil.

8 Add the meatballs to the boiling stock, reduce the heat and cook gently for 20–25 minutes.

9 Add the noodles, enoki mushrooms and cabbage to the wok and cook gently for 4–5 minutes. Serve ladled into wide shallow bowls. Drizzle with sesame oil and chilli oil, if liked.

Energy 548Kcal/2279kJ; Protein 36.8g; Carbohydrate 24.9g, of which sugars 3g; Fat 33.3g, of which saturates 12.4g;
Cholesterol 101mg; Calcium 52mg; Fibre 1.7g; Sodium 161mg.

STEAMED OYSTERS WITH ZESTY TOMATO AND CUCUMBER SALSA

A PLATE OF LIGHTLY STEAMED FRESH OYSTERS MAKES A DELICIOUS AND IMPRESSIVE APPETIZER FOR A SPECIAL OCCASION, AND IS EASY TO PREPARE. THE FRESH, ZESTY, AROMATIC SALSA COMPLEMENTS THE DELICATE FLAVOUR AND TEXTURE OF THE OYSTERS PERFECTLY, AND EACH IRRESISTIBLE MOUTHFUL FEELS LIKE THE ULTIMATE INDULGENCE.

SERVES FOUR

INGREDIENTS
  30ml/2 tbsp sunflower oil
  1 garlic clove, crushed
  15ml/1 tbsp light soy sauce
  12–16 oysters
  sea salt, to serve
For the salsa
  1 ripe plum tomato, seeds removed
  ½ small cucumber
  ¼ small red onion
  15ml/1 tbsp very finely chopped
    coriander (cilantro)
  1 small red chilli, seeded and very
    finely chopped
  juice of 1–2 limes
  salt and ground black pepper

1 First prepare the salsa. Finely dice the tomato, cucumber and red onion. Place in a bowl with the chopped coriander and red chilli.

2 Add the lime juice to the bowl and season to taste. Set aside (at room temperature) for 15–20 minutes.

3 In a separate bowl, mix together the sunflower oil, garlic and soy sauce.

COOK'S TIP
To de-seed the tomato, cut it in half around the middle rather than over the top, and then scoop out the seeds using a teaspoon.

4 Carefully open the oysters using a special oyster knife or a strong knife with a short, blunt blade. Arrange the oysters in their half shells in a bamboo steamer and spoon over the sauce.

5 Cover the steamer and place over a wok of simmering water. Steam the oysters for 2–3 minutes.

6 Arrange the oysters on a bed of sea salt, top each with a teaspoonful of the salsa and serve.

Energy 82Kcal/339kJ; Protein 4.5g; Carbohydrate 2.4g, of which sugars 1.3g; Fat 6.1g, of which saturates 0.8g; Cholesterol 21mg; Calcium 60mg; Fibre 0.4g; Sodium 461mg.

LEMON, CHILLI AND HERB STEAMED RAZOR CLAMS

RAZOR CLAMS HAVE BEAUTIFUL STRIPED GOLD AND BROWN TUBULAR SHELLS AND MAKE A WONDERFUL AND UNUSUAL APPETIZER. HERE THEY ARE LIGHTLY STEAMED AND TOSSED IN A FRAGRANT ITALIAN-STYLE DRESSING OF CHILLI, LEMON, GARLIC AND PARSLEY. SERVE WITH CRUSTY BREAD FOR MOPPING UP THE JUICES. FOR A MAIN COURSE, DOUBLE THE QUANTITY.

SERVES FOUR

INGREDIENTS
    12 razor clams
    90–120ml/6–8 tbsp extra virgin
        olive oil
    finely grated rind and juice of
        1 small lemon
    2 garlic cloves, very finely grated
    1 red chilli, seeded and very
        finely chopped
    60ml/4 tbsp chopped flat leaf parsley
    salt and ground black pepper
    mixed salad leaves and crusty bread,
        to serve

1 Wash the razor clams well in plenty of cold running water. Drain and arrange half the clams in a steamer, with the hinge side down.

2 Pour 5cm/2in water into a wok and bring to the boil. Carefully balance the steamer over the water and cover tightly. Steam for 3–4 minutes until the clams have opened.

3 Remove the clams from the wok and keep warm while you steam the remaining clams in the same way.

4 In a bowl, mix together the olive oil, grated lemon rind and juice, garlic, red chilli and flat leaf parsley.

5 Season the dressing well with salt and pepper. Spoon the mixture over the steamed razor clams on plates and serve immediately with a crisp mixed-leaf salad and crusty bread.

Energy 188Kcal/775kJ; Protein 6.1g; Carbohydrate 2.9g, of which sugars 0.5g; Fat 16.9g, of which saturates 2.4g; Cholesterol 20mg; Calcium 47mg; Fibre 1.1g; Sodium 364mg.

STIR-FRIED CLAMS <u>WITH</u> ORANGE <u>AND</u> GARLIC

ZESTY ORANGE JUICE COMBINED WITH PUNGENT GARLIC AND SHALLOTS MAKE SURPRISINGLY GOOD PARTNERS FOR THE SWEET-TASTING SHELLFISH. FRESH, PLUMP CLAMS WILL RELEASE PLENTY OF JUICES WHILE THEY ARE COOKING, SO SERVE THIS TANGY DISH WITH A SPOON, OR WITH SOME CRUSTY BREAD SO YOU CAN MOP UP ALL THE DELICIOUS SAUCE.

SERVES FOUR

INGREDIENTS
  1kg/2¼lb fresh clams
  15ml/1 tbsp sunflower oil
  30ml/2 tbsp finely chopped garlic
  4 shallots, finely chopped
  105ml/7 tbsp vegetable or fish stock
  finely grated rind and
    juice of 1 orange
  salt and ground black pepper
  a large handful of roughly
    chopped flat leaf parsley

COOK'S TIP
To avoid the risk of food poisoning, it is essential that the clams are live before cooking. Tap any open clams with the back of a knife. Any that do not close are dead and so must be discarded; and any that remain closed after cooking should also be thrown away.

1 Wash and scrub the clams under cold running water. Check carefully and discard any that are open and do not close when tapped lightly.

2 Heat a wok over a high heat and add the sunflower oil. When hot, add the garlic, shallots and clams and stir-fry for 4–5 minutes.

3 Add the stock and orange rind and juice to the wok and season well. Cover and cook for 3–4 minutes, or until all the clams have opened. (Discard any unopened clams.)

4 Stir the chopped flat leaf parsley into the clams, then remove from the heat and serve immediately.

Energy 142Kcal/596kJ; Protein 21.4g; Carbohydrate 5.9g, of which sugars 1.6g; Fat 3.8g, of which saturates 0.6g; Cholesterol 84mg; Calcium 121mg; Fibre 1.2g; Sodium 1506mg.

CRAB DIM SUM WITH CHINESE CHIVES

THESE DELECTABLE CHINESE-STYLE DUMPLINGS HAVE A WONDERFULLY STICKY TEXTURE AND MAKE A PERFECT APPETIZER. YOU CAN MAKE THEM IN ADVANCE, STORING THEM IN THE REFRIGERATOR UNTIL READY TO COOK. STEAM THEM JUST BEFORE SERVING, THEN ENJOY THE SENSATION AS YOUR TEETH SINK THROUGH THE SOFT WRAPPER INTO THE FILLING.

SERVES FOUR

INGREDIENTS
150g/5oz fresh white crab meat
115g/4oz minced (ground) pork
30ml/2 tbsp chopped Chinese chives
15ml/1 tbsp finely chopped red
  (bell) pepper
30ml/2 tbsp sweet chilli sauce
30ml/2 tbsp hoisin sauce
24 fresh dumpling wrappers
  (available from Asian stores)
Chinese chives, to garnish
chilli oil and soy sauce, to serve

1 Place the crab meat, pork and chopped chives in a bowl. Add the red pepper, sweet chilli and hoisin sauces.

VARIATION
Use chopped raw tiger prawns (jumbo shrimp) in place of the crab.

2 Working with 2–3 wrappers at a time, put a spoonful of the mixture on to each wrapper. Brush the edges of a wrapper with water and fold over to form a half-moon shape. Press and pleat the edges to seal, and flatten. Cover with a clean, damp dish towel and make the rest.

3 Arrange the dumplings on 3 lightly oiled plates and fit inside 3 tiers of a bamboo steamer.

4 Cover the steamer and place over a wok of simmering water (making sure the water does not touch the steamer). Steam for 8–10 minutes, or until the dumplings are cooked through and become slightly translucent.

5 Divide the dumplings among four plates. Garnish with Chinese chives and serve immediately with chilli oil and soy sauce for dipping.

Energy 166Kcal/700kJ; Protein 14.7g; Carbohydrate 20.5g, of which sugars 1.4g; Fat 3.3g, of which saturates 1.1g; Cholesterol 46mg; Calcium 83mg; Fibre 0.8g; Sodium 287mg.

PARCHMENT-WRAPPED PRAWNS

THESE SUCCULENT PINK PRAWNS COATED IN A FRAGRANT SPICE PASTE MAKE THE PERFECT DISH FOR INFORMAL ENTERTAINING. SERVE THE PRAWNS IN THEIR PAPER PARCELS AND ALLOW YOUR GUESTS TO UNWRAP THEM AT THE TABLE AND ENJOY THE AROMA OF THAI SPICES AS THE PARCEL IS OPENED.

SERVES FOUR

INGREDIENTS

2 lemon grass stalks, very
   finely chopped
5ml/1 tsp galangal, very finely
   chopped
4 garlic cloves, finely chopped
finely grated rind and juice
   of 1 lime
4 spring onions (scallions), chopped
10ml/2 tsp palm sugar
15ml/1 tbsp soy sauce
5ml/1 tsp Thai fish sauce
5ml/1 tsp chilli oil
45ml/3 tbsp chopped fresh coriander
   (cilantro) leaves
30ml/2 tbsp chopped fresh Thai
   basil leaves
1kg/2¼lb raw tiger prawns (jumbo
   shrimp), heads and shells removed
   but with tails left on
basil leaves and lime wedges,
   to garnish

1 Place the lemon grass, galangal, garlic, lime rind and juice and spring onions in a food processor or blender. Blend in short bursts until the mixture forms a coarse paste.

2 Transfer the paste to a large bowl and stir in the palm sugar, soy sauce, fish sauce, chilli oil and chopped herbs.

3 Add the prawns to the paste and toss to coat evenly. Cover and marinate in the refrigerator for 30 minutes–1 hour.

4 Cut out eight 20cm/8in squares of baking parchment. Place one-eighth of the prawn mixture in the centre of each one, then fold over the edges and twist together to make a sealed parcel.

5 Place the parcels in a large bamboo steamer, cover and steam over a wok of simmering water for 10 minutes, or until the prawns are just cooked through. Serve immediately garnished with basil leaves and lime wedges.

Energy 169Kcal/713kJ; Protein 35.4g; Carbohydrate 2.4g, of which sugars 2.4g; Fat 2g, of which saturates 0.3g; Cholesterol 390mg; Calcium 163mg; Fibre 0.2g; Sodium 381mg.

SEAWEED-WRAPPED PRAWN ROLLS

JAPANESE NORI SEAWEED IS USED TO ENCLOSE THE FRAGRANT FILLING OF PRAWNS, WATER CHESTNUTS, AND FRESH HERBS AND SPICES IN THESE PRETTY STEAMED ROLLS. IDEAL FOR ENTERTAINING, THE ROLLS CAN BE PREPARED IN ADVANCE AND STORED IN THE REFRIGERATOR UNTIL READY TO STEAM.

SERVES FOUR

INGREDIENTS

675g/1 ½lb raw tiger prawns (jumbo shrimp), peeled and deveined
5ml/1 tsp finely chopped kaffir lime leaves
1 red chilli, seeded and chopped
5ml/1 tsp finely grated garlic clove
5ml/1 tsp finely grated root ginger
5ml/1 tsp finely grated lime rind
60ml/4 tbsp very finely chopped fresh coriander (cilantro)
1 egg white, lightly beaten
30ml/2 tbsp chopped water chestnuts
4 sheets of nori
salt and ground black pepper
ketjap manis or soy sauce, to serve

1 Place the prawns in a food processor with the lime leaves, red chilli, garlic, ginger, lime rind and coriander. Process until smooth, add the egg white and water chestnuts, season and process again until combined. Transfer the mixture to a bowl, cover and chill for 3–4 hours.

2 Lay the nori sheets on a clean, dry surface and spread the prawn mixture over each sheet, leaving a 2cm/¾in border at one end. Roll up to form tight rolls, wrap in clear film (plastic wrap) and chill for 2–3 hours.

3 Unwrap the rolls and place on a board. Using a sharp knife, cut each roll into 2cm/¾in lengths. Place the slices in a baking parchment-lined bamboo steamer, cover and place over a wok of simmering water (making sure the water does not touch the steamer).

4 Steam the rolls for 6–8 minutes, or until cooked through. Serve warm or at room temperature with a dish of ketjap manis or soy sauce for dipping.

Energy 136Kcal/574kJ; Protein 30.8g; Carbohydrate 0.4g, of which sugars 0.4g; Fat 1.2g, of which saturates 0.2g; Cholesterol 329mg; Calcium 162mg; Fibre 0.7g; Sodium 345mg.

HERB AND CHILLI FISH CUSTARDS

THESE PRETTY LITTLE CUSTARDS MAKE AN UNUSUAL, BEAUTIFULLY PRESENTED AND RATHER EXOTIC
APPETIZER FOR A DINNER PARTY, AND THEY COOK PERFECTLY IN THE WOK.

SERVES FOUR

INGREDIENTS
    2 eggs
    200ml/7fl oz/scant 1 cup
        coconut cream
    60ml/4 tbsp chopped fresh
        coriander (cilantro)
    1 fresh red chilli, seeded and sliced
    15ml/1 tbsp finely chopped
        lemon grass
    2 kaffir lime leaves, finely shredded
    30ml/2 tbsp Thai red curry paste
    1 garlic clove, crushed
    5ml/1 tsp finely grated ginger
    2 spring onions (scallions),
        finely sliced
    300g/11oz mixed firm white fish fillets
        (cod, halibut or haddock), skinned
    200g/7oz raw tiger prawns (jumbo
        shrimp), peeled and deveined
    4–6 pandanus leaves
    salt and ground black pepper
    shredded cucumber, steamed rice
        and soy sauce, to serve

1 Beat the eggs in a bowl, then stir in
the coconut cream, coriander, chilli,
lemon grass, lime leaves, curry paste,
garlic, ginger and spring onions. Finely
chop the fish and roughly chop the
prawns and add to the egg mixture. Stir
well and season.

COOK'S TIP
Pandanus leaves keep the custards from
drying out, and have a floral flavour that
is transferred to the food, but they are
not edible and should be discarded after
the cooking.

2 Grease 4 ramekins and line them with
the pandanus leaves. Divide the fish
mixture between them, then arrange in
a bamboo steamer.

3 Pour 5cm/2in water into a wok and
bring to the boil. Suspend the steamer
over the water, cover, reduce the heat to
low and steam for 25–30 minutes, or
until the fish is cooked through.

4 Serve the custards immediately with
shredded cucumber, a little steamed
rice and soy sauce.

Energy 150Kcal/632kJ; Protein 26.2g; Carbohydrate 2.8g, of which sugars 2.8g; Fat 3.9g, of which saturates 1g; Cholesterol 227mg; Calcium 100mg; Fibre 0.6g; Sodium 234mg.

FISH CAKES WITH CUCUMBER RELISH

THESE WONDERFUL SMALL FISH CAKES ARE A VERY FAMILIAR AND POPULAR APPETIZER IN THAILAND AND INCREASINGLY THROUGHOUT SOUTH-EAST ASIA. THEY ARE USUALLY SERVED WITH THAI BEER.

MAKES ABOUT TWELVE

INGREDIENTS
8 kaffir lime leaves
300g/11oz cod fillet, cut into chunks
30ml/2 tbsp Thai red curry paste
1 egg
30ml/2 tbsp Thai fish sauce
5ml/1 tsp granulated sugar
30ml/2 tbsp cornflour (cornstarch)
15ml/1 tbsp chopped fresh
   coriander (cilantro)
50g/2oz/½ cup green beans,
   thinly sliced
vegetable oil, for deep-frying
For the cucumber relish
60ml/4 tbsp coconut or rice vinegar
50g/2oz/¼ cup granulated sugar
60ml/4 tbsp water
1 head pickled garlic
1cm/½in piece fresh root
   ginger, peeled
1 cucumber, cut into thin batons
4 shallots, thinly sliced

1 Make the cucumber relish. Mix the coconut or rice vinegar, sugar and water in a small pan. Heat gently, stirring constantly until the sugar has completely dissolved. Remove the pan from the heat and leave to cool.

2 Separate the pickled garlic into cloves. Chop the cloves finely, along with the ginger, and place in a bowl. Add the cucumber batons and shallots, pour over the vinegar mixture and mix lightly. Cover and set aside.

3 Reserve five kaffir lime leaves for the garnish and thinly slice the remainder. Put the chunks of fish, curry paste and egg in a food processor and process to a smooth paste. Transfer the mixture to a bowl and stir in the fish sauce, sugar, cornflour, sliced kaffir lime leaves, coriander and green beans. Mix well, then shape the mixture into about twelve 5mm/¼in thick cakes, each measuring about 5cm/2in in diameter.

4 Heat the oil in a wok to 190°C/375°F or until a cube of bread, added to the oil, browns in about 40 seconds. Fry the fish cakes, a few at a time, for about 4–5 minutes, until cooked and evenly brown.

5 Lift out the fish cakes and drain them on kitchen paper. Keep each batch hot while frying successive batches. Garnish with the reserved kaffir lime leaves and serve with the cucumber relish.

Energy 83Kcal/346kJ; Protein 5.5g; Carbohydrate 5.8g, of which sugars 5.6g; Fat 4.4g, of which saturates 0.6g; Cholesterol 27mg; Calcium 15mg; Fibre 0.3g; Sodium 111mg.

SALMON, SESAME AND GINGER FISH CAKES

THESE LIGHT FISH CAKES ARE SCENTED WITH THE EXOTIC FLAVOURS OF SESAME, LIME AND GINGER.
THEY MAKE A TEMPTING APPETIZER SERVED SIMPLY WITH A WEDGE OF LIME FOR SQUEEZING OVER, BUT
ARE ALSO PERFECT FOR A LIGHT LUNCH OR SUPPER, SERVED WITH A CRUNCHY, REFRESHING SALAD.

MAKES TWENTY-FIVE

INGREDIENTS

500g/1¼lb salmon fillet,
  skinned and boned
45ml/3 tbsp dried breadcrumbs
30ml/2 tbsp mayonnaise
30ml/2 tbsp sesame seeds
30ml/2 tbsp light soy sauce
finely grated rind of 2 limes
10ml/2 tsp finely grated
  fresh root ginger
4 spring onions (scallions),
  finely sliced
vegetable oil, for frying
salt and ground black pepper
spring onions (scallions), to garnish
lime wedges, to serve

1 Finely chop the salmon and place
in a bowl. Add the breadcrumbs,
mayonnaise, sesame seeds, soy sauce,
lime rind, ginger and spring onions
and use your fingers to mix well.

2 With wet hands, divide the mixture
into 25 portions and shape each into a
small round cake. Place the cakes on a
baking sheet, lined with baking
parchment, cover and chill for at least
two hours. They can be left overnight.

3 When you are ready to cook the fish
cakes, heat about 5cm/2in vegetable oil
in a wok and fry the fish cakes in
batches, over a medium heat, for 2–3
minutes on each side.

4 Drain the fish cakes well on kitchen
paper and serve warm or at room
temperature, garnished with spring
onion slivers and plenty of lime wedges
for squeezing over.

Energy 83Kcal/343kJ; Protein 4.6g; Carbohydrate 1.6g, of which sugars 0.2g; Fat 6.5g, of which saturates 0.9g; Cholesterol 11mg; Calcium 16mg; Fibre 0.2g; Sodium 117mg.

LETTUCE PARCELS

KNOWN AS SANG CHOY *IN* HONG KONG, *THIS IS A POPULAR* "ASSEMBLE-IT-YOURSELF" *TREAT. THE FILLING — AN IMAGINATIVE BLEND OF TEXTURES AND FLAVOURS — IS SERVED WITH CRISP LETTUCE LEAVES, WHICH ARE SPREAD WITH HOISIN SAUCE AND USED AS WRAPPERS.*

SERVES SIX

INGREDIENTS

2 boneless chicken breast portions,
  total weight about 350g/12oz
4 Chinese dried mushrooms, soaked
  for 30 minutes in warm water
  to cover
30ml/2 tbsp vegetable oil
2 garlic cloves, crushed
6 drained canned water chestnuts,
  thinly sliced
30ml/2 tbsp light soy sauce
5ml/1 tsp Sichuan peppercorns, dry
  fried and crushed
4 spring onions (scallions), finely
  chopped
5ml/1 tsp sesame oil
vegetable oil, for deep-frying
50g/2oz cellophane noodles
salt and ground black pepper
  (optional)
1 crisp lettuce and 60ml/4 tbsp
  hoisin sauce, to serve

1 Remove the skin from the chicken breasts, pat dry and set aside. Chop the chicken into thin strips. Drain the soaked mushrooms. Cut off and discard the mushroom stems; slice the caps finely and set aside.

2 Heat the oil in a wok. Add the garlic, then add the chicken and stir-fry until the pieces are cooked through and no longer pink. Check by lifting one of the thicker chicken strips out of the wok and cutting it in half.

3 Add the sliced mushrooms, water chestnuts, soy sauce and peppercorns. Toss for 2–3 minutes, then season, if needed. Stir in half of the spring onions, then the sesame oil. Remove from the heat and keep warm.

4 Heat the oil for deep-frying to 190°C/375°F. Cut the chicken skin into strips, deep-fry until very crisp and drain on kitchen paper. Add the noodles to the hot oil, deep-fry until crisp. Transfer to a plate lined with kitchen paper.

5 Crush the noodles and put in a serving dish. Top with the chicken skin, chicken mixture and the remaining spring onions. Arrange the lettuce leaves on a large platter.

6 Toss the chicken and noodles to mix. Invite guests to take one or two lettuce leaves, spread the inside with hoisin sauce and add a spoonful of filling, turning in the sides of the leaves and rolling them into a parcel. The parcels are traditionally eaten in the hand.

Energy 195Kcal/821kJ; Protein 28.7g; Carbohydrate 7.5g, of which sugars 0.6g; Fat 5.5g, of which saturates 0.9g; Cholesterol 82mg; Calcium 11mg; Fibre 0.1g; Sodium 428mg.

STEAMED PORK BUNS

THESE DELICIOUSLY LIGHT STUFFED BUNS ARE A POPULAR STREET SNACK SOLD THROUGHOUT CHINA. THE SOFT TEXTURE OF THE BUN CONTRASTS WONDERFULLY WITH THE SPICED MEAT FILLING INSIDE. THEY MAKE AN UNUSUAL ALTERNATIVE TO RICE AND, ONCE COOKED, CAN BE REHEATED IN THE STEAMER.

SERVES FOUR

INGREDIENTS
30ml/2 tbsp golden caster
  (superfine) sugar
10ml/2 tsp dried yeast
300g/11oz/2¾ cups plain
  (all-purpose) flour
30ml/2 tbsp sunflower oil
10ml/2 tsp baking powder
For the filling
250g/9oz pork sausages
15ml/1 tbsp barbecue sauce
30ml/2 tbsp oyster sauce
15ml/1 tbsp sweet chilli sauce
15ml/1 tbsp Chinese rice wine
15ml/1 tbsp hoisin sauce
5ml/1 tsp chilli oil

1 To make the dough pour 250ml/ 8fl oz/1 cup warm water into a mixing bowl. Add the sugar and stir to dissolve. Stir in the yeast, cover and leave in a warm place for 15 minutes.

2 Sift the flour into a large mixing bowl and make a well in the centre. Add the sugar and yeast mixture to it with the sunflower oil. Stir the mixture together using your fingers and turn out on to a lightly floured surface.

3 Knead the dough for 8–10 minutes until smooth and elastic. Place in a lightly oiled bowl, cover with a dish towel and leave to rise in a warm place for 3–4 hours.

4 When risen, place the dough on a lightly floured surface, punch down and shape into a large circle. Sprinkle the baking powder in the centre, bring all the edges towards the centre and knead for 6–8 minutes. Divide the dough into 12 balls, cover with a clean, damp dish towel and set aside.

5 Squeeze the sausage meat from the casings into a large bowl and stir in the barbecue sauce, oyster sauce, sweet chilli sauce, rice wine, hoisin sauce and chilli oil. Mix thoroughly, using your fingers to combine.

6 Press each dough ball to form a round, 12cm/4½in in diameter. Place a large spoonful of the pork mixture in the centre of each round and bring the edges up to the centre, press together to seal and form a bun shape.

7 Arrange the buns on several layers of a large bamboo steamer, cover and steam over a wok of simmering water for 20–25 minutes, or until they are puffed up and the pork is cooked through. Serve immediately.

VARIATION
You can replace the sausage meat with cooked, peeled prawns. Place the same quantity of prawns in a food blender and process with the other ingredients until you have a rough paste.

Energy 588Kcal/2468kJ; Protein 14g; Carbohydrate 76.4g, of which sugars 14g; Fat 27.3g, of which saturates 8.5g; Cholesterol 29mg; Calcium 137mg; Fibre 2.8g; Sodium 722mg.

STUFFED THAI OMELETTES

OMELETTES ARE USUALLY COOKED IN A FLAT PAN, BUT A WOK WORKS EQUALLY WELL. THE HOT CHILLI IN THIS RECIPE MAKES AN INTERESTING CONTRASTING FLAVOUR TO THE DELICATE EGG.

3 To make the omelettes, put the eggs and Thai fish sauce in a bowl and beat together lightly with a fork.

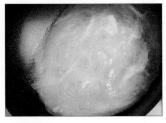

4 Heat 15ml/1 tbsp of the oil in an omelette pan or wok over a medium heat. When the oil is very hot, but not smoking, add half the beaten egg mixture and immediately tilt the pan or wok to spread the egg into a thin, even layer over the base. Cook over a medium heat until the omelette is just set and the underside is golden.

5 Spoon half the filling into the centre of the omelette. Fold into a neat square parcel by bringing the opposite sides of the omelette towards each other. Slide the parcel on to a serving dish, folded side down. Make another omelette parcel in the same way. Garnish with the coriander sprigs and chillies. Cut each omelette in half to serve.

COOK'S TIP
Making the omelette in a wok is actually easier than in a regular frying pan, since the sloping sides make it simple to flip the omelette over the filling.

SERVES FOUR

INGREDIENTS
 30ml/2 tbsp groundnut
  (peanut) oil
 2 garlic cloves, finely chopped
 1 small onion, finely chopped
 225g/8oz minced (ground) pork
 30ml/2 tbsp Thai fish sauce
 5ml/1 tsp granulated sugar
 2 tomatoes, peeled and chopped
 15ml/1 tbsp chopped fresh
  coriander (cilantro)
 ground black pepper
 fresh coriander (cilantro)
  sprigs and sliced fresh red
  chillies, to garnish
For the omelettes
 5 eggs
 15ml/1 tbsp Thai fish sauce
 30ml/2 tbsp groundnut
  (peanut) oil

1 Heat the oil in a wok, add the garlic and onion, and cook over a medium heat, for 3–4 minutes, until soft. Add the pork and cook until lightly browned.

2 Stir in the Thai fish sauce, sugar and tomatoes, season with pepper and simmer over a low heat until thickened. Mix in the coriander. Remove the wok from the heat, cover to keep warm and set aside while you make the omelettes.

Energy 305Kcal/1267kJ; Protein 19.2g; Carbohydrate 4.8g, of which sugars 4.5g; Fat 23.6g, of which saturates 5.7g; Cholesterol 275mg; Calcium 48mg; Fibre 0.7g; Sodium 130mg.

GOLDEN CORN CAKES WITH AIOLI

EAST MEETS WEST IN THESE CRISP, MOUTHWATERING CAKES THAT BRING TOGETHER CREAMY GOAT'S CHEESE AND TANGY MEDITERRANEAN PEPPERS IN THE ASIAN WOK.

SERVES FOUR

INGREDIENTS
    300g/11oz/scant 2 cups fresh
      corn kernels
    200g/7oz/scant 1 cup ricotta cheese
    200g/7oz/scant 1 cup goat's
      cheese, crumbled
    30ml/2 tbsp thyme leaves
    50g/2oz/½ cup plain
      (all-purpose) flour
    1 large (US extra large) egg,
      lightly beaten
    150g/5oz natural dried breadcrumbs
    vegetable oil, for deep-frying
    salt and ground black pepper
For the aioli
    2 red (bell) peppers, halved
      and seeded
    2 garlic cloves, crushed
    250ml/8fl oz/1 cup mayonnaise

3 Place the breadcrumbs on a plate. Roll 15ml/1 tbsp of the corn mixture into a ball, flatten slightly and coat in the breadcrumbs. Place on baking parchment and chill for 30 minutes.

4 Fill a wok one-third full of oil and heat to 180°C/350°F (or until a cube of bread, dropped into the oil, browns in 45 seconds). Working in batches, deep-fry the corn cakes for 1–2 minutes, until golden. Drain well on kitchen paper and serve with the aioli.

COOK'S TIP
If you deep-fry regularly, you will soon learn to judge when the oil has reached optimum temperature. If you need reassurance, buy a deep-fat thermometer. The safest and most reliable are those that can be clipped to the side of the wok before the oil is hot.

1 Make the aioli. Preheat the grill (broiler) to medium-high and cook the peppers, skin-side up, for 8–10 minutes, until the skins blister. Place the peppers in a plastic bag for 10 minutes and then peel away the skin. Place the flesh in a food processor with the garlic and mayonnaise and blend until fairly smooth. Transfer to a bowl and chill.

2 In a bowl, combine the corn, cheeses and thyme, then stir in the flour and egg and season well.

COOK'S TIP
If you're short on time, make the aioli with bottled peppers.

Energy 1048Kcal/4363kJ; Protein 26.1g; Carbohydrate 68.2g, of which sugars 17.3g; Fat 76.5g, of which saturates 22g; Cholesterol 162mg; Calcium 156mg; Fibre 3.9g; Sodium 1091mg.

THAI TEMPEH CAKES <u>WITH</u> DIPPING SAUCE

*MADE FROM SOYA BEANS, TEMPEH IS SIMILAR TO TOFU BUT HAS A NUTTIER TASTE. HERE, IT IS
COMBINED WITH A FRAGRANT BLEND OF LEMON GRASS, CORIANDER AND GINGER TO MAKE TASTY
LITTLE RISSOLES THAT GO VERY WELL WITH THE LIGHT DIPPING SAUCE THAT ACCOMPANIES THEM.*

MAKES EIGHT

INGREDIENTS

1 lemon grass stalk, outer leaves
   removed and inside finely chopped
2 garlic cloves, chopped
2 spring onions (scallions),
   finely chopped
2 shallots, finely chopped
2 fresh red chillies, seeded and
   finely chopped
2.5cm/1in piece fresh root ginger,
   finely chopped
60ml/4 tbsp chopped fresh coriander
   (cilantro), plus extra to garnish
250g/9oz/2¼ cups tempeh, thawed if
   frozen, sliced
15ml/1 tbsp fresh lime juice
5ml/1 tsp granulated sugar
45ml/3 tbsp plain (all-purpose) flour
1 large (US extra large) egg,
   lightly beaten
salt and freshly ground black pepper
vegetable oil, for frying

For the dipping sauce
45ml/3 tbsp mirin (see Cook's Tip)
45ml/3 tbsp white wine vinegar
2 spring onions (scallions),
   thinly sliced
15ml/1 tbsp granulated sugar
2 fresh red chillies, seeded and
   finely chopped
30ml/2 tbsp chopped fresh
   coriander (cilantro)
large pinch of salt

1 Make the dipping sauce. Mix together
the mirin, vinegar, spring onions, sugar,
chillies, coriander and salt in a small
bowl. Cover with clear film (plastic
wrap) and set aside until ready to serve.

COOK'S TIP

Mirin is a sweet rice wine from Japan. It
has quite a delicate flavour and is used
for cooking. Rice wine for drinking,
called sake, is rather more expensive.
Both are available from Asian food
stores. If you cannot locate mirin, dry
sherry can be used instead, although the
results will not be quite the same.

2 Place the lemon grass, garlic, spring
onions, shallots, chillies, ginger and
coriander in a food processor or
blender, then process to a coarse paste.
Add the tempeh, lime juice and sugar
and process until combined. Add the
flour and egg, with salt and pepper to
taste. Process again until the mixture
forms a coarse, sticky paste.

3 Scrape the paste into a bowl. Take
one-eighth of the mixture at a time and
form it into rounds with your hands.

4 Heat a little oil in a wok, then fry the
tempeh cakes for 5–6 minutes, turning
once, until golden. Drain on kitchen
paper. Transfer to a platter, garnish and
serve with the sauce.

Energy 79Kcal/332kJ; Protein 4.5g; Carbohydrate 9.1g, of which sugars 4.3g; Fat 2.3g, of which saturates 0.4g; Cholesterol 26mg; Calcium 192mg; Fibre 0.8g; Sodium 15mg.

SON-IN-LAW EGGS

THE FASCINATING NAME FOR THIS DISH COMES FROM A STORY ABOUT A PROSPECTIVE BRIDEGROOM WHO VERY MUCH WANTED TO IMPRESS HIS FUTURE MOTHER-IN-LAW AND DEVISED A NEW RECIPE BASED ON THE ONLY DISH HE KNEW HOW TO MAKE — BOILED EGGS.

SERVES FOUR TO SIX

INGREDIENTS
30ml/2 tbsp vegetable oil
6 shallots, thinly sliced
6 garlic cloves, thinly sliced
6 fresh red chillies, sliced
oil, for deep-frying
6 hard-boiled eggs, shelled
salad leaves, to serve
sprigs of fresh coriander (cilantro),
  to garnish

For the sauce
75g/3oz/6 tbsp palm sugar or light
  muscovado (brown) sugar
75ml/5 tbsp Thai fish sauce
90ml/6 tbsp tamarind paste mixed
  with a little warm water

COOK'S TIP
Chillies' heat depends on which type is used and whether you include the seeds.

1 Make the sauce. Put the sugar, fish sauce and tamarind juice in a pan. Bring to the boil, stirring until the sugar dissolves, lower the heat and simmer for 5 minutes. Taste and add more sugar, fish sauce or tamarind juice, if needed. Transfer the sauce to a bowl.

2 Heat the vegetable oil in a frying pan and cook the shallots, garlic and chillies for 5 minutes. Transfer to a bowl.

3 Heat the oil in a wok to 190°C/375°F or until a cube of bread, added to the oil, browns in about 40 seconds. Deep-fry the eggs until golden. Remove and drain on kitchen paper.

4 Cut the eggs in quarters and arrange them on a bed of leaves. Drizzle with the sauce and sprinkle over the shallot mixture. Garnish with coriander sprigs and serve immediately.

Energy 180Kcal/752kJ; Protein 7.3g; Carbohydrate 18g, of which sugars 17.1g; Fat 9.4g, of which saturates 2g; Cholesterol 190mg; Calcium 50mg; Fibre 0.5g; Sodium 666mg.

RICE PAPER PARCELS WITH WILTED CHOI SUM

TRANSLUCENT RICE PAPER MAKES A WONDERFULLY CRISP WRAPPING FOR THE LIGHTLY SPICED VEGETABLE AND TOFU FILLING. TAKE CARE, AS THE PAPERS ARE VERY BRITTLE AND EASILY DAMAGED.

SERVES FOUR

INGREDIENTS

30ml/2 tbsp sunflower oil
90g/3½oz shiitake mushrooms, stalks
  discarded and finely chopped
30ml/2 tbsp chopped garlic
90g/3½oz water chestnuts,
  finely chopped
90g/3½oz firm tofu, finely chopped
2 spring onions (scallions),
  finely chopped
½ red (bell) pepper, seeded and
  finely chopped
50g/2oz mangetouts (snow peas),
  finely chopped
15ml/1 tbsp light soy sauce
15ml/1 tbsp sweet chilli sauce
45ml/3 tbsp chopped fresh
  coriander (cilantro)
30ml/2 tbsp chopped fresh
  mint leaves
90ml/6 tbsp plain
  (all-purpose) flour
12 medium rice paper wrappers
sunflower oil, for deep-frying
500g/1¼lb choi sum or Chinese
  greens, roughly sliced or chopped
egg fried rice, to serve

1 Heat the oil in a large wok over a high heat and add the chopped mushrooms. Stir-fry for 3–4 minutes, add the garlic and fry for 1 minute.

2 Add the water chestnuts, tofu, spring onions, red pepper and mangetout to the wok, and stir-fry for 2–3 minutes.

3 Add the soy and sweet chilli sauces to the wok. Remove from the heat and stir in the chopped coriander and mint. Leave to cool completely.

4 Place the flour in a bowl and stir in 105ml/7 tbsp of cold water to make a thick, smooth paste.

5 Fill a large bowl with warm water and dip a rice paper wrapper in it for a few minutes until softened. Remove and drain on a dish towel.

6 Divide the filling into 12 portions and spoon one portion on to the softened rice wrapper. Fold in each side and roll up tightly. Seal the ends with a little of the flour paste. Repeat with the remaining wrappers and filling.

7 Fill a wok one-third full with the oil and heat to 180ºC/350ºF or until a cube of bread, dropped into the oil, browns in 40 seconds. Working in batches of 2–3, deep-fry the parcels for 3 minutes until crisp and lightly browned. Drain well on kitchen paper and keep warm.

8 Pour off most of the oil, reserving 30ml/2 tbsp. Place the wok over a medium heat and add the choi sum. Stir-fry for 3–4 minutes. Divide among four warmed bowls and top with the parcels. Serve immediately with egg fried rice.

Energy 252Kcal/1051kJ; Protein 10.2g; Carbohydrate 34.6g, of which sugars 6.6g; Fat 8.5g, of which saturates 1g; Cholesterol 0mg; Calcium 448mg; Fibre 6.8g; Sodium 313mg.

POULTRY DISHES

The wok is an excellent cooking vessel for chicken and

poultry dishes, as its fast cooking ability retains the flavour

and moistness of the meat. Poultry's mild taste also makes

it a good protein to mix with robust oriental spices and

flavours. This chapter ranges from fast and simple stir-fries

such as Cashew Chicken to slow-cooked dishes like

Southern Thai Chicken Curry and Adobo of Chicken and

Pork. The wok doubles as a deep-fryer when Lemon and

Sesame Chicken is on the menu, a dish children will love,

and serves as a steamer for Lotus-leaf Parcels filled with

Chicken, Rice and Vegetables, or Orange and Ginger

Glazed Poussins, both of which are perfect for a

sophisticated supper party.

CHICKEN AND LEMON GRASS CURRY

QUICK-COOK CURRIES, SUCH AS THIS THAI SPECIALITY, WORK WELL IN A WOK, ESPECIALLY IF YOU USE AN ELECTRIC APPLIANCE, WHICH ALLOWS YOU TO ADJUST THE HEAT FOR SUCCESSFUL SIMMERING.

SERVES FOUR

INGREDIENTS
45ml/3 tbsp vegetable oil
2 garlic cloves, crushed
500g/1¼lb skinless, chicken thighs, boned and chopped into small pieces
45ml/3 tbsp Thai fish sauce
120ml/4fl oz/½ cup chicken stock
5ml/1 tsp granulated sugar
1 lemon grass stalk, chopped into 4 sticks and lightly crushed
5 kaffir lime leaves, rolled into cylinders and thinly sliced across, plus extra to garnish
chopped roasted peanuts and chopped fresh coriander (cilantro), to garnish
For the curry paste
1 lemon grass stalk, coarsely chopped
2.5cm/1in piece fresh galangal, peeled and coarsely chopped
2 kaffir lime leaves, chopped
3 shallots, coarsely chopped
6 coriander (cilantro) roots, coarsely chopped
2 garlic cloves
2 fresh green chillies, seeded and coarsely chopped
5ml/1 tsp shrimp paste
5ml/1 tsp ground turmeric

1 Make the curry paste. Place all the ingredients in a large mortar, or food processor, and pound with the pestle or process to a smooth paste.

2 Heat the vegetable oil in a wok or large, heavy frying pan, add the garlic and cook over a low heat, stirring frequently, until golden brown. Be careful not to let the garlic burn or it will taste bitter. Add the curry paste and stir-fry with the garlic for about 30 seconds more.

3 Add the chicken pieces to the pan and stir until thoroughly coated with the curry paste. Stir in the Thai fish sauce and chicken stock, with the sugar, and cook, stirring constantly, for 2 minutes more.

4 Add the lemon grass and lime leaves, reduce the heat and simmer for 10 minutes. If the mixture begins to dry out, add a little more stock or water.

5 Remove the lemon grass, if you like. Spoon the curry into four dishes, garnish with the lime leaves, peanuts and coriander and serve immediately.

Energy 229Kcal/959kJ; Protein 31.3g; Carbohydrate 4.3g, of which sugars 3.4g; Fat 9.7g, of which saturates 1.4g; Cholesterol 94mg; Calcium 32mg; Fibre 0.5g; Sodium 397mg.

YELLOW CHICKEN CURRY

*THE PAIRING OF SLIGHTLY SWEET COCONUT MILK AND FRUIT WITH SAVOURY CHICKEN AND SPICES
IS AT ONCE A COMFORTING, REFRESHING AND EXOTIC COMBINATION.*

SERVES FOUR

INGREDIENTS
- 300ml/½ pint/1¼ cups
  chicken stock
- 30ml/2 tbsp tamarind paste mixed
  with a little warm water
- 15ml/1 tbsp granulated sugar
- 200ml/7fl oz/scant 1 cup
  coconut milk
- 1 green papaya, peeled, seeded and
  thinly sliced
- 250g/9oz skinless chicken breast
  fillets, diced
- juice of 1 lime
- lime slices, to garnish

For the curry paste
- 1 fresh red chilli, seeded and
  coarsely chopped
- 4 garlic cloves, coarsely chopped
- 3 shallots, coarsely chopped
- 2 lemon grass stalks, sliced
- 5cm/2in piece fresh turmeric,
  coarsely chopped, or 5ml/1 tsp
  ground turmeric
- 5ml/1 tsp shrimp paste
- 5ml/1 tsp salt

2 Pour the stock into a wok or medium pan and bring it to the boil. Stir in the curry paste. Bring back to the boil and add the tamarind juice, sugar and coconut milk. Add the papaya and chicken and cook over a medium to high heat for about 15 minutes, stirring frequently, until the chicken is cooked.

3 Stir in the lime juice, transfer to a warm dish and serve immediately, garnished with lime slices.

1 Make the yellow curry paste. Put the red chilli, garlic, shallots, lemon grass and turmeric in a mortar or food processor. Add the shrimp paste and salt. Pound or process to a paste, adding a little water if necessary.

COOK'S TIP
Fresh turmeric resembles root ginger in appearance and is a member of the same family. When preparing it, wear gloves to protect your hands from staining.

Energy 149Kcal/633kJ; Protein 17.2g; Carbohydrate 18.9g, of which sugars 17.2g; Fat 1.1g, of which saturates 0.3g; Cholesterol 50mg; Calcium 70mg; Fibre 2.8g; Sodium 153mg.

SOUTHERN THAI CHICKEN CURRY

THIS IS A MILD COCONUT CURRY FLAVOURED WITH TURMERIC, CORIANDER AND CUMIN SEEDS, WHICH COMBINES THE CULINARY INFLUENCES OF MALAYSIA AND NEIGHBOURING THAILAND.

SERVES FOUR

INGREDIENTS
  60ml/4 tbsp vegetable oil
  1 large garlic clove, crushed
  1 chicken, weighing about 1.5kg/
    3–3½lb, chopped into
    12 large pieces
  400ml/14fl oz/1⅔ cups
    coconut cream
  250ml/8fl oz/1 cup chicken stock
  30ml/2 tbsp Thai fish sauce
  30ml/2 tbsp sugar
  juice of 2 limes
To garnish
  2 small fresh red chillies, seeded and
    finely chopped
  1 bunch spring onions (scallions),
    thinly sliced
For the curry paste
  5ml/1 tsp dried chilli flakes
  2.5ml/½ tsp salt
  5cm/2in piece fresh turmeric or
    5ml/1 tsp ground turmeric
  2.5ml/½ tsp coriander seeds
  2.5ml/½ tsp cumin seeds
  5ml/1 tsp shrimp paste

1 First make the curry paste. Put all the ingredients in a mortar, food processor or spice grinder and pound, process or grind to a smooth paste.

2 Heat the oil in a wok or frying pan and cook the garlic until golden. Add the chicken and cook until golden. Remove the chicken and set aside.

3 Reheat the oil and add the curry paste and then half the coconut cream. Cook for a few minutes until fragrant.

4 Return the chicken to the wok or pan, add the stock, mixing well, then add the remaining coconut cream, the fish sauce, sugar and lime juice. Stir well and bring to the boil, then lower the heat and simmer for 15 minutes.

5 Turn the curry into four warm serving bowls and sprinkle with the chopped fresh chillies and spring onions to garnish. Serve immediately.

COOK'S TIP
Shrimp paste has a very powerful flavour and should always be cooked before eating. Its strong, salty flavour mellows when cooked, but it still has a powerful kick, and should be used with care. Store, well wrapped, in the fridge.

Energy 686Kcal/2849kJ; Protein 46.8g; Carbohydrate 12.8g, of which sugars 12.8g; Fat 50g, of which saturates 12.8g; Cholesterol 246mg; Calcium 67mg; Fibre 0g; Sodium 352mg.

STIR-FRIED CHICKEN WITH BASIL AND CHILLI

THIS QUICK AND EASY CHICKEN DISH FROM THAILAND OWES ITS SPICY FLAVOUR TO FRESH CHILLIES
AND ITS PUNGENCY TO THAI BASIL, WHICH HAS A LOVELY AROMA WITH HINTS OF LIQUORICE.

2 Add the pieces of chicken to the wok or pan, in batches if necessary, and stir-fry until the chicken changes colour.

3 Stir in the fish sauce, soy sauce and sugar. Continue to stir-fry the mixture for 3–4 minutes, or until the chicken is fully cooked and golden brown.

4 Stir in the fresh Thai basil leaves. Spoon the mixture on to a warm platter, or into individual dishes. Garnish with the chopped chillies and deep-fried Thai basil and serve immediately.

SERVES FOUR TO SIX

INGREDIENTS
45ml/3 tbsp vegetable oil
4 garlic cloves, thinly sliced
2–4 fresh red chillies, seeded and
finely chopped
450g/1lb skinless chicken breast
fillets, cut into bitesize pieces
45ml/3 tbsp Thai fish sauce
10ml/2 tsp dark soy sauce
5ml/1 tsp granulated sugar
10–12 fresh Thai basil leaves
2 fresh red chillies, seeded and
finely chopped, and about 20 deep-
fried Thai basil leaves, to garnish

1 Heat the oil in a wok or large, heavy frying pan. Add the garlic and chillies and stir-fry over a medium heat for 1–2 minutes until the garlic is golden. Take care not to let the garlic burn, otherwise it will taste bitter.

COOK'S TIP
To deep-fry Thai basil leaves, first make sure that the leaves are completely dry or they will splutter when added to the oil. Heat vegetable or groundnut (peanut) oil in a wok or deep-fryer to 190°C/375°F or until a cube of bread, added to the oil, browns in about 40 seconds. Add the leaves and deep-fry them briefly until they are crisp and translucent – this will take only about 30–40 seconds, so watch them carefully. Lift out the leaves using a slotted spoon or wire basket and leave them to drain on kitchen paper before using.

Energy 138Kcal/576kJ; Protein 18.3g; Carbohydrate 1.9g, of which sugars 1.8g; Fat 6.4g, of which saturates 0.9g; Cholesterol 53mg; Calcium 6mg; Fibre 0.1g; Sodium 579mg.

CASHEW CHICKEN

ONE OF THE MOST POPULAR ITEMS ON ANY CHINESE RESTAURANT MENU, CASHEW CHICKEN IS EASY TO RECREATE AT HOME. IT IS IMPORTANT TO HAVE THE WOK VERY HOT BEFORE ADDING THE CHICKEN OR IT WILL STEW RATHER THAN STIR-FRY. A CARBON STEEL WOK WILL GIVE GOOD RESULTS.

SERVES FOUR TO SIX

INGREDIENTS
  450g/1lb skinless chicken breast
    fillets
  1 red (bell) pepper
  2 garlic cloves
  4 dried red chillies
  30ml/2 tbsp vegetable oil
  30ml/2 tbsp oyster sauce
  15ml/1 tbsp soy sauce
  pinch of granulated sugar
  1 bunch spring onions (scallions), cut
    into 5cm/2in lengths
  175g/6oz/1½ cups cashews, roasted
  coriander (cilantro) leaves,
    to garnish

1 Remove and discard the skin from the chicken breasts and trim off any excess fat. With a sharp knife, cut the chicken into bitesize pieces and set aside.

2 Halve the red pepper, scrape out the seeds and membranes and discard, then cut the flesh into 2cm/¾in dice. Peel and thinly slice the garlic and chop the dried red chillies.

3 Preheat a wok and then heat the oil. The best way to do this is to drizzle a "necklace" of oil around the inner rim of the wok, so that it drops down to coat the entire inner surface. Make sure the coating is even by swirling the wok.

4 Add the garlic and dried chillies to the wok and stir-fry over a medium heat until golden. Do not let the garlic burn, otherwise it will taste bitter.

5 Add the chicken to the wok and stir-fry until it is cooked through, then add the red pepper. If the mixture is very dry, add a little water.

6 Stir in the oyster sauce, soy sauce and sugar. Add the spring onions and cashew nuts. Stir-fry for 1–2 minutes more, until heated through. Spoon into a warm dish and serve immediately, garnished with the coriander leaves.

COOK'S TIP
Cashews are also valued for the "fruit" under which each nut grows. Although they are known as cashew apples, these so-called fruits are actually bulbous portions of the stem. They may be pink, red or yellow in colour and the crisp, sweet flesh can be eaten raw or made into a refreshing drink. Cashew apples – and undried nuts – are rarely seen outside their growing regions.

Energy 314Kcal/1307kJ; Protein 24.7g; Carbohydrate 10.2g, of which sugars 6.2g; Fat 19.6g, of which saturates 3.7g; Cholesterol 53mg; Calcium 24mg; Fibre 1.7g; Sodium 268mg.

CRISPY FIVE-SPICE CHICKEN

TENDER STRIPS OF CHICKEN FILLET, WITH A DELICATELY SPICED RICE FLOUR COATING, BECOME DELICIOUSLY CRISP AND GOLDEN WHEN SHALLOW-FRIED IN A HOT WOK. THEY MAKE A GREAT MEAL SERVED ON A BED OF STIR-FRIED NOODLES WITH SWEET PEPPERS AND BROCCOLI.

SERVES FOUR

INGREDIENTS
200g/7oz thin egg noodles
30ml/2 tbsp sunflower oil
2 garlic cloves, very thinly sliced
1 fresh red chilli, seeded and sliced
½ red (bell) pepper, seeded and very
  thinly sliced
300g/11oz carrots, peeled and
  cut into thin strips
300g/11oz Chinese broccoli
  or Chinese greens, roughly sliced
45ml/3 tbsp hoisin sauce
45ml/3 tbsp soy sauce
15ml/1 tbsp caster (superfine) sugar
4 skinless chicken breast fillets,
  cut into strips
2 egg whites, lightly beaten
115g/4oz/1 cup rice flour
15ml/1 tbsp five-spice powder
salt and ground black pepper
vegetable oil, for frying

1 Cook the noodles in boiling water for 2–4 minutes, or according to the packet instructions, drain and set aside.

2 Heat a wok, add the sunflower oil, and when it is hot add the garlic, chilli, red pepper, carrots and the broccoli or greens. Stir-fry over a high heat for 2–3 minutes.

3 Add the sauces and sugar to the wok and cook for a further 2–3 minutes. Add the drained noodles, toss to combine, then remove from the heat, cover and keep warm.

4 Dip the chicken strips into the egg white. Combine the rice flour and five-spice powder in a shallow dish and season. Add the chicken strips to the flour mixture and toss to coat.

5 Heat about 2.5cm/1in oil in a clean wok. When hot, shallow-fry the chicken for 3–4 minutes until crisp and golden.

6 To serve, divide the noodle mixture between warmed plates or bowls and top each serving with the chicken.

VARIATION
The coating also works well on thin strips of fish. When frying the fish, it is best to cook just a few pieces at once, so the oil stays hot. Use a draining rack clipped to the side of the wok, and drain each batch while cooking the next.

Energy 679Kcal/2849kJ; Protein 43.9g; Carbohydrate 75.8g, of which sugars 17g; Fat 23.2g, of which saturates 3.7g; Cholesterol 103mg; Calcium 96mg; Fibre 6.3g; Sodium 1207mg.

LEMON AND SESAME CHICKEN

*THESE DELICATE STRIPS OF CHICKEN ARE AT THEIR BEST IF YOU
HAVE TIME TO LEAVE THEM TO MARINATE OVERNIGHT SO THAT
THEY CAN REALLY SOAK UP THE FLAVOURS. THE SUBTLE FRAGRANCE
OF LEMON PERFECTLY COMPLEMENTS THE RICH TASTE OF FRIED
CHICKEN AND THE NUTTY SESAME SEEDS.*

SERVES FOUR

INGREDIENTS

4 large chicken breast portions,
   skinned and cut into strips
15ml/1 tbsp light soy sauce
15ml/1 tbsp Chinese rice wine
2 garlic cloves, crushed
10ml/2 tsp finely grated fresh
   root ginger
1 egg, lightly beaten
150g/5oz cornflour (cornstarch)
sunflower oil, for deep-frying
toasted sesame seeds, to sprinkle
rice or noodles, to serve

For the sauce

15ml/1 tbsp sunflower oil
2 spring onions (scallions),
   finely sliced
1 garlic clove, crushed
10ml/2 tsp cornflour (cornstarch)
90ml/6 tbsp chicken stock
10ml/2 tsp finely grated lemon rind
30ml/2 tbsp lemon juice
10ml/2 tsp sugar
2.5ml/½ tsp sesame oil
salt

1 Place the chicken strips in a large,
non-metallic bowl. Mix together the light
soy sauce, rice wine, garlic and ginger
and pour over the chicken. Toss
together to combine.

2 Cover the bowl of chicken with clear
film (plastic wrap) and place in the
refrigerator for 8–10 hours, or overnight
if that is more convenient.

3 When ready to cook, add the beaten
egg to the chicken and mix well, then
tip the mixture into a colander to drain
off any excess marinade and egg.

4 Place the cornflour in a large plastic
bag and add the chicken pieces. Shake
it vigorously to coat the chicken strips
thoroughly.

5 Fill a wok one-third full of sunflower
oil and heat to 180ºC/350ºF (or until a
cube of bread, dropped into the oil,
browns in 45 seconds).

6 Deep-fry the chicken, in batches,
for 3–4 minutes. Lift out the chicken
using a slotted spoon and drain on
kitchen paper. Reheat the oil and deep-
fry the chicken once more, in batches,
for 2–3 minutes. Remove with a slotted
spoon and drain on kitchen paper. Pour
the oil out and wipe out the wok with
kitchen paper.

7 To make the sauce, heat the wok,
then add the sunflower oil. When the oil
is hot add the spring onions and garlic
and stir-fry for 1–2 minutes. Mix
together the cornflour, stock, lemon rind
and juice, sugar, sesame oil and salt
and pour into the wok.

8 Cook over a high heat for 2–3 minutes
until thickened. Return the chicken to
the wok, toss lightly to coat with sauce,
and sprinkle over the toasted sesame
seeds. Serve with rice or noodles.

Energy 229Kcal/959kJ; Protein 31.3g; Carbohydrate 4.3g, of which sugars 3.4g; Fat 9.7g, of which saturates 1.4g;
Cholesterol 94mg; Calcium 32mg; Fibre 0.5g; Sodium 397mg.

SICHUAN CHICKEN WITH KUNG PO SAUCE

THIS RECIPE, WHICH HAILS FROM THE SICHUAN REGION OF WESTERN CHINA, HAS BECOME ONE OF THE CLASSIC RECIPES IN THE CHINESE REPERTOIRE. THE COMBINATION OF YELLOW SALTED BEANS AND HOISIN, SPIKED WITH CHILLI, MAKES FOR A VERY TASTY AND SPICY SAUCE.

SERVES THREE

INGREDIENTS

2–3 skinless chicken breast fillets,
  cut into neat pieces
1 egg white
10ml/2 tsp cornflour
2.5ml/½ tsp salt
30ml/2 tbsp yellow salted beans
15ml/1 tbsp hoisin sauce
5ml/1 tsp light brown sugar
15ml/1 tbsp rice wine or
  medium-dry sherry
15ml/1 tbsp wine vinegar
4 garlic cloves, crushed
150ml/¼ pint/⅔ cup chicken stock
45ml/3 tbsp sunflower oil
2–3 dried chillies, broken into
  small pieces
115g/4oz roasted cashew nuts
fresh coriander (cilantro), to garnish

1 Lightly whisk the egg white in a dish, whisk in the cornflour and salt, then add the chicken and stir until coated.

2 In a separate bowl, mash the salted beans with a spoon. Stir in the hoisin sauce, brown sugar, rice wine or sherry, vinegar, garlic and stock.

COOK'S TIP
Peanuts are the classic ingredient in this dish, but cashew nuts have an even better flavour and have become popular both in home cooking and in restaurants. Use roasted peanuts if you prefer.

3 Heat a wok, add the oil and then stir-fry the chicken, turning constantly, for about 2 minutes until tender. Either drain the chicken over a bowl to collect excess oil, or lift out each piece with a slotted spoon, leaving the oil in the wok.

4 Heat the reserved oil and fry the chilli pieces for 1 minute. Return the chicken to the wok and pour in the bean sauce mixture. Bring to the boil and stir in the cashew nuts. Spoon into a heated serving dish and garnish with coriander leaves.

Energy 490Kcal/2040kJ; Protein 37.7g; Carbohydrate 12.4g, of which sugars 2.6g; Fat 31.9g, of which saturates 5.6g; Cholesterol 82mg; Calcium 24mg; Fibre 1.9g; Sodium 204mg.

FRAGRANT TARRAGON CHICKEN

CHICKEN THIGHS HAVE A PARTICULARLY GOOD FLAVOUR AND STAND UP WELL TO THE ROBUST INGREDIENTS USED IN THIS DISH. FEW PEOPLE THINK OF USING A WOK FOR BRAISING, BUT IT WORKS EXTREMELY WELL, PROVIDED YOU HAVE A SUITABLE LID THAT FITS SNUGLY.

SERVES FOUR

INGREDIENTS

3 heads of garlic, cloves separated
but still in their skins
2 onions, quartered
8 chicken thighs
90ml/6 tbsp chopped fresh
tarragon leaves
8 small pickled lemons,
30–45ml/2–3 tbsp olive oil
750ml/1¼ pints/3 cups
dessert wine
250ml/8fl oz/1 cup chicken stock
sea salt and ground black pepper
sautéed potatoes and steamed yellow
or green beans, to serve

1 Arrange the garlic cloves and quartered onions in the base of a large wok and lay the chicken thighs over the top in a single layer. Sprinkle the tarragon over the top of the chicken, season well with salt and ground black pepper and drizzle over the olive oil.

2 Chop the pickled lemons and add to the wok. Pour the wine and stock over and bring to the boil. Cover the wok tightly, reduce the heat to low and simmer gently for 1½ hours. Remove from the heat, and leave to stand, covered, for 10 minutes. Serve with sautéed potatoes and steamed beans.

Energy 390Kcal/1630kJ; Protein 24g; Carbohydrate 21.8g, of which sugars 17.2g; Fat 8.8g, of which saturates 1.6g; Cholesterol 105mg; Calcium 86mg; Fibre 2.7g; Sodium 122mg.

SPICED COCONUT CHICKEN WITH CARDAMOM

YOU NEED TO PLAN AHEAD TO MAKE THIS LUXURIOUS CHICKEN CURRY. THE CHICKEN LEGS ARE MARINATED OVERNIGHT IN AN AROMATIC BLEND OF YOGURT AND SPICES BEFORE BEING GENTLY SIMMERED WITH HOT GREEN CHILLIES IN CREAMY COCONUT MILK. SERVE WITH RICE.

SERVES FOUR

INGREDIENTS

1.6kg/3½lb large chicken drumsticks
30ml/2 tbsp sunflower oil
400ml/14fl oz/1⅔ cups coconut milk
4–6 large green chillies, halved
45ml/3 tbsp finely chopped
  coriander (cilantro)
salt and ground black pepper
natural (plain) yogurt, to drizzle

For the marinade
15ml/1 tbsp cardamom pods
15ml/1 tbsp grated fresh root ginger
10ml/2 tsp crushed garlic
105ml/7 tbsp natural (plain) yogurt
2 fresh green chillies, seeded and
  chopped
5ml/1 tsp ground cumin
5ml/1 tsp ground coriander
5ml/1 tsp ground turmeric
finely grated rind and juice of 1 lime

1 Make the marinade. Smash the cardamom pods in a pestle so the seeds separate from the husks. Discard the husks. Put the cardamom seeds, ginger, garlic, half the yogurt, green chillies, cumin, coriander, turmeric and lime rind and juice in a blender. Process until smooth, season and pour into a large glass bowl.

2 Add the chicken to the bowl and toss to coat. Cover and marinate in the refrigerator for 6–8 hours, or overnight.

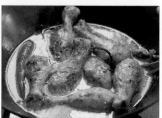

3 Heat the oil in a large, non-stick wok over a low heat. Add the chicken, reserving the marinade. Add the chicken to the wok and brown all over, then add the coconut milk, remaining yogurt, reserved marinade and green chillies and bring to the boil.

4 Reduce the heat and simmer gently, uncovered, for 30–35 minutes. Check the seasoning, adding more if needed. Stir in the coriander, ladle into warmed bowls and serve drizzled with yogurt.

Energy 691Kcal/2906kJ; Protein 107.7g; Carbohydrate 6.2g, of which sugars 6.1g; Fat 26.5g, of which saturates 6.5g; Cholesterol 540mg; Calcium 142mg; Fibre 0.6g; Sodium 805mg.

ADOBO OF CHICKEN AND PORK

FOUR INGREDIENTS ARE ESSENTIAL IN AN ADOBO, ONE OF THE BEST-LOVED RECIPES IN THE FILIPINO REPERTOIRE. THEY ARE VINEGAR, GARLIC, PEPPERCORNS AND BAY LEAVES. THE PLANTAIN CHIPS ARE THE TRADITIONAL ACCOMPANIMENT BUT SWEET POTATO CHIPS CAN BE SERVED INSTEAD.

SERVES FOUR

INGREDIENTS
1 chicken, about 1.4kg/3lb, or
   4 chicken quarters
350g/12oz pork leg steaks (with fat)
10ml/2 tsp sugar
60ml/4 tbsp sunflower oil
75ml/5 tbsp wine or cider vinegar
4 plump garlic cloves, crushed
1/2 tsp black peppercorns,
   crushed lightly
15ml/1 tbsp light soy sauce
4 bay leaves
2.5ml/1/2 tsp annatto seeds, soaked
   in 30ml/2 tbsp boiling water, or
   2.5ml/1/2 tsp ground turmeric
salt
For the plantain chips
1–2 large plantains and/or
   1 sweet potato
vegetable oil, for deep-frying

3 Add the vinegar, garlic, peppercorns, soy sauce and bay leaves and stir well. Strain the annatto seed liquid and stir it into the wok, stir in the turmeric. Add salt to taste. Bring to the boil, cover, lower the heat and simmer the chicken for 30–35 minutes. When the chicken is cooked through, remove the lid and simmer for 10 minutes more to reduce the liquid a little.

4 Meanwhile, prepare the plantain chips. Heat the oil in a wok or deep-fryer to 195°C/390°F. Peel the plantains and slice them into rounds or chips. Deep-fry them, in batches if necessary, until cooked but not brown. Drain on kitchen paper. When ready to serve, reheat the oil and refry the plantains until crisp – it will take only seconds. Drain and serve with the adobo.

1 Wipe the chicken and cut into eight even-size pieces, or halve the chicken quarters, if using. Cut the pork into neat pieces. Spread out all the meat on a board, sprinkle lightly with sugar and set aside.

2 Heat the oil in a wok and fry the chicken and pork pieces, in batches if necessary, until they are golden on both sides.

COOK'S TIP
Sprinkling the chicken lightly with sugar turns the skin beautifully brown when fried, but do not have the oil too hot to begin with or they will over-brown.

Energy 676Kcal/2825kJ; Protein 60.2g; Carbohydrate 28.8g, of which sugars 8.1g; Fat 36.2g, of which saturates 6g; Cholesterol 178mg; Calcium 38mg; Fibre 1.7g; Sodium 503mg.

Chicken Rendang

THIS SPICY RECIPE MAKES A MARVELLOUS DISH FOR A BUFFET. SERVE IT WITH PRAWN CRACKERS OR WITH BOILED RICE AND DEEP-FRIED ANCHOVIES, ACAR PICKLE OR A SELECTION OF SAMBALS.

SERVES FOUR

INGREDIENTS
1 chicken, about 1.4kg/3lb
5ml/1 tsp sugar
75g/3oz/1 cup desiccated (dry,
  unsweeted, shredded) coconut
4 small red or white onions,
  roughly chopped
2 garlic cloves, chopped
2.5cm/1in piece fresh root ginger,
  peeled and sliced
1–2 lemon grass stalks, root trimmed
2.5cm/1in piece fresh galangal,
  peeled and sliced
75ml/5 tbsp groundnut (peanut) oil
  or vegetable oil
10–15ml/2–3 tsp chilli powder, or
  to taste
400ml/14fl oz can coconut milk
10ml/2 tsp salt
fresh chives and deep-fried
  anchovies, to garnish

1 Joint the chicken into 8 pieces and remove the skin, sprinkle with the sugar and leave to stand for 1 hour.

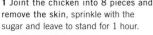

2 Dry-fry the coconut in a wok or large frying pan over medium to low heat, turning all the time until it is crisp and golden. Place the fried coconut in a food processor and process to an oily paste. Transfer to a bowl and reserve.

3 Add the onions, garlic and ginger to the processor. Cut off the lower 5cm/2in of the lemon grass, chop and add to the processor with the galangal. Process to a fine paste.

4 Heat the oil in a wok or large pan and fry the onion mixture for a few minutes. Reduce the heat, stir in the chilli powder and cook for 2–3 minutes, stirring constantly. Spoon in 120ml/4fl oz/½ cup of the coconut milk and add salt to taste.

5 As soon as the mixture bubbles, add the chicken pieces, turning them until they are well coated with the spices. Pour in the remaining coconut milk, stirring constantly to prevent curdling.

6 Bruise the top of the lemon grass stalks and add to the wok or pan. Cover and cook gently for 40–45 minutes until the chicken is tender.

7 Just before serving, stir in the coconut paste. Bring to just below boiling point, then simmer for 5 minutes. Transfer to a serving bowl and garnish with fresh chives and deep-fried anchovies.

Energy 501Kcal/2098kJ; Protein 55.4g; Carbohydrate 7.2g, of which sugars 7.2g; Fat 28.1g, of which saturates 12.5g; Cholesterol 158mg; Calcium 45mg; Fibre 2.6g; Sodium 1233mg.

TANGY CHICKEN SALAD

*WHEN YOU'VE GOT A WOK, MAKING A FRESH AND LIVELY DISH LIKE THIS ONE IS EASY. THE SALAD IS
IDEAL FOR A LIGHT LUNCH ON A HOT AND LAZY SUMMER'S DAY. THE DRESSING IS DELICIOUS.*

SERVES FOUR TO SIX

INGREDIENTS
    4 skinless chicken breast fillets
    2 garlic cloves, crushed
    30ml/2 tbsp soy sauce
    30ml/2 tbsp vegetable oil
    115g/4oz/½ cup water
      chestnuts, sliced
    50g/2oz/½ cup cashew nuts, roasted
      and coarsely chopped
    4 shallots, thinly sliced
    4 kaffir lime leaves, thinly sliced
    1 lemon grass stalk, thinly sliced
    5ml/1 tsp chopped fresh galangal
    1 large fresh red chilli, seeded and
      finely chopped
    2 spring onions (scallions),
      thinly sliced
    10–12 fresh mint leaves, torn
    1 lettuce, separated into leaves,
      to serve
    2 fresh red chillies to garnish
For the dressing
    120ml/4fl oz/½ cup coconut
      cream
    30ml/2 tbsp Thai fish sauce
    juice of 1 lime
    30ml/2 tbsp palm sugar or light
      muscovado (brown) sugar

1 Place the chicken in a large dish. Rub
with the garlic and soy sauce and
drizzle with 15ml/1 tbsp of the oil.
Cover and marinate for 1–2 hours.

2 Heat the remaining oil in a wok or
frying pan and stir-fry the chicken for
3–4 minutes on each side, or until
cooked. Remove and set aside to cool.

3 In a pan, heat the coconut cream,
fish sauce, lime juice and sugar. Stir
until the sugar has dissolved; set aside.

4 Tear the cooked chicken into strips
and put it in a bowl. Add the water
chestnuts, cashew nuts, shallots, kaffir
lime leaves, lemon grass, galangal, red
chilli, spring onions and mint leaves.

5 Pour the coconut dressing over the
mixture and toss well. Serve the chicken
on a bed of lettuce leaves and garnish
with seeded and sliced red chillies.

Energy 216Kcal/905kJ; Protein 26.2g; Carbohydrate 7.8g, of which sugars 6.6g; Fat 9.1g, of which saturates 1.6g; Cholesterol 70mg; Calcium 23mg; Fibre 0.7g; Sodium 453mg.

LOTUS LEAF PARCELS FILLED WITH CHICKEN, RICE AND VEGETABLES

THE LOTUS LEAVES IMPART A DELICIOUS SMOKY FLAVOUR TO THE RICE IN THIS DISH. YOU CAN BUY THE DRIED LEAVES FROM ASIAN SUPERMARKETS. THE PARCELS MAKE A GREAT LUNCH OR SUPPER.

SERVES FOUR

INGREDIENTS

2 large lotus leaves
300g/11oz/1½ cups Thai jasmine
  rice
400ml/14fl oz/1⅔ cups vegetable
  or chicken stock
8 dried shiitake mushrooms
15ml/1 tbsp sunflower oil
200g/7oz skinless chicken thigh
  fillets, cut into small cubes
50g/2oz pancetta, cubed
3 garlic cloves, finely sliced
10ml/2 tsp finely grated
  fresh root ginger
50g/2oz carrots, cut into thin batons
50g/2oz mangetouts (snow peas),
  sliced down the middle
60ml/4 tbsp light soy sauce
15ml/1 tbsp Chinese rice wine
5ml/1 tsp cornflour (cornstarch)

1 Place the lotus leaves in a large bowl and pour over enough hot water to cover. Leave to soak for 1½ hours. Drain and cut in half, then set aside.

2 Place the rice in a wok and pour over the stock. Bring to the boil, then reduce the heat, cover and cook gently for 10 minutes. Remove from the heat.

3 Soak the mushrooms in boiling water for 15 minutes, drain, reserving the liquid. Squeeze them dry, discard the stems and thinly slice the caps.

4 Add the oil to a clean wok and place over a high heat. Add the chicken and pancetta and stir-fry for 2–3 minutes, until lightly browned. Add the garlic, ginger, carrots, mangetout and mushrooms and stir-fry for 30 seconds.

5 Add half the soy sauce, the rice wine and 60ml/4 tbsp of the reserved mushroom liquid to the wok.

6 Combine the cornflour with 15ml/1 tbsp cold water, add to the wok and cook for a few minutes until the mixture thickens. Add the rice and the remaining soy sauce and mix well.

7 Place the lotus leaves on a clean work surface (brown side down) and divide the chicken mixture among them. Fold in the sides of the leaves, then roll up and place the parcels, seam side down, in a baking parchment-lined bamboo steamer.

8 Cover the steamer and place over a wok of simmering water for about 20 minutes (replenishing the water in the wok if necessary). Serve the parcels immediately and unwrap at the table.

VARIATION
Use cooked broad (fava) beans instead of mangetouts, popping them out of their skins before adding to the wok.

Energy 377Kcal/1581kJ; Protein 20.7g; Carbohydrate 63.7g, of which sugars 2.4g; Fat 4g, of which saturates 1.2g; Cholesterol 43mg; Calcium 31mg; Fibre 0.8g; Sodium 1082mg.

SCENTED CHICKEN WRAPS

FOR SHEER SOPHISTICATION, THESE LEAF-WRAPPED CHICKEN BITES TAKE A LOT OF BEATING. THEY ARE SURPRISINGLY EASY TO MAKE AND CAN BE DEEP-FRIED IN MINUTES IN THE WOK.

SERVES FOUR

INGREDIENTS
   400g/14oz skinless chicken thighs,
      boned
   45ml/3 tbsp soy sauce
   30ml/2 tbsp finely grated garlic
   15ml/1 tbsp cumin
   15ml/1 tbsp ground coriander
   15ml/1 tbsp golden caster
      (superfine) sugar
   5ml/1 tsp finely grated fresh
      root ginger
   1 fresh bird's eye chilli
   30ml/2 tbsp oyster sauce
   15ml/1 tbsp Thai fish sauce
   1 bunch of pandanus leaves, to wrap
   vegetable oil, for deep-frying
   sweet chilli sauce, to serve

1 Using a cleaver or sharp knife, cut the chicken into bitesize pieces and place in a large mixing bowl.

2 Place the soy sauce, garlic, cumin, coriander, sugar, ginger, chilli, oyster sauce and fish sauce in a blender and process until smooth. Pour over the chicken, cover and leave to marinate in the refrigerator for 6-8 hours.

3 When ready to cook, drain the chicken from the marinade and wrap each piece in a pandanus leaf (you will need to cut the leaves to size) and secure with a cocktail stick (toothpick).

4 Fill a wok one-third full of oil and heat to 180°C/350°F or until a cube of bread, dropped into the oil, browns in 45 seconds. Carefully add the chicken parcels, 3–4 at a time, and deep-fry for 3–4 minutes, or until cooked through. Drain on kitchen paper and serve with the chilli sauce. (Do not eat the leaves!)

COOK'S TIP
Pandanus leaves are usually available from Asian supermarkets.

Energy 159Kcal/669kJ; Protein 24.5g; Carbohydrate 6.8g, of which sugars 6.6g; Fat 3.9g, of which saturates 0.6g; Cholesterol 70mg; Calcium 10mg; Fibre 0.1g; Sodium 1055mg.

HIJIKI SEAWEED AND CHICKEN

THE TASTE OF HIJIKI IS SOMEWHERE BETWEEN RICE AND VEGETABLE. IT GOES WELL WITH MEAT OR TOFU PRODUCTS, ESPECIALLY WHEN IT'S STIR-FRIED IN THE WOK FIRST WITH A LITTLE OIL.

SERVES TWO

INGREDIENTS

90g/3½oz dried hijiki seaweed
150g/5oz chicken breast portion
½ small carrot, about 5cm/2in
15ml/1 tbsp vegetable oil
100ml/3fl oz/scant ½ cup instant
  dashi powder plus 1.5ml/¼ tsp
  dashi-no-moto
30ml/2 tbsp sake
30ml/2 tbsp caster (superfine) sugar
45ml/3 tbsp shoyu
a pinch of cayenne pepper

1 Soak the hijiki in cold water for about 30 minutes. When ready to cook, it is easily crushed between the fingers. Pour into a sieve and wash under running water. Drain.

2 Peel the skin from the chicken and par-boil the skin in rapidly boiling water for 1 minute, then drain. With a sharp knife, shave off all the yellow fat from the skin. Discard the clear membrane between the fat and the skin as well. Cut the skin into thin strips about 5mm/¼in wide and 2.5cm/1in long. Cut the meat into small, bitesize chunks.

3 Peel and chop the carrot into long, narrow matchsticks.

4 Heat the oil in a wok or frying pan and stir-fry the strips of chicken skin for 5 minutes, or until golden and curled up. Add the chicken meat and keep stirring until the colour changes.

5 Add the hijiki and carrot, then stir-fry for a further minute. Add the remaining ingredients. Lower the heat and toss over the heat for 5 minutes more.

6 Remove the wok from the heat and leave to stand for about 10 minutes. Serve in small individual bowls. Sprinkle with cayenne pepper.

COOK'S TIP
Chicken skin is sometimes discarded because of its high calorie content. However, in this dish the thick yellow fat is removed from the skin before cooking, thus greatly reducing the fat content. The skin curls and becomes crisp when fried, rather like pork crackling. It tastes good but can be omitted if preferred.

Energy 224Kcal/942kJ; Protein 19g; Carbohydrate 19.8g, of which sugars 19.4g; Fat 6.4g, of which saturates 1g; Cholesterol 52mg; Calcium 24mg; Fibre 0.6g; Sodium 1658mg.

CHIANG MAI NOODLES

AN INTERESTING NOODLE DISH FROM THAILAND THAT COMBINES SOFT, BOILED NOODLES WITH CRISP DEEP-FRIED ONES AND ADDS THE CLASSIC THAI CONTRAST OF SWEET, HOT AND SOUR FLAVOURS.

SERVES FOUR

INGREDIENTS
  250ml/8fl oz/1 cup coconut cream
  15ml/1 tbsp magic paste
  5ml/1 tsp Thai red curry paste
  450g/1lb chicken thigh meat,
    chopped into small pieces
  30ml/2 tbsp dark soy sauce
  2 red (bell) peppers, seeded and
    finely diced
  600ml/1 pint/2½ cups chicken or
    vegetable stock
  90g/3½oz fresh or dried rice noodles
For the garnishes
  vegetable oil, for deep-frying
  90g/3½oz fine dried rice noodles
  2 pickled garlic cloves, chopped
  small bunch fresh coriander
    (cilantro), chopped
  2 limes, cut into wedges

1 Pour the coconut cream into a large wok and bring to the boil over a medium heat. Continue to boil, stirring frequently, for 8–10 minutes, until the milk separates and an oily sheen appears on the surface.

2 Add the magic paste and red curry paste and cook, stirring constantly, for 3–5 seconds, until fragrant.

3 Add the chicken and toss over the heat until sealed on all sides. Stir in the soy sauce and the diced peppers and stir-fry for 3–4 minutes. Pour in the stock. Bring to the boil, then lower the heat and simmer for 10–15 minutes, until the chicken is fully cooked.

4 Meanwhile, make the noodle garnish. Heat the oil in a wok to 190°C/375°F or until a cube of bread, added to the oil, browns in 40 seconds. Break all the noodles in half, then divide them into four portions. Add one portion at a time to the hot oil. They will puff up on contact. As soon as they are crisp, lift the noodles out with a slotted spoon and drain on kitchen paper.

5 Bring a large pan of water to the boil and cook the fresh or dried noodles until tender, following the instructions on the packet. Drain well, divide among four warmed individual dishes, then spoon the curry sauce over them. Top each portion with a cluster of fried noodles. Sprinkle the chopped pickled garlic and coriander over the top and serve immediately, offering lime wedges for squeezing.

COOK'S TIP
Magic paste is a commercial product sold in jars in Asian stores. It is a blend of garlic, coriander (cilantro) root and white pepper. This combination of flavours is widely used in Thai home cooking. When mixed with red curry paste, magic paste gives a great flavour to this combination of chicken, red (bell) peppers and noodles.

Energy 245Kcal/1034kJ; Protein 29.4g; Carbohydrate 27.6g, of which sugars 9g; Fat 1.8g, of which saturates 0.6g; Cholesterol 79mg; Calcium 35mg; Fibre 1.4g; Sodium 677mg.

SOUTHERN CURRIED NOODLES

CHICKEN OR PORK CAN BE USED IN THIS TASTY DISH. IT IS SO QUICK AND EASY TO PREPARE AND COOKS IN NEXT TO NO TIME, MAKING IT THE PERFECT SNACK FOR BUSY PEOPLE.

SERVES TWO

INGREDIENTS
  30ml/2 tbsp vegetable oil
  10ml/2 tsp magic paste
  1 lemon grass stalk, finely chopped
  5ml/1 tsp Thai red curry paste
  90g/3½oz skinless chicken breast
    fillets or pork fillet (tenderloin),
    sliced into slivers
  30ml/2 tbsp light soy sauce
  400ml/14fl oz/1⅔ cups coconut milk
  2 kaffir lime leaves, rolled into
    cylinders and thinly sliced
  250g/9oz dried medium egg noodles
  90g/3½oz Chinese leaves (Chinese
    cabbage), shredded
  90g/3½oz spinach or watercress,
    shredded
  juice of 1 lime
  small bunch fresh coriander
    (cilantro), chopped

1 Heat the oil in a wok or large, heavy frying pan. Add the magic paste and lemon grass and stir-fry over a low to medium heat for 4–5 seconds, until they give off their aroma.

2 Stir in the curry paste, then add the chicken or pork. Stir-fry over a medium to high heat for 2 minutes, until the chicken or pork is coated in the paste and seared on all sides.

3 Add the soy sauce, coconut milk and sliced lime leaves. Bring to a simmer, then add the noodles. Simmer gently for 4 minutes, tossing the mixture occasionally to make sure that the noodles cook evenly.

4 Add the Chinese leaves and the spinach or watercress. Stir well. Add the lime juice. Spoon into a warmed bowl, sprinkle with the coriander and serve.

Energy 709Kcal/2989kJ; Protein 29.5g; Carbohydrate 102.1g, of which sugars 14.6g; Fat 23.1g, of which saturates 4.8g; Cholesterol 69mg; Calcium 251mg; Fibre 5.5g; Sodium 1666mg.

CURRIED CHICKEN AND RICE

THIS SIMPLE ONE-WOK MEAL IS PERFECT FOR CASUAL ENTERTAINING. IT CAN BE MADE USING VIRTUALLY ANY TENDER PIECES OF MEAT OR STIR-FRY VEGETABLES THAT YOU HAVE TO HAND.

SERVES FOUR

INGREDIENTS

  60ml/4 tbsp vegetable oil
  4 garlic cloves, finely chopped
  1 chicken (about 1.5kg/3–3½ lb)
    or chicken pieces, skinned and
    boned and cut into bitesize pieces
  5ml/1 tsp garam masala
  450g/1lb/2⅔ cups jasmine rice,
    rinsed and drained
  10ml/2 tsp salt
  1 litre/1¾ pints/4 cups
    chicken stock
  small bunch fresh coriander
    (cilantro), chopped, to garnish

COOK'S TIP
You will probably need to brown the chicken in batches, so don't be tempted to add too much chicken at once.

1 Heat the oil in a wok or flameproof casserole, which has a lid. Add the garlic and cook over a low to medium heat until golden brown. Add the chicken, increase the heat and brown the pieces on all sides (see Cook's Tip).

2 Add the garam masala, stir well to coat the chicken all over in the spice, then tip in the drained rice. Add the salt and stir to mix.

3 Pour in the stock, stir well, then cover the wok or casserole and bring to the boil. Reduce the heat to low and simmer gently for 10 minutes, until the rice is cooked and tender.

4 Lift the wok or casserole off the heat, leaving the lid on, and leave for 10 minutes. Fluff up the rice grains with a fork and spoon on to a platter. Sprinkle with the coriander and serve immediately.

Energy 715Kcal/2994kJ; Protein 56.3g; Carbohydrate 89.8g, of which sugars 0g; Fat 13.8g, of which saturates 1.9g; Cholesterol 140mg; Calcium 32mg; Fibre 0g; Sodium 1103mg.

THAI FRIED RICE

*THIS SUBSTANTIAL AND TASTY DISH IS BASED ON THAI JASMINE RICE COOKED IN COCONUT MILK.
DICED CHICKEN, RED PEPPER AND CORN KERNELS ADD COLOUR AND EXTRA FLAVOUR.*

SERVES FOUR

INGREDIENTS
  475ml/16fl oz/2 cups water
  50g/2oz/½ cup coconut milk powder
  350g/12oz/1¾ cups Thai jasmine
    rice, rinsed
  30ml/2 tbsp groundnut (peanut) oil
  2 garlic cloves, chopped
  1 small onion, finely chopped
  2.5cm/1in piece fresh root ginger,
    peeled and grated
  225g/8oz skinned chicken breast
    fillets, cut into 1cm/½in pieces
  1 red (bell) pepper, seeded
    and sliced
  115g/4oz/1 cup drained canned
    whole kernel corn
  5ml/1 tsp chilli oil
  5ml/1 tsp hot curry powder
  2 eggs, beaten
  salt
  spring onion (scallion) shreds,
    to garnish

1 Pour the water into a pan and whisk in the coconut milk powder. Add the rice and bring to the boil. Reduce the heat, cover and cook for 12 minutes, or until the rice is tender and the liquid has been absorbed. Spread the rice on a baking sheet and leave until cold.

2 Heat the oil in a wok, add the garlic, onion and ginger and stir-fry over a medium heat for 2 minutes.

COOK'S TIP
It is important that the rice is completely cold before being fried.

3 Push the onion mixture to the sides of the wok, add the chicken to the centre and stir-fry for 2 minutes. Add the rice and toss well. Stir-fry over a high heat for about 3 minutes more, until the chicken is cooked through.

4 Stir in the sliced red pepper, corn, chilli oil and curry powder, with salt to taste. Toss over the heat for 1 minute. Stir in the beaten eggs and cook for 1 minute more. Garnish with the spring onion shreds and serve.

Energy 563Kcal/2358kJ; Protein 26.7g; Carbohydrate 88.9g, of which sugars 13.9g; Fat 11.2g, of which saturates 2.1g; Cholesterol 139mg; Calcium 77mg; Fibre 1.8g; Sodium 284mg.

ORANGE AND GINGER GLAZED POUSSINS

THESE MOIST, SUCCULENT POUSSINS COATED IN A SPICED CITRUS AND HONEY GLAZE MAKE A GREAT ALTERNATIVE TO A TRADITIONAL ROAST. BE SURE TO PLAN AHEAD BECAUSE THEY NEED TO BE MARINATED FOR AT LEAST 6 HOURS, BEFORE BEING COOKED IN THE WOK.

SERVES FOUR

INGREDIENTS

4 poussins, 300–350g/11–12oz each
juice and finely grated rind
  of 2 oranges
2 garlic cloves, crushed
15ml/1 tbsp grated fresh root ginger
90ml/6 tbsp soy sauce
75ml/5 tbsp clear honey
2–3 star anise
30ml/2 tbsp Chinese rice wine
about 20 kaffir lime leaves
a large bunch of spring onions
  (scallions), shredded
60ml/4 tbsp butter
1 large orange, segmented

1 Place the poussins in a deep, non-metallic dish. Combine the orange rind and juice, garlic, ginger, half the soy sauce, half the honey, star anise and rice wine, then pour the mixture over the poussins. Turn the poussins so they are coated all over in the marinade. Cover the dish with clear film (plastic wrap), and place in the refrigerator for at least 6 hours to marinate.

2 To cook the poussins, line a large, heatproof plate with the kaffir lime leaves and spring onions. Lift the poussins out of the marinade and place on top of the layer of leaves. Reserve the marinade in a jug (pitcher).

3 Place a trivet or steamer rack in the base of a large wok and pour in 5cm/2in water. Bring to the boil and carefully lower the plate of poussins on to the trivet or rack. Cover, reduce the heat to low and steam for 45 minutes–1 hour, or until the poussins are cooked through and tender. (Check the water level regularly and add more when necessary.)

4 Remove the poussins from the wok and keep warm while you make the glaze. Wipe out the wok and pour in the reserved marinade, butter and the remaining soy sauce and honey. Bring to the boil, reduce the heat and cook gently for 10–15 minutes, or until thick.

5 Spoon the glaze over the poussins and serve immediately, garnished with the orange segments.

COOK'S TIP
You can make easily make this for fewer people. Just use one poussin and reduce the amount of glaze accordingly. A single bird can be cooked in a steamer basket wrapped with banana leaves.

Energy 568Kcal/2378kJ; Protein 67.3g; Carbohydrate 18.7g, of which sugars 18.5g; Fat 25.3g, of which saturates 11.1g; Cholesterol 32mg; Calcium 110mg; Fibre 0.7g; Sodium 1344mg.

JUNGLE CURRY OF GUINEA FOWL

*A TRADITIONAL WILD FOOD COUNTRY CURRY FROM THE NORTH-CENTRAL REGION OF THAILAND, THIS
DISH CAN BE MADE USING ANY GAME, FISH OR CHICKEN. GUINEA FOWL IS NOT TYPICAL OF THAI
CUISINE, BUT IS A POPULAR AND WIDELY AVAILABLE GAME BIRD IN THE WEST.*

SERVES FOUR

INGREDIENTS
 1 guinea fowl or similar game bird
 15ml/1 tbsp vegetable oil
 10ml/2 tsp Thai green curry paste
 15ml/1 tbsp Thai fish sauce
 2.5cm/1in piece fresh galangal,
  peeled and finely chopped
 15ml/1 tbsp fresh green peppercorns
 3 kaffir lime leaves, torn
 15ml/1 tbsp whisky,
  preferably Mekhong
 300ml/½ pint/1¼ cups
  chicken stock
 50g/2oz snake beans or yard-long
  beans, cut into 2.5cm/1in lengths
  (about ½ cup)
 225g/8oz/3¼ cups chestnut
  mushrooms, sliced
 1 piece drained canned bamboo
  shoot, about 50g/2oz, shredded
 5ml/1 tsp dried chilli flakes, to
  garnish (optional)

1 Cut up the guinea fowl, remove and
discard the skin, then take all the meat
off the bones. Chop the meat into
bitesize pieces and set aside.

2 Heat the oil in a wok or frying pan
and add the curry paste. Stir-fry over a
medium heat for 30 seconds, until the
paste gives off its aroma.

3 Add the fish sauce and the guinea
fowl meat and stir-fry until the meat is
browned all over. Add the galangal,
peppercorns, lime leaves and whisky,
then pour in the stock.

4 Bring to the boil. Add the vegetables,
return to a simmer and cook gently for
2–3 minutes, until they are just cooked.
Spoon into a dish, sprinkle with chilli
flakes, if you like, and serve.

COOK'S TIPS
• Guinea fowl originated in West Africa
and was regarded as a game bird.
However, it has been domesticated in
Europe for over 500 years. They range
in size from 675g/1½ lb to 2kg/4½ lb,
but about 1.2kg/2½lb is average.
American readers could substitute two or
three Cornish hens, depending on size.
• Fresh green peppercorns are simply
unripe berries. They are sold on the stem
and look rather like miniature Brussels
sprout stalks. Look for them at Thai
supermarkets. If unavailable, substitute
bottled green peppercorns, but rinse well
and drain them first.

Energy 321Kcal/1345kJ; Protein 42.2g; Carbohydrate 1.1g, of which sugars 0.7g; Fat 15g, of which saturates 4.4g; Cholesterol 0mg; Calcium 73mg; Fibre 1.1g; Sodium 127mg.

CHINESE DUCK CURRY

THIS RICHLY SPICED CURRY ILLUSTRATES HOW HARMONIOUSLY FIVE-SPICE POWDER MARRIES THE FLAVOURS OF DUCK, GINGER AND BUTTERNUT SQUASH. THE DUCK IS BEST MARINATED FOR AS LONG AS POSSIBLE, ALTHOUGH IT TASTES GOOD EVEN IF YOU ONLY HAVE TIME TO MARINATE IT BRIEFLY.

SERVES FOUR

INGREDIENTS

  4 duck breast portions, skinned
  30ml/2 tbsp five-spice powder
  30ml/2 tbsp sesame oil
  grated rind and juice of 1 orange
  1 medium butternut squash, peeled
    and cubed
  10ml/2 tsp Thai red curry paste
  30ml/2 tbsp Thai fish sauce
  15ml/1 tbsp palm sugar or light
    muscovado (brown) sugar
  300ml/½ pint/1¼ cups coconut milk
  2 fresh red chillies, seeded
  4 kaffir lime leaves, torn
  small bunch coriander (cilantro),
    chopped, to garnish

1 Cut the duck meat into bitesize pieces and place in a bowl with the five-spice powder, sesame oil and orange rind and juice. Stir well to mix all the ingredients and coat the duck in the marinade. Cover the bowl with clear film (plastic wrap) and set aside in a cool place to marinate for at least 15 minutes.

2 Meanwhile, bring a pan of water to the boil. Add the squash and cook for 10–15 minutes, until just tender. Drain well and set aside.

3 Pour the marinade from the duck into a wok and heat until boiling. Stir in the curry paste and cook for 2–3 minutes, until well blended and fragrant. Add the duck and cook for 3–4 minutes, stirring constantly, until browned on all sides.

4 Add the fish sauce and palm sugar and cook for 2 minutes more. Stir in the coconut milk until the mixture is smooth, then add the cooked squash, with the chillies and lime leaves.

5 Simmer gently, stirring frequently, for 5 minutes, then spoon into a dish, sprinkle with the coriander and serve with noodles.

Energy 295Kcal/1241kJ; Protein 31.4g; Carbohydrate 13.3g, of which sugars 12.3g; Fat 15.9g, of which saturates 3.1g; Cholesterol 165mg; Calcium 102mg; Fibre 2g; Sodium 427mg.

RED DUCK CURRY <u>WITH</u> PEA AUBERGINES

THIS TASTY CURRY NEEDS TO BE SIMMERED AND THEN LEFT TO STAND TO ALLOW THE FLAVOURS TO BLEND BEAUTIFULLY. USE AN ELECTRIC WOK IF YOU HAVE ONE TO MAINTAIN THE STEADY TEMPERATURE NEEDED FOR GENTLE SIMMERING.

SERVES FOUR

INGREDIENTS

    4 duck breast portions
    400ml/14fl oz can coconut milk
    200ml/7fl oz/scant 1 cup chicken
      stock
    30ml/2 tbsp red Thai curry paste
    8 spring onions (scallions), finely
      sliced
    10ml/2 tsp grated fresh root ginger
    30ml/2 tbsp Chinese rice wine
    15ml/1 tbsp fish sauce
    15ml/1 tbsp soy sauce
    2 lemon grass stalks, halved
      lengthways
    3–4 kaffir lime leaves
    300g/11oz pea aubergines
      (eggplants)
    10ml/2 tsp sugar
    salt and ground black pepper
    10–12 fresh basil and mint leaves, to
      garnish
    steamed jasmine rice, to serve

1 Using a sharp knife, cut the duck breast portions into neat bitesize pieces.

2 Place a wok over a low heat and add the coconut milk, stock, curry paste, spring onions, ginger, rice wine, fish and soy sauces, lemon grass and lime leaves. Stir well to mix, then bring to the boil over a medium heat.

3 Add the duck, aubergines and sugar to the wok and gently simmer for 25–30 minutes, stirring occasionally.

4 Remove the wok from the heat and leave to stand, covered, for about 15 minutes. Season to taste

5 Serve the duck curry ladled into shallow bowls, garnished with fresh mint and basil leaves. Serve with steamed jasmine rice.

COOK'S TIP
Tiny pea aubergines (eggplants) are sold in Asian stores. If you can't find them, use regular aubergines cut into chunks

Energy 241Kcal/1017kJ; Protein 31.1g; Carbohydrate 10.2g, of which sugars 10g; Fat 10.5g, of which saturates 2.3g; Cholesterol 165mg; Calcium 65mg; Fibre 1.8g; Sodium 546mg.

SHREDDED DUCK AND NOODLE SALAD

THIS REFRESHING, PIQUANT SALAD MAKES A MOUTHWATERING FIRST COURSE OR LIGHT MEAL. THE MARINATED DUCK IS LOVELY AND MOIST, HAVING BEEN STEAMED IN THE WOK, AND TASTES SUPERB WITH THE FRESH RAW VEGETABLES, NOODLES AND ZESTY DRESSING.

SERVES FOUR

INGREDIENTS

4 duck breast portions
30ml/2 tbsp Chinese rice wine
10ml/2 tsp finely grated fresh
   root ginger
60ml/4 tbsp soy sauce
15ml/1 tbsp sesame oil
15ml/1 tbsp clear honey
10ml/2 tsp Chinese five-spice powder
toasted sesame seeds, to sprinkle
For the noodles
150g/5oz bean-thread noodles
a small handful of fresh mint leaves
a small handful of coriander
   (cilantro) leaves
1 red (bell) pepper, seeded and
   finely sliced
4 spring onions (scallions), finely
   shredded or sliced
50g/2oz mixed salad leaves
For the dressing
45ml/3 tbsp light soy sauce
30ml/2 tbsp mirin
10ml/2 tsp golden caster
   (superfine) sugar
1 garlic clove, crushed
10ml/2 tsp chilli oil

1 Place the duck breast portions in a non-metallic bowl. Mix together the rice wine, ginger, soy sauce, sesame oil, clear honey and five-spice powder. Toss to coat, cover and marinate in the refrigerator for 3–4 hours.

VARIATIONS
If you prefer, you can use shredded chicken in place of the duck.

2 Double over a large sheet of heavy foil. Place the foil on a heatproof plate. Place the duck breast portions on it and spoon the marinade over. Fold the foil to enclose the duck and juices and scrunch the edges to seal.

3 Place a trivet or steamer rack in a large wok and pour in water to a depth of about 5cm/2in. Bring to the boil and place the plate on to the trivet or rack. Cover tightly, reduce the heat and steam gently for 50–60 minutes. Remove the plate from the wok and leave to rest for 15 minutes.

4 Place the noodles in a large bowl and pour over boiling water to cover. Cover and soak for 5–6 minutes. Drain, refresh under cold water and drain again. Put in a bowl with the herbs, red pepper, spring onions and salad leaves.

5 Mix together all the dressing ingredients. Remove the skin from the duck breasts and roughly shred the flesh using a fork. Divide the noodle salad among four plates and top with the shredded duck. Spoon over the dressing, sprinkle with the sesame seeds and serve immediately.

Energy 398Kcal/1671kJ; Protein 32.8g; Carbohydrate 41.7g, of which sugars 10.8g; Fat 11.6g, of which saturates 2.2g; Cholesterol 165mg; Calcium 40mg; Fibre 1g; Sodium 1688mg.

DUCK AND SESAME STIR-FRY

THIS RECIPE COMES FROM NORTHERN THAILAND AND IS INTENDED FOR GAME BIRDS, AS FARMED DUCK WOULD HAVE TOO MUCH FAT. USE WILD DUCK IF YOU CAN GET IT, OR EVEN PARTRIDGE, PHEASANT OR PIGEON. IF YOU DO USE FARMED DUCK, YOU SHOULD REMOVE THE SKIN AND FAT LAYER.

SERVES FOUR

INGREDIENTS
    250g/9oz boneless wild duck meat
    15ml/1 tbsp sesame oil
    15ml/1 tbsp vegetable oil
    4 garlic cloves, finely sliced
    2.5ml/½ tsp dried chilli flakes
    15ml/1 tbsp Thai fish sauce
    15ml/1 tbsp light soy sauce
    120ml/4fl oz/½ cup water
    1 head broccoli, cut into small florets
    coriander (cilantro) and 15ml/1 tbsp
        toasted sesame seeds, to garnish

VARIATIONS
Pak choi (bok choy) or Chinese flowering cabbage can be used instead of broccoli.

1 Cut the duck meat into bitesize pieces. Heat the wok, add the oils and, when hot, stir-fry the garlic over a medium heat until it is golden brown – do not let it burn. Add the duck to the pan and stir-fry for a further 2 minutes, until the meat begins to brown.

2 Stir in the chilli flakes, fish sauce, soy sauce and water. Add the broccoli and continue to stir-fry for about 2 minutes, until the duck is just cooked through.

3 Serve on warmed plates, garnished with coriander and sesame seeds.

Energy 192Kcal/798kJ; Protein 18.7g; Carbohydrate 2.7g, of which sugars 2.3g; Fat 12.9g, of which saturates 2.1g; Cholesterol 69mg; Calcium 104mg; Fibre 3.6g; Sodium 436mg.

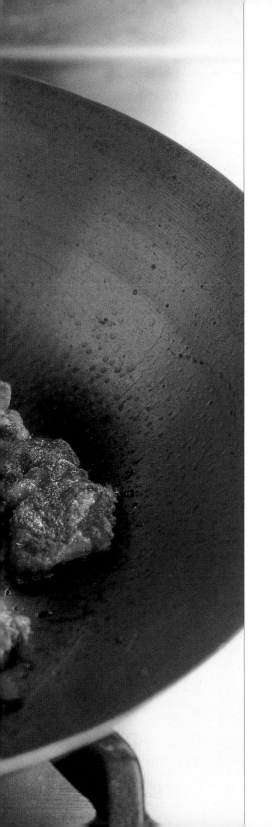

MEAT
DISHES

Rich meat curries and gently simmered dishes lend
themselves perfectly to wok cooking, with great depths of
flavour coming from ingredients such as chillies, garlic,
shallots, ginger or galangal. Fresh lemon grass and coriander
are often included, and smooth, sweet coconut milk is often
the liquid that marries these robust tastes together and
tames their stridency. From this chapter try Beef Rendang
for a typically intense dish, or you could opt for a
milder dish such as Fried Rice with Pork, which is
quick and easy to prepare.

GREEN BEEF CURRY WITH THAI AUBERGINES

THIS IS A VERY QUICK CURRY SO BE SURE TO USE GOOD QUALITY MEAT. SIRLOIN IS RECOMMENDED,
BUT TENDER RUMP STEAK COULD BE USED INSTEAD. IF YOU BUY THE CURRY PASTE, THERE'S VERY
LITTLE ADDITIONAL PREPARATION, BUT YOU COULD MAKE IT FROM SCRATCH IF YOU PREFER.

SERVES FOUR TO SIX

INGREDIENTS
    450g/1lb sirloin steak
    15ml/1 tbsp vegetable oil
    45ml/3 tbsp Thai green curry paste
    600ml/1 pint/2½ cups coconut milk
    4 kaffir lime leaves, torn
    15–30ml/1–2 tbsp Thai fish sauce
    5ml/1 tsp palm sugar or light
      muscovado (brown) sugar
    150g/5oz small Thai aubergines
      (eggplant), halved
    small handful of fresh Thai basil
    2 fresh green chillies, to garnish

1 Trim off any excess fat from the beef.
Using a sharp knife, cut it into long,
thin strips. This is easiest to do if it is
well chilled. Set it aside.

2 Heat the oil in a wok. Add the curry
paste and cook for 1–2 minutes, until it
you can smell the fragrances.

3 Stir in half the coconut milk, a little at
a time. Cook, stirring frequently, for
about 5–6 minutes, until an oily sheen
appears on the surface of the liquid.

4 Add the beef to the pan with the kaffir
lime leaves, Thai fish sauce, sugar and
aubergine halves. Cook for 2–3 minutes,
then stir in the remaining coconut milk.

5 Bring back to a simmer and cook
until the meat and aubergines are
tender. Stir in the Thai basil just before
serving. Finely shred the green chillies
and use to garnish the curry.

GREEN CURRY PASTE
To make the curry paste from scratch,
put 15 fresh green chillies, 2 chopped
lemon grass stalks, 3 sliced shallots, 2
garlic cloves, 15ml/1 tbsp chopped
galangal, 4 chopped kaffir lime leaves,
2.5ml/½ tsp grated kaffir lime rind,
5ml/1 tsp chopped coriander root, 6
black peppercorns, 5ml/1 tsp each
roasted coriander and cumin seeds,
15ml/1 tbsp granulated sugar, 5ml/1 tsp
salt and 5ml/1 tsp shrimp paste into a
food processor and process until smooth.
Gradually add 30ml/2 tbsp vegetable oil,
processing after each addition.

Energy 146Kcal/615kJ; Protein 18.2g; Carbohydrate 6.2g, of which sugars 6.1g; Fat 5.6g, of which saturates 1.9g; Cholesterol 38mg; Calcium 36mg; Fibre 0.5g; Sodium 163mg.

DRY BEEF CURRY WITH PEANUT AND LIME

ALTHOUGH THIS IS CALLED A DRY CURRY, THE DESCRIPTION SIMPLY MEANS THE MEAT ISN'T SWIMMING IN LIQUID. THE METHOD OF COOKING IN THE WOK ENSURES THAT THE BEEF ABSORBS THE COCONUT MILK AND PEANUT BUTTER MIXTURE AND STAYS SUCCULENT.

SERVES FOUR TO SIX

INGREDIENTS

400g/14oz can coconut milk
900g/2lb stewing steak,
  finely chopped
300ml/½ pint/1¼ cups beef stock
30ml/2 tbsp crunchy peanut butter
juice of 2 limes
lime slices, shredded coriander
  (cilantro) and fresh red chilli slices,
  to garnish

For the red curry paste

30ml/2 tbsp coriander seeds
5ml/1 tsp cumin seeds
seeds from 6 green cardamom pods
2.5ml/½ tsp grated or ground nutmeg
1.5ml/¼ tsp ground cloves
2.5ml/½ tsp ground cinnamon
20ml/4 tsp paprika
pared rind of 1 mandarin orange,
  finely chopped
4–5 small fresh red chillies, seeded
  and finely chopped
25ml/1½ tsp granulated sugar
2.5ml/½ tsp salt
1 piece lemon grass, about 10cm/4in
  long, shredded
3 garlic cloves, crushed
2cm/¾in piece fresh galangal,
  peeled and finely chopped
4 red shallots, finely chopped
1 piece shrimp paste,
  2cm/¾in square
50g/2oz coriander (cilantro) root or
  stem, chopped
juice of ½ lime
30ml/2 tbsp vegetable oil

1 Strain the coconut milk into a bowl, retaining the thicker coconut milk in the strainer or sieve.

2 Pour the thin coconut milk from the bowl into a large, heavy pan, then scrape in half the residue from the sieve. Reserve the remaining thick coconut milk. Add the chopped steak. Pour in the beef stock and bring to the boil. Reduce the heat, cover the pan and simmer gently for 50 minutes.

3 Make the curry paste. Dry-fry all the seeds for 1–2 minutes. Tip into a bowl and add the nutmeg, cloves, cinnamon, paprika and orange rind. Pound the chillies with the sugar and salt. Add the spice mixture, lemon grass, garlic, galangal, shallots and shrimp paste and pound to a paste. Work in the coriander, lime juice and oil.

4 Strain the beef, reserving the cooking liquid, and place a cupful of liquid in a wok. Stir in 30–45ml/2–3 tbsp of the curry paste, according to taste. Boil rapidly until all the liquid has evaporated. Stir in the reserved thick coconut milk, the peanut butter and the beef. Simmer, uncovered, for 15–20 minutes, adding a little more cooking liquid if the mixture starts to stick to the pan, but keep the curry dry.

5 Just before serving, stir in the lime juice. Serve in warmed bowls, garnished with the lime slices, shredded coriander and sliced red chillies.

VARIATION
The curry is equally delicious made with lean leg or shoulder of lamb.

Energy 296Kcal/1238kJ; Protein 35.2g; Carbohydrate 4.9g, of which sugars 4.5g; Fat 15.2g, of which saturates 4.8g; Cholesterol 103mg; Calcium 66mg; Fibre 0.7g; Sodium 262mg.

STIR-FRIED BEEF IN OYSTER SAUCE

This is another simple but delicious recipe. It is often made with just one type of mushroom, such as oyster, but using a mixture makes the dish more interesting. Oyster sauce adds a savoury depth to the dish and is an essential ingredient.

3 Heat half the oil in a wok or large, heavy frying pan. Add the garlic and ginger and cook for 1–2 minutes, until fragrant. Drain the steak, add it to the wok or pan and stir well to separate the strips. Cook, stirring frequently, for a further 1–2 minutes, until the steak is browned all over and tender. Remove from the wok or pan and set aside.

4 Heat the remaining oil in the wok or pan. Add the shiitake, oyster and straw mushrooms. Stir-fry over a medium heat until golden brown.

5 Return the steak to the wok and mix it with the mushrooms. Spoon in the oyster sauce and sugar, mix well, then add ground black pepper to taste. Toss over the heat until all the ingredients are thoroughly combined.

6 Stir in the spring onions. Tip the mixture on to a serving platter, garnish with the strips of red chilli and serve.

SERVES FOUR TO SIX

INGREDIENTS

- 450g/1lb rump (round) or sirloin steak
- 30ml/2 tbsp soy sauce
- 15ml/1 tbsp cornflour (cornstarch)
- 45ml/3 tbsp groundnut (peanut) oil or vegetable oil for stir-frying
- 15ml/1 tbsp chopped garlic
- 15ml/1 tbsp chopped fresh root ginger
- 225g/8oz/3¼ cups mixed mushrooms such as shiitake, oyster and straw
- 30ml/2 tbsp oyster sauce
- 5ml/1 tsp granulated sugar
- 4 spring onions (scallions), cut into short lengths
- ground black pepper
- 2 fresh red chillies, seeded and cut into strips, to garnish

1 Place the steak in the freezer for 30–40 minutes, until firm, then, using a sharp knife, slice it on the diagonal into long thin strips.

2 Mix together the soy sauce and cornflour in a large bowl. Add the steak, turning to coat well, cover with clear film (plastic wrap) and leave to marinate at room temperature for 1–2 hours.

Energy 160Kcal/670kJ; Protein 17.6g; Carbohydrate 2.9g, of which sugars 2.7g; Fat 8.8g, of which saturates 2g; Cholesterol 44mg; Calcium 10mg; Fibre 0.6g; Sodium 485mg.

THAI CRISPY NOODLES WITH BEEF

WHEN IT COMES TO VALUE FOR MONEY, RICE VERMICELLI IS SOMETHING SPECIAL — WHEN IT IS ADDED TO THE HOT OIL IT EXPANDS TO AT LEAST FOUR TIMES ITS ORIGINAL SIZE. THE STRANDS ALSO BECOME CRISP AND CRUNCHY, ADDING A GREAT CONTRAST TO THE BEEF AND VEGETABLE STIR-FRY.

SERVES FOUR

INGREDIENTS

450g/1lb rump (round) steak
teriyaki sauce, for brushing
175g/6oz rice vermicelli
groundnut (peanut) oil, for deep-
    frying and stir-frying
8 spring onions (scallions),
    diagonally sliced
2 garlic cloves, crushed
4–5 carrots, cut into julienne strips
1–2 fresh red chillies, seeded and
    finely sliced
2 small courgettes (zucchini),
    diagonally sliced
5ml/1 tsp grated fresh root ginger
60ml/4 tbsp rice vinegar
90ml/6 tbsp light soy sauce
about 475ml/16fl oz/2 cups
    beef stock

1 Beat the steak to about 2.5cm/1in thick. Place in a shallow dish, brush generously with the teriyaki sauce and set aside for 2–4 hours to marinate.

2 Separate the rice vermicelli into manageable loops. Pour oil into a large wok to a depth of about 5cm/2in, and heat until a strand of vermicelli cooks as soon as it is lowered into the oil.

3 Carefully add a loop of vermicelli to the oil. Almost immediately, turn to cook on the other side, then remove and drain on kitchen paper. Repeat with the remaining loops. Transfer the cooked noodles to a deep serving bowl and keep them warm.

4 Strain the oil from the wok into a heatproof bowl and set it aside. Return 15ml/1 tbsp oil to a clean wok. When it sizzles, fry the steak for about 30 seconds on each side, until browned. Transfer to a board and cut into thick slices. The meat should be well browned on the outside but still pink inside. Set aside.

5 Add a little extra oil to the wok, add the spring onions, garlic and carrots and stir-fry over a medium heat for 5–6 minutes, until the carrots are slightly soft and have a glazed appearance. Add the chillies, courgettes and ginger and stir-fry for 1–2 minutes.

6 Stir in the rice vinegar, soy sauce and stock. Cook for 4 minutes, or until the sauce has thickened slightly. Return the slices of steak to the wok and cook for a further 1–2 minutes.

7 Spoon the steak, vegetables and sauce over the noodles and toss lightly and carefully to mix. Serve immediately.

COOK'S TIP
As soon as you add the meat mixture to the noodles, they will begin to soften in the sauce. If you wish to keep a few crispy noodles, leave some on the surface so that they do not come into contact with the hot liquid.

Energy 410Kcal/1712kJ; Protein 30.7g; Carbohydrate 41.4g, of which sugars 6.6g; Fat 13.5g, of which saturates 3g; Cholesterol 66mg; Calcium 49mg; Fibre 1.9g; Sodium 1687mg.

BEEF RENDANG

IN INDONESIA, WHERE THIS SPICY DISH ORIGINATED, IT IS USUALLY SERVED WITH THE MEAT QUITE DRY; IF YOU PREFER MORE SAUCE, SIMPLY ADD MORE WATER WHEN STIRRING IN THE POTATOES. THE DEEP FRIED ONIONS, TRADITIONALLY SERVED WITH THE BEEF, ADD A DELICIOUS, CRISPY CONTRAST.

SERVES SIX–EIGHT

INGREDIENTS
2 onions or 5–6 shallots, chopped
4 garlic cloves, chopped
2.5cm/1in piece fresh galangal,
  peeled and sliced, or 15ml/1 tbsp
  galangal paste
2.5cm/1in piece fresh root ginger,
  peeled and sliced
4–6 fresh red chillies, seeded
  and roughly chopped
lower part only of 1 lemon grass
  stem, sliced
2.5cm/1in piece fresh turmeric,
  peeled and sliced, or 5ml/1 tsp
  ground turmeric
1kg/2¼lb prime beef in one piece
5ml/1 tsp coriander seeds,
  dry-fried
5ml/1 tsp cumin seeds, dry-fried
2 kaffir lime leaves, torn into
  pieces
2 x 400ml/14fl oz cans coconut
  milk
300ml/½ pint/1¼ cups water
30ml/2 tbsp dark soy sauce
5ml/1 tsp tamarind pulp, soaked in
  60ml/4 tbsp warm water
8–10 small new potatoes, well
  scrubbed and eyed
salt and ground black pepper
deep-fried onions (see below),
  sliced fresh red chillies and spring
  onions (scallions), to garnish

1 Put the onions or shallots in a food processor. Add the garlic, galangal, ginger, chillies, sliced lemon grass and fresh or ground turmeric. Process to a fine paste or grind in a mortar, using a pestle.

2 Cut the meat into cubes using a large sharp knife, then place the cubes in a bowl.

3 Grind the dry-fried coriander and cumin seeds, then add to the meat with the onion, chilli paste and kaffir lime leaves; stir well. Cover and leave in a cool place to marinate while you prepare the other ingredients.

COOK'S TIP
This dish is even better if you can cook it a day or two in advance of serving, which allows the flavours to mellow beautifully. Add the potatoes on reheating and simmer until tender.

4 Pour the coconut milk and water into a wok, then stir in the spiced meat and the soy sauce. Strain the tamarind water and add to the wok. Stir over medium heat until the liquid boils, then simmer gently, half-covered, for 1½ hours.

5 Add the potatoes and simmer for 20–25 minutes, or until the meat and the potatoes are tender. Add water if you prefer. Season and serve, garnished with the deep-fried onions, chillies and spring onions.

DEEP-FRIED ONIONS

KNOWN AS BAWANG GORENG, THESE ARE A TRADITIONAL GARNISH AND ACCOMPANY MANY INDONESIAN DISHES. ORIENTAL STORES SELL THEM READY-PREPARED, BUT IT IS EASY TO MAKE THEM. THE SMALL RED ONIONS SOLD IN ASIAN SHOPS ARE EXCELLENT BECAUSE THEY CONTAIN LESS WATER.

MAKES 450G/1LB

INGREDIENTS
450g/1lb onions
vegetable oil, for deep-frying

1 Thinly slice the onions with a sharp knife or in a food processor. Spread the slices out in a single layer on several sheets of kitchen paper and leave them to dry, in an airy place, for no less than 30 minutes and up to 2 hours.

2 Heat the oil in a wok to 190°C/375°F. Fry the onions in batches, until crisp and golden, turning all the time. Drain well on kitchen paper, cool and store in an airtight container, unless you are using them immediately.

Energy 289Kcal/1210kJ; Protein 30.2g; Carbohydrate 15.4g, of which sugars 8.6g; Fat 12.2g, of which saturates 5g; Cholesterol 73mg; Calcium 63mg; Fibre 1.4g; Sodium 465mg.
Energy 854Kcal/3521kJ; Protein 5.4g; Carbohydrate 35.5g, of which sugars 25.2g; Fat 77.8g, of which saturates 9g; Cholesterol 0mg; Calcium 113mg; Fibre 6.3g; Sodium 14mg.

BEEF AND BUTTERNUT SQUASH WITH CHILLI

STIR-FRIED BEEF AND SWEET, ORANGE-FLESHED SQUASH FLAVOURED WITH WARM SPICES, OYSTER SAUCE AND FRESH HERBS MAKES A ROBUST MAIN COURSE WHEN SERVED WITH RICE OR EGG NOODLES. THE ADDITION OF CHILLI AND FRESH ROOT GINGER GIVES THE DISH A WONDERFUL VIGOROUS BITE.

SERVES FOUR

INGREDIENTS
  30ml/2 tbsp sunflower oil
  2 onions, cut into thick slices
  500g/1¼lb butternut squash,
    peeled, seeded and cut into thin
    strips
  675g/1½lb fillet steak
    (beef tenderloin)
  60ml/4 tbsp soy sauce
  90g/3½oz/½ cup golden caster
    (superfine) sugar
  1 fresh bird's eye chilli, seeded
    and chopped
  15ml/1 tbsp finely shredded fresh
    root ginger
  30ml/2 tbsp Thai fish sauce
  5ml/1 tsp ground star anise
  5ml/1 tsp five-spice powder
  15ml/1 tbsp oyster sauce
  4 spring onions (scallions), shredded
  a small handful of sweet basil leaves
  a small handful of mint leaves

1 Heat a wok over a medium-high heat and add the oil, trickling it down just below the rim so that it coats the surface. When hot, stir in the onions and squash. Stir-fry for 2–3 minutes, then reduce the heat, cover and cook gently for 5–6 minutes, or until the vegetables are just tender.

2 Place the beef between 2 sheets of clear film (plastic wrap) and beat, with a mallet or rolling pin, until thin. Using a sharp knife, cut into thin strips.

3 In a separate wok, mix the soy sauce, sugar, chilli, ginger, fish sauce, star anise, five-spice powder and oyster sauce. Stir-fry for 3–4 minutes.

4 Add the beef to the soy sauce mixture in the wok and cook over a high heat for 3–4 minutes. Remove from the heat. Add the onion and squash slices to the beef and toss well with the spring onions and herbs. Serve immediately.

Energy 500Kcal/2093kJ; Protein 41.3g; Carbohydrate 36.9g, of which sugars 33.8g; Fat 21.7g, of which saturates 7.2g; Cholesterol 98mg; Calcium 91mg; Fibre 2.9g; Sodium 1243mg.

SPICY SHREDDED BEEF

THE ESSENCE OF THIS RECIPE IS THAT THE BEEF IS CUT INTO VERY FINE STRIPS BEFORE BEING STIR-FRIED. THIS IS EASIER TO ACHIEVE IF THE PIECE OF BEEF IS PLACED IN THE FREEZER FOR 30 MINUTES UNTIL IT IS VERY FIRM BEFORE BEING SLICED WITH A SHARP KNIFE.

SERVES TWO

INGREDIENTS

225g/8oz rump (round) steak
15ml/1 tbsp each light and dark
   soy sauce
15ml/1 tbsp rice wine or
   medium-dry sherry
5ml/1 tsp dark brown soft sugar or
   golden granulated sugar
90ml/6 tbsp vegetable oil
1 large onion, thinly sliced
2.5cm/1in piece fresh root ginger,
   peeled and grated
1–2 carrots, cut into matchsticks
2–3 fresh or dried chillies, halved,
   seeded (optional) and chopped
salt and ground black pepper
fresh chives, to garnish

3 Heat a wok and add half the oil. When it is hot, stir-fry the onion and ginger for 3–4 minutes, then transfer to a plate. Add the carrot, stir-fry for 3–4 minutes until slightly softened, then transfer to a plate and keep warm.

4 Heat the remaining oil in the wok, then quickly add the beef, with the marinade, followed by the chillies.

5 Cook over high heat for 2 minutes, stirring all the time. Return the fried onion and ginger to the wok and stir-fry for 1 minute more.

6 Season with salt and pepper to taste, cover and cook for 30 seconds. Spoon the meat into two warmed bowls and add the strips of carrots. Garnish with fresh chives and serve.

1 With a sharp knife, slice the well-chilled beef very thinly, then cut each slice into fine strips or shreds.

2 Mix together the light and dark soy sauces with the rice wine or sherry and sugar in a bowl. Add the strips of beef and stir well to ensure they are evenly coated with the marinade.

COOK'S TIP
Remove and discard the seeds from the chillies before you chop them – unless, of course, you like really fiery food. In which case, you could add some or all of the seeds with the chopped chillies.

Energy 532Kcal/2207kJ; Protein 27.3g; Carbohydrate 19.3g, of which sugars 15.4g; Fat 38.1g, of which saturates 5.8g; Cholesterol 66mg; Calcium 59mg; Fibre 3.3g; Sodium 1154mg.

Spicy Meat Balls

A WOK IS GREAT FOR COOKING MEAT BALLS BECAUSE YOU CAN PUSH THE COOKED ONES UP THE SIDES. CHILLI SAMBAL IS FIERCELY HOT, SO BE CAREFUL HOW MUCH YOU ADD TO YOUR MOUTHFUL.

SERVES FOUR TO SIX

INGREDIENTS
1cm/¹/₂in cube shrimp paste
1 large onion, roughly chopped
1–2 fresh red chillies, seeded
  and chopped
2 garlic cloves, crushed
15ml/1 tbsp coriander seeds
5ml/1 tsp cumin seeds
450g/1lb lean minced beef
10ml/2 tsp dark soy sauce
5ml/1 tsp dark brown sugar
juice of 1¹/₂ lemons
a little beaten egg
vegetable oil, for shallow frying
salt and ground black pepper
1 green and 2 fresh red chillies,
  to garnish
Chilli Sambal, to serve

1 Wrap the shrimp paste in a piece of foil and warm in a frying pan for 5 minutes, turning a few times. Unwrap and put in a food processor.

COOK'S TIP
When processing the shrimp paste (blachan), onion, chillies and garlic, do not process for too long, otherwise the onion will become too wet and spoil the consistency of the meat balls.

2 Add the onion, chillies and garlic to the food processor and process until finely chopped. Set aside. Dry fry the coriander and cumin seeds in a hot frying pan for 1 minute, to release the aroma. Tip the seeds into a mortar and grind with a pestle.

3 Put the meat in a large bowl. Stir in the onion mixture. Add the ground spices, soy sauce, brown sugar, lemon juice and beaten egg. Season to taste.

4 Shape the meat mixture into small, even-size balls, and chill these for 5–10 minutes to firm them up.

5 Heat the oil in a wok or large frying pan and fry the meat balls for 4–5 minutes, turning often, until cooked through and browned. You may have to do this in batches.

6 Drain the meat balls on kitchen paper, and then pile them on to a warm serving platter or into a large serving bowl. Finely slice the green chilli and one of the red chillies and scatter over the meat balls. Garnish with the remaining red chilli, if you like. Serve with the Chilli Sambal (see below) handed round separately.

VARIATION
Minced beef is traditionally used for this dish, but pork, lamb – or even turkey – mince would also be good.

Chilli Sambal

THIS FIERCE CONDIMENT IS BOTTLED AS SAMBAL OELEK, BUT IT IS EASY TO PREPARE AND WILL KEEP FOR SEVERAL WEEKS IN A WELL-SEALED JAR IN THE REFRIGERATOR. USE A STAINLESS-STEEL OR PLASTIC SPOON TO MEASURE; IF SAUCE DRIPS ON YOUR FINGERS, WASH WELL IN SOAPY WATER IMMEDIATELY.

MAKES 450G/1LB

INGREDIENTS
450g/1lb fresh red chillies, seeded
10ml/2 tsp salt

1 Bring a saucepan of water to the boil, add the seeded chillies and cook them for 5–8 minutes.

2 Drain the chillies and then grind them in a food processor, without making the paste too smooth. Stir in the salt.

3 Spoon into small individual dishes, to serve with the Spicy Meat Balls. Alternatively, transfer to a screw-topped glass jar, and cover with a piece of greaseproof paper or clear film (plastic wrap). Screw on the lid and store in the refrigerator for up to 3 weeks.

Energy 255Kcal/1057kJ; Protein 15.8g; Carbohydrate 4.1g, of which sugars 3.2g; Fat 19.6g, of which saturates 6.1g; Cholesterol 49mg; Calcium 28mg; Fibre 0.6g; Sodium 216mg.
Energy 90Kcal/374kJ; Protein 13.1g; Carbohydrate 3.1g, of which sugars 3.1g; Fat 2.7g, of which saturates 0g; Cholesterol 0mg; Calcium 136mg; Fibre 0g; Sodium 3962mg.

FRIED RICE <u>WITH</u> BEEF

ONE OF THE JOYS OF WOK COOKING IS THE EASE AND SPEED WITH WHICH A REALLY GOOD MEAL CAN BE PREPARED. THIS DELECTABLE BEEF AND RICE STIR-FRY CAN BE ON THE TABLE IN 15 MINUTES.

SERVES FOUR

INGREDIENTS

200g/7oz beef steak, chilled
15ml/1 tbsp vegetable oil
2 garlic cloves,
   finely chopped
1 egg
250g/9oz/2¼ cups cooked
   jasmine rice
½ medium head broccoli,
   coarsely chopped
30ml/2 tbsp dark soy sauce
15ml/1 tbsp light soy sauce
5ml/1 tsp palm sugar or light
   muscovado (brown) sugar
15ml/1 tbsp Thai fish sauce
ground black pepper
chilli sauce, to serve

1 Trim the steak and cut into very thin strips with a sharp knife.

2 Heat the oil in a wok or frying pan and cook the garlic over a low to medium heat until golden. Do not let it burn. Increase the heat to high, add the steak and stir-fry for 2 minutes.

3 Move the pieces of beef to the edges of the wok or pan and break the egg into the centre. When the egg starts to set, stir-fry it with the meat.

4 Add the rice and toss all the contents of the wok together, scraping up any residue on the base, then add the broccoli, soy sauces, sugar and fish sauce and stir-fry for 2 minutes more. Season to taste with pepper and serve immediately with chilli sauce.

COOK'S TIP
Soy sauce is made from fermented soya beans. The first extraction is sold as light soy sauce and has a delicate, "beany" fragrance. Dark soy sauce has been allowed to mature for longer.

Energy 385Kcal/1606kJ; Protein 20.7g; Carbohydrate 52.7g, of which sugars 2.5g; Fat 9.8g, of which saturates 2.8g; Cholesterol 81mg; Calcium 59mg; Fibre 1.6g; Sodium 590mg.

FRIED RICE WITH PORK

THIS IS GREAT FOR USING UP LAST NIGHT'S LEFTOVER RICE, BUT FOR SAFETY'S SAKE, IT MUST HAVE BEEN COOLED QUICKLY AND KEPT IN THE REFRIGERATOR, THEN FRIED UNTIL THOROUGHLY HEATED.

SERVES FOUR TO SIX

INGREDIENTS
45ml/3 tbsp vegetable oil
1 onion, chopped
15ml/1 tbsp chopped garlic
115g/4oz pork, cut into small cubes
2 eggs, beaten
500g/2¼lb/4 cups cooked rice
30ml/2 tbsp Thai fish sauce
15ml/1 tbsp dark soy sauce
2.5ml/½ tsp caster (superfine) sugar
4 spring onions (scallions),
    finely sliced, sliced fresh red
    chillies, and 1 lime, cut into
    wedges, to serve

COOK'S TIP
To make 1kg/2¼lb/4 cups cooked rice, you will need approximately 400g/14oz/2 cups uncooked rice.

1 Heat the oil in a wok or large frying pan. Add the onion and garlic and cook for about 2 minutes until softened.

2 Add the pork to the softened onion and garlic. Stir-fry until the pork changes colour and is cooked.

3 Add the eggs and cook until scrambled into small lumps.

4 Add the rice and continue to stir and toss, to coat it with the oil and prevent it from sticking.

5 Add the fish sauce, soy sauce and sugar and mix well. Continue to fry until the rice is thoroughly heated. Spoon into warmed individual bowls and serve, with sliced spring onions, chillies and lime wedges.

Energy 343Kcal/1448kJ; Protein 11.2g; Carbohydrate 54.3g, of which sugars 2.2g; Fat 10.6g, of which saturates 2g; Cholesterol 82mg; Calcium 51mg; Fibre 0.6g; Sodium 220mg.

PORK CHOPS WITH FIELD MUSHROOMS

EVEN THOUGH THE PORK CHOPS AND MUSHROOMS ARE COOKED ON THE BARBECUE OR GRIDDLE, THE WOK IS USED FOR MAKING THE QUICK, EASY SAUCE THAT IS SPOONED OVER THEM. SERVE THE PORK AND MUSHROOMS OVER NOODLES OR WITH THAI JASMINE RICE.

SERVES FOUR

INGREDIENTS
    4 pork chops
    4 large field (portabello) mushrooms
    45ml/3 tbsp vegetable oil
    4 fresh red chillies, seeded and
       thinly sliced
    45ml/3 tbsp Thai fish sauce
    90ml/6 tbsp fresh lime juice
    4 shallots, chopped
    5ml/1 tsp roasted ground rice
    30ml/2 tbsp spring onions
       (scallions), chopped, plus shredded
       spring onions to garnish
    coriander (cilantro) leaves, to garnish
For the marinade
    2 garlic cloves, chopped
    15ml/1 tbsp granulated sugar
    15ml/1 tbsp Thai fish sauce
    30ml/2 tbsp soy sauce
    15ml/1 tbsp sesame oil
    15ml/1 tbsp whisky or dry sherry
    2 lemon grass stalks, finely chopped
    2 spring onions (scallions), chopped

1 Make the marinade. Combine the garlic, sugar, sauces, oil and whisky or sherry in a large, shallow dish. Stir in the lemon grass and spring onions.

2 Add the pork chops, turning to coat them in the marinade. Cover and leave to marinate for 1–2 hours.

3 Lift the chops out of the marinade and place them on a barbecue grid over hot coals or on a grill (broiler) rack. Add the mushrooms and brush them with 15ml/1 tbsp of the oil. Cook the pork chops for 5–7 minutes on each side and the mushrooms for about 2 minutes. Brush both with the marinade while cooking.

4 Heat the remaining oil in a wok or small frying pan, then remove the pan from the heat and stir in the chillies, fish sauce, lime juice, shallots, ground rice and chopped spring onions. Put the pork chops and mushrooms on a large serving plate and spoon over the sauce. Garnish with the coriander leaves and shredded spring onion.

Energy 293Kcal/1229kJ; Protein 44.4g; Carbohydrate 2.9g, of which sugars 1.4g; Fat 11.1g, of which saturates 3.3g; Cholesterol 126mg; Calcium 24mg; Fibre 0.9g; Sodium 411mg.

CURRIED PORK WITH PICKLED GARLIC

THIS VERY RICH CURRY IS BEST ACCOMPANIED BY LOTS OF PLAIN RICE AND PERHAPS A LIGHT VEGETABLE DISH. IT COULD SERVE FOUR WITH A VEGETABLE CURRY. ASIAN STORES SELL PICKLED GARLIC. IT IS WELL WORTH INVESTING IN A JAR, AS THE TASTE IS SWEET AND DELICIOUS.

SERVES TWO

INGREDIENTS

130g/4½oz lean pork steaks
30ml/2 tbsp vegetable oil
1 garlic clove, crushed
15ml/1 tbsp Thai red curry paste
130ml/4½fl oz/generous ½ cup
  coconut cream
2.5cm/1in piece fresh root ginger,
  finely chopped
30ml/2 tbsp vegetable or
  chicken stock
30ml/2 tbsp Thai fish sauce
5ml/1 tsp granulated sugar
2.5ml/½ tsp ground turmeric
10ml/2 tsp lemon juice
4 pickled garlic cloves,
  finely chopped
strips of lemon and lime rind,
  to garnish

1 Place the pork steaks in the freezer for 30–40 minutes, until firm, then, using a sharp knife, cut the meat into fine slivers, trimming off any excess fat.

2 Heat the oil in a wok or large, heavy frying pan and cook the garlic over a low to medium heat until golden brown. Do not let it burn. Add the curry paste and stir it in well.

3 Add the coconut cream and stir until the liquid begins to reduce and thicken. Stir in the pork. Cook for 2 minutes more, until the pork is cooked through.

4 Add the ginger, stock, fish sauce, sugar and turmeric, stirring constantly, then add the lemon juice and pickled garlic and heat through. Serve in bowls, garnished with strips of rind.

Energy 227Kcal/947kJ; Protein 16.3g; Carbohydrate 9.8g, of which sugars 6.1g; Fat 14g, of which saturates 2.4g; Cholesterol 41mg; Calcium 30mg; Fibre 1g; Sodium 474mg.

SWEET AND SOUR PORK

THIS CLASSIC CHINESE-STYLE DISH, WITH ITS STUNNING COLOURS, PIQUANT SWEET AND SOUR SAUCE AND GLORIOUSLY STICKY TEXTURE MAKES A TASTY SUPPER DISH. SERVE WITH FRIED RICE AND STEAMED ASIAN GREENS TO CREATE AN AUTHENTIC CHINESE MEAL.

SERVES FOUR

INGREDIENTS

1 carrot
1 red (bell) pepper
4 spring onions (scallions)
45ml/3 tbsp light soy sauce
15ml/1 tbsp Chinese rice wine
15ml/1 tbsp sesame oil
5ml/1 tsp freshly ground
  black pepper
500g/1¼lb pork loin, cut into
  1cm/½in cubes
65g/2½oz/9 tbsp cornflour
  (cornstarch)
65g/2½oz/9 tbsp plain
  (all-purpose) flour
5ml/1 tsp bicarbonate of soda
  (baking soda)
sunflower oil, for deep-frying
10ml/2 tsp finely grated garlic
5ml/1 tsp finely grated fresh
  root ginger
60ml/4 tbsp tomato ketchup
30ml/2 tbsp caster (superfine) sugar
15ml/1 tbsp rice vinegar
15ml/1 tbsp cornflour (cornstarch)
  blended with 120ml/4fl oz/
  ½ cup water
egg fried rice or noodles, to serve
salt

1 Using a sharp knife or cleaver, chop the carrots in half, then in slices, and then into thin shreds. Cut the pepper into sections and shred into similar sized pieces. Cut the spring onions in half, then cut each half into shreds.

2 In a large mixing bowl, combine 15ml/1 tbsp of the soy sauce with the rice wine, sesame oil and pepper. Add the pork and toss to mix. Cover and chill for 3–4 hours.

3 Combine the cornflour, plain flour and bicarbonate of soda in a bowl. Add a pinch of salt and mix in 150ml/¼ pint/⅔ cup cold water to make a thick batter. Add the pork to the batter and mix well with your hands to coat evenly.

4 Fill a wok one-third full with the sunflower oil and heat to 180°C/350°F or until a cube of bread browns in 45 seconds. Separate the pork cubes and deep-fry them, in batches, for 1–2 minutes, or until golden. Remove and drain on kitchen paper.

5 Mix together the garlic, ginger, tomato ketchup, sugar, the remaining soy sauce, rice vinegar and cornflour mixture. Place a small pan over a medium heat. Add the mixture and heat for 2–3 minutes, until thickened. Add the carrot, red pepper and spring onions, stir and remove from the heat.

6 Reheat the deep-frying oil in the wok to 180°C/350°F and then re-fry the pork pieces in batches for 1–2 minutes, until golden and crisp. Drain and add to the sauce and toss to mix well. Serve with egg-fried rice or noodles.

Energy 445Kcal/1873kJ; Protein 29.8g; Carbohydrate 52.2g, of which sugars 17.4g; Fat 13.9g, of which saturates 2.9g; Cholesterol 79mg; Calcium 55mg; Fibre 2g; Sodium 1154mg.

SWEET AND SOUR PORK, THAI-STYLE

IT WAS THE CHINESE WHO ORIGINALLY CREATED SWEET AND SOUR COOKING, BUT THE THAIS ALSO DO IT VERY WELL. THIS VERSION HAS A FRESHER AND CLEANER FLAVOUR THAN THE ORIGINAL. IT MAKES A SUBSTANTIAL MEAL WHEN SERVED WITH RICE.

SERVES FOUR

INGREDIENTS
350g/12oz lean pork
30ml/2 tbsp vegetable oil
4 garlic cloves, thinly sliced
1 small red onion, sliced
30ml/2 tbsp Thai fish sauce
15ml/1 tbsp granulated sugar
1 red (bell) pepper, seeded and diced
½ cucumber, seeded and sliced
2 plum tomatoes, cut into wedges
115g/4oz piece of fresh pineapple, cut into small chunks
2 spring onions (scallions), cut into short lengths
ground black pepper
coriander (cilantro) leaves and spring onions (scallions), shredded to garnish

1 Place the pork in the freezer for 30–40 minutes, until firm. Using a sharp knife, cut it into thin strips.

2 Heat the oil in a wok or large frying pan. Add the garlic. Cook over a medium heat until golden, then add the pork and stir-fry for 4–5 minutes. Add the onion slices and toss to mix.

3 Add the fish sauce, sugar and ground black pepper to taste. Toss the mixture over the heat for 3–4 minutes more.

4 Stir in the red pepper, cucumber, tomatoes, pineapple and spring onions. Stir-fry for 3–4 minutes more, then spoon into a bowl. Garnish with the coriander and spring onions and serve.

Energy 211Kcal/881kJ; Protein 20.3g; Carbohydrate 11.8g, of which sugars 10.7g; Fat 9.5g, of which saturates 2g; Cholesterol 55mg; Calcium 31mg; Fibre 2g; Sodium 70mg.

STIR-FRIED PORK WITH DRIED SHRIMP

YOU MIGHT EXPECT THE DRIED SHRIMPS TO GIVE THIS DISH A FISHY FLAVOUR, BUT INSTEAD THEY SIMPLY IMPART A DELICIOUS SAVOURY TASTE, WHICH GOES VERY WELL WITH THE PORK AND WILTED GREENS. THIS IS GOOD JUST AS IT IS, BUT COULD BE SERVED WITH NOODLES OR JASMINE RICE.

SERVES FOUR

INGREDIENTS

  250g/9oz pork fillet
    (tenderloin), sliced
  30ml/2 tbsp vegetable oil
  2 garlic cloves, finely chopped
  45ml/3 tbsp dried shrimps
  10ml/2 tsp dried shrimp paste
  30ml/2 tbsp soy sauce
  juice of 1 lime
  15ml/1 tbsp palm sugar or light
    muscovado (brown) sugar
  1 small fresh red or green chilli,
    seeded and finely chopped
  4 pak choi (bok choy) or 450g/1lb
    spring greens (collards), shredded

1 Place the pork in the freezer for about 30 minutes, until firm. Using a sharp knife, cut it into thin slices.

2 Heat the oil in a wok or frying pan and cook the garlic until golden brown. Add the pork and stir-fry for about 4 minutes, until just cooked through.

3 Add the dried shrimp, then stir in the shrimp paste, with the soy sauce, lime juice and sugar. Add the chilli and pak choi or spring greens and toss over the heat until the vegetables are just wilted.

4 Transfer the stir-fry to warm individual bowls and serve immediately.

Energy 200Kcal/833kJ; Protein 23.1g; Carbohydrate 6.3g, of which sugars 6.2g; Fat 9.2g, of which saturates 1.7g; Cholesterol 96mg; Calcium 334mg; Fibre 2.4g; Sodium 1223mg.

LEMON GRASS PORK

CHILLIES AND LEMON GRASS FLAVOUR THIS SIMPLE STIR-FRY, WHILE CHOPPED, UNSALTED PEANUTS ADD AN INTERESTING CONTRAST IN TEXTURE. LOOK OUT FOR JARS OF CHOPPED LEMON GRASS, WHICH ARE HANDY WHEN THE FRESH VEGETABLE ISN'T AVAILABLE, AND WILL KEEP IN THE REFRIGERATOR.

SERVES FOUR

INGREDIENTS
  675g/1½lb boneless
    pork loin
  2 lemon grass stalks,
    finely chopped
  4 spring onions (scallions),
    thinly sliced
  5ml/1 tsp salt
  12 black peppercorns,
    coarsely crushed
  30ml/2 tbsp groundnut
    (peanut) oil
  2 garlic cloves, chopped
  2 fresh red chillies, seeded
    and chopped
  5ml/1 tsp soft light brown sugar
  30ml/2 tbsp Thai fish sauce
  25g/1oz/¼ cup roasted unsalted
    peanuts, chopped
  ground black pepper
  coarsely torn coriander (cilantro)
    leaves, to garnish
  cooked rice noodles, to serve

1 Trim any excess fat from the pork. Cut the meat across into 5mm/¼in thick slices, then cut each slice into 5mm/¼in strips. Put the pork into a bowl with the lemon grass, spring onions, salt and crushed peppercorns; mix well. Cover with clear film (plastic wrap) and leave to marinate in a cool place for 30 minutes.

2 Preheat a wok, add the oil and swirl it around. Add the pork mixture and stir-fry over a medium heat for about 3 minutes, until browned all over.

3 Add the garlic and red chillies and stir-fry for a further 5–8 minutes over a medium heat, until the pork is cooked through and tender.

4 Add the sugar, fish sauce and chopped peanuts and toss to mix, then season to taste with black pepper. Serve immediately on a bed of rice noodles, garnished with the coarsely torn coriander leaves.

COOK'S TIP
The most intense heat in chillies is in the membrane surrounding the seeds, so make sure you remove it all.

Energy 297Kcal/1240kJ; Protein 37.9g; Carbohydrate 2.1g, of which sugars 1.7g; Fat 15.2g, of which saturates 3.6g; Cholesterol 106mg; Calcium 20mg; Fibre 0.5g; Sodium 119mg.

PAN-FRIED PORK WITH GINGER SAUCE

REPUTEDLY CREATED BY A CANTEEN DINNER LADY AT A TOKYO UNIVERSITY DURING THE 1970s, THIS DISH, KNOWN AS BUTA-NIKU SHOGA YAKI, IS PARTICULARLY POPULAR WITH YOUNGSTERS.

SERVES FOUR

INGREDIENTS
  450g/1lb pork chops, boned
    and trimmed
  15ml/1 tbsp vegetable oil
  1 small onion, thinly sliced
    lengthways
  50g/2oz/1 cup beansprouts
  50g/2oz mangetouts (snow peas),
    trimmed
  salt
For the marinade
  15ml/1 tbsp shoyu
  15ml/1 tbsp sake
  15ml/1 tbsp mirin
  4cm/1½in piece fresh root ginger,
    very finely grated,
    plus juice

1 Wrap the pork chops in clear film (plastic wrap) and freeze for 2 hours. Cut into 3mm/⅛in slices, then into 4cm/1½in wide strips.

2 To make the marinade, mix all the ingredients in a plastic container. Add the pork and marinate for 15 minutes.

3 Heat the vegetable oil in a wok on a medium-high heat. Add the onion and stir-fry for 3 minutes.

4 Take half of the pork slices out of the marinade and add to the wok. Transfer the meat to a plate when its colour changes; this will take only about 2–3 minutes. Repeat the process with the rest of the meat and reserve the marinade. Transfer all the cooked pork slices and onions to the plate.

5 Pour the reserved marinade into the wok and simmer until it has reduced by one-third. Add the beansprouts and mangetouts, then the pork and increase the heat to medium-high for 2 minutes.

6 Heap the beansprouts on individual serving plates and lean the meat, onions and mangetouts against them. Serve immediately.

DEEP-FRIED PORK FILLET

THIS INVIGORATING JAPANESE DISH IS SO GOOD THAT SOME RESTAURANTS SERVE NOTHING ELSE. THE PORK IS ALWAYS GARNISHED WITH A HEAP OF VERY FINELY SHREDDED WHITE CABBAGE.

SERVES FOUR

INGREDIENTS
  1 white cabbage
  4 pork loin chops or cutlets, boned
  plain (all-purpose) flour, to dust
  vegetable oil, for deep-frying
  2 eggs, beaten
  50g/2oz/1 cup dried
    white breadcrumbs
  salt and ready-ground mixed pepper
  prepared English (hot) mustard,
    to garnish
  Japanese pickles, to serve
For the sauce
  60ml/4 tbsp Worcestershire sauce
  30ml/2 tbsp good-quality
    tomato ketchup
  5ml/1 tsp shoyu

1 Quarter the cabbage and remove the central core. Slice the wedges very finely with a vegetable slicer or a sharp knife.

2 Make a few deep cuts horizontally across the fat of the meat. This prevents the meat curling up while cooking. Rub a little salt and pepper into the meat and dust with the flour, then shake off any excess.

3 Heat the oil to 180°C/350°F, or until a cube of bread browns in 45 seconds.

4 Dip the meat in the beaten eggs, then coat with breadcrumbs. Deep-fry two pieces at a time for 8–10 minutes, or until golden brown. Drain on a wire rack or on kitchen paper. Repeat until all the pieces of pork are deep-fried.

5 Heap the cabbage on four individual serving plates. Cut the pork crossways into 2cm/¾in thick strips and arrange them to your liking on the cabbage.

6 To make the *ton-katsu* sauce, mix the Worcestershire sauce, ketchup and shoyu in a jug (pitcher) or gravy boat. Serve the pork and cabbage immediately, with the sauce, mustard and Japanese pickles. Pickles can also be served in separate dishes, if you like.

Energy 179Kcal/747kJ; Protein 25.3g; Carbohydrate 2.8g, of which sugars 2.1g; Fat 7.4g, of which saturates 1.9g; Cholesterol 71mg; Calcium 21mg; Fibre 0.7g; Sodium 614mg.
Energy 311Kcal/1304kJ; Protein 31.1g; Carbohydrate 21.7g, of which sugars 12g; Fat 11.6g, of which saturates 2.9g; Cholesterol 166mg; Calcium 141mg; Fibre 3.5g; Sodium 522mg.

CHINESE BRAISED PORK BELLY WITH GREENS

PORK BELLY BECOMES MELTINGLY TENDER IN THIS SLOW-BRAISED DISH FLAVOURED WITH ORANGE, CINNAMON, STAR ANISE AND GINGER. THE FLAVOURS MELD AND MELLOW DURING COOKING TO PRODUCE A RICH, COMPLEX, ROUNDED TASTE. SERVE SIMPLY WITH RICE AND STEAMED GREENS.

<u>SERVES FOUR</u>

INGREDIENTS

800g/1¾lb pork belly, trimmed
  and cut into 12 pieces
400ml/14fl oz/1⅔ cups beef stock
75ml/5 tbsp soy sauce
finely grated rind and juice
  of 1 large orange
15ml/1 tbsp finely shredded fresh
  root ginger
2 garlic cloves, sliced
15ml/1 tbsp hot chilli powder
15ml/1 tbsp muscovado sugar
  (molasses)
3 cinnamon sticks
3 cloves
10 black peppercorns
2–3 star anise
steamed greens and rice, to serve

1 Place the pork in a wok and pour over water to cover. Bring the water to the boil. Cover, reduce the heat and cook gently for 30 minutes. Drain the pork and return to the wok with the stock, soy sauce, orange rind and juice, ginger, garlic, chilli powder, muscovado sugar, cinnamon sticks, cloves, peppercorns and star anise.

2 Pour over water to just cover the pork belly pieces and cook on a high heat until the mixture comes to a boil.

3 Cover the wok tightly with a lid, then reduce the heat to low and cook gently for 1½ hours, stirring occasionally to prevent the pork from sticking to the base of the wok.

Energy 543Kcal/2260kJ; Protein 38.9g; Carbohydrate 6.6g, of which sugars 6.4g; Fat 40.4g, of which saturates 14.6g; Cholesterol 142mg; Calcium 19mg; Fibre 0g; Sodium 1475mg.

AROMATIC PORK WITH BASIL

THE COMBINATION OF MOIST, JUICY PORK AND MUSHROOMS, CRISP GREEN MANGETOUTS AND FRAGRANT BASIL IN THIS GINGER- AND GARLIC-INFUSED STIR-FRY IS ABSOLUTELY DELICIOUS. SERVED WITH SIMPLE STEAMED JASMINE RICE, IT MAKES A PERFECT QUICK SUPPER DURING THE WEEK.

SERVES FOUR

INGREDIENTS
  40g/1½oz cornflour (cornstarch)
  500g/1¼lb pork fillet (tenderloin),
    thinly sliced
  15ml/1 tbsp sunflower oil
  10ml/2 tsp sesame oil
  15ml/1 tbsp very finely shredded
    fresh root ginger
  3 garlic cloves, thinly sliced
  200g/7oz mangetouts (snow peas),
    halved lengthways
  300g/11oz/generous 4 cups mixed
    mushrooms, such as shiitake,
    button (white) or oyster, sliced if
    large
  120ml/4fl oz/½ cup Chinese
    cooking wine
  45ml/3 tbsp soy sauce
  a small handful of sweet basil leaves
  salt and ground black pepper
  steamed jasmine rice, to serve

1 Place the cornflour in a strong plastic bag. Season well and add the sliced pork. Shake the bag to coat the pork in flour and then remove the pork and shake off any excess flour. Set aside.

2 Preheat the wok over a high heat and add the oils. When very hot, stir in the ginger and garlic and cook for 30 seconds. Add the pork and cook over a high heat for about 5 minutes, stirring often, until sealed.

3 Add the mangetouts and mushrooms to the wok and stir-fry for 2–3 minutes. Add the Chinese cooking wine and soy sauce, stir-fry for 2–3 minutes and remove from the heat.

4 Just before serving, stir the sweet basil leaves into the pork. Serve with steamed jasmine rice.

Energy 298Kcal/1248kJ; Protein 30.4g; Carbohydrate 14.6g, of which sugars 4.8g; Fat 9.8g, of which saturates 2.4g; Cholesterol 79mg; Calcium 41mg; Fibre 2g; Sodium 903mg.

CELLOPHANE NOODLES WITH PORK

SIMPLE, SPEEDY AND SATISFYING, THIS IS THE SORT OF DISH THE WOK WAS MADE FOR. IT LOOKS SPECTACULAR, WITH THE CLEAR, GLASS-LIKE NOODLES CURLING OVER THE COLOURFUL VEGETABLE MIXTURE. A POPULAR THAI DISH, IT IS NOW SERVED ALL OVER THE WORLD.

SERVES TWO

INGREDIENTS

  200g/7oz cellophane noodles
  30ml/2 tbsp vegetable oil
  15ml/1 tbsp magic paste
  200g/7oz minced (ground) pork
  1 fresh green or red chilli, seeded
    and finely chopped
  300g/11oz/3½ cups beansprouts
  bunch spring onions (scallions),
    finely chopped
  30ml/2 tbsp soy sauce
  30ml/2 tbsp Thai fish sauce
  30ml/2 tbsp sweet chilli sauce
  15ml/1 tbsp palm sugar or light
    muscovado (brown) sugar
  30ml/2 tbsp rice vinegar
  30ml/2 tbsp roasted peanuts,
    chopped and small bunch fresh
    coriander (cilantro), chopped,
    to garnish

1 Place the noodles in a large bowl, cover with boiling water and soak for 10 minutes. Drain the noodles and set aside until ready to use.

2 Heat the oil in a wok or large, heavy frying pan. Add the magic paste and stir-fry for 2–3 seconds, then add the pork. Stir-fry the meat, breaking it up with a wooden spatula, for 2–3 minutes, until browned all over.

3 Add the chopped chilli to the meat and stir-fry for 3–4 seconds, then add the beansprouts and chopped spring onions, stir-frying for a few seconds after each addition.

4 Snip the noodles into 5cm/2in lengths and add to the wok, with the soy sauce, Thai fish sauce, sweet chilli sauce, sugar and rice vinegar.

5 Toss the ingredients together over the heat until well combined and the noodles have warmed through. Pile on to a platter or into a large bowl. Sprinkle over the peanuts and coriander and serve immediately.

VARIATION
This dish is also very good made with chicken. Replace the pork with the same quantity of minced (ground) chicken.

Energy 755Kcal/3153kJ; Protein 39.8g; Carbohydrate 96.8g, of which sugars 14.6g; Fat 23.3g, of which saturates 4.2g; Cholesterol 63mg; Calcium 94mg; Fibre 4g; Sodium 1158mg.

FIVE-FLAVOUR NOODLES

THE JAPANESE NAME FOR THIS DISH TRANSLATES AS "FIVE DIFFERENT INGREDIENTS"; HOWEVER, THERE'S NOTHING TO STOP YOU ADDING AS MANY DIFFERENT INGREDIENTS AS YOU LIKE TO MAKE AN EXCITING AND TASTY NOODLE STIR-FRY. THE SEASONING MIX IMPARTS A GREAT FLAVOUR.

SERVES FOUR

INGREDIENTS

300g/11oz dried Chinese thin egg
   noodles or 500g/1¼lb fresh yaki-
   soba noodles
200g/7oz lean boneless pork,
   thinly sliced
22ml/4 tsp sunflower oil
10g/¼oz grated fresh root ginger
1 garlic clove, crushed
200g/7oz green cabbage,
   roughly chopped
115g/4oz/2 cups beansprouts
1 green (bell) pepper, seeded and cut
   into fine strips
1 red (bell) pepper, seeded and cut
   into fine strips
salt and ground black pepper
20ml/4 tsp ao-nori seaweed, to
   garnish (optional)
For the seasoning mix
60ml/4 tbsp Worcestershire sauce
15ml/1 tbsp Japanese soy sauce
15ml/1 tbsp oyster sauce
15ml/1 tbsp sugar
2.5ml/½ tsp salt
ground white pepper

3 Heat 7.5ml/1½ tsp of the oil in a wok. Stir fry the pork until just cooked, then remove it from the pan.

4 Wipe the wok with kitchen paper, and heat the remaining oil in it. Add the ginger, garlic and cabbage and stir-fry for 1 minute.

5 Add the beansprouts, stir until softened, then add the peppers and stir-fry for 1 minute more.

6 Return the pork to the pan and add the noodles. Stir in all the ingredients for the seasoning mix and stir-fry for 2–3 minutes. Serve immediately, sprinkled with ao-nori seaweed (if using).

1 Cook the noodles according to the instructions on the packet. Drain well and set aside.

2 Cut the pork into 3–4cm/1¼–1½in strips and season with salt and pepper.

VARIATION
Try this with strips of tender chicken breast instead of pork.

Energy 471Kcal/1988kJ; Protein 22.8g; Carbohydrate 71g, of which sugars 17.4g; Fat 12.6g, of which saturates 3g; Cholesterol 54mg; Calcium 95mg; Fibre 5.2g; Sodium 652mg.

SPICY FRIED NOODLES

THIS IS A WONDERFULLY VERSATILE DISH BECAUSE YOU CAN ADAPT IT TO INCLUDE YOUR FAVOURITE
INGREDIENTS — JUST AS LONG AS YOU KEEP A BALANCE OF FLAVOURS, TEXTURES AND COLOURS.

SERVES FOUR

INGREDIENTS
225g/8oz egg thread noodles
60ml/4 tbsp vegetable oil
2 garlic cloves, finely chopped
175g/6oz pork fillet (tenderloin),
  sliced into thin strips
1 skinless, boneless chicken breast
  portion (about 175g/6oz), sliced
  into thin strips
115g/4oz/1 cup cooked peeled
  prawns (shrimp)
juice of half a lemon
45ml/3 tbsp Thai fish sauce
30ml/2 tbsp soft light brown sugar
2 eggs, beaten
½ fresh red chilli, seeded and
  finely chopped
50g/2oz/⅔ cup beansprouts
60ml/4 tbsp roasted
  peanuts, chopped
3 spring onions (scallions), cut into
  5cm/2in lengths and shredded
45ml/3 tbsp chopped fresh
  coriander (cilantro)

1 Bring a large pan of water to the boil.
Add the noodles, remove the pan from
the heat and leave for 5 minutes.

2 Meanwhile, heat 45ml/3 tbsp of the
oil in a wok or large frying pan, add the
garlic and cook for 30 seconds. Add the
pork and chicken and stir-fry until
lightly browned, then add the prawns
and stir-fry for 2 minutes.

3 Add the lemon juice, then add
the fish sauce and sugar. Stir-fry
until the sugar has dissolved.

4 Drain the noodles and add to the wok
or pan with the remaining 15ml/1 tbsp
oil. Toss all the ingredients together.

5 Pour the beaten eggs over the
noodles and stir-fry until almost set,
then add the chilli and beansprouts.

6 Divide the roasted peanuts, spring
onions and coriander leaves into two
equal portions, add one portion to the
pan and stir-fry for about 2 minutes.

7 Tip the noodles on to a serving platter.
Sprinkle on the remaining roasted
peanuts, spring onions and chopped
coriander and serve immediately.

COOK'S TIP
Store beansprouts in the refrigerator and
use within a day of purchase, as they
tend to lose their crispness and become
slimy and unpleasant quite quickly. The
most commonly used beansprouts are
sprouted mung beans, but you could use
other types of beansprouts instead.

Energy 597Kcal/2504kJ; Protein 39.3g; Carbohydrate 50.8g, of which sugars 10.3g; Fat 27.8g, of which saturates 5.5g; Cholesterol 226mg; Calcium 76mg; Fibre 2.9g; Sodium 250mg.

NASI GORENG

ONE OF THE MOST POPULAR AND BEST-KNOWN DISHES FROM INDONESIA, THIS IS A MARVELLOUS WAY TO USE UP LEFTOVER RICE, AND MEATS SUCH AS PORK AND CHICKEN.

SERVES FOUR TO SIX

INGREDIENTS
    350g/12oz/1¾ cups basmati rice
      (dry weight), cooked and cooled
    2 eggs
    30ml/2 tbsp water
    105ml/7 tbsp sunflower oil
    225g/8oz pork fillet or fillet of beef
    2–3 fresh red chillies
    10ml/2 tsp shrimp paste
    2 garlic cloves, crushed
    1 onion, sliced
    115g/4oz cooked, peeled prawns
      (shrimp)
    225g/8oz cooked chicken, chopped
    30ml/2 tbsp dark soy sauce
    salt and freshly ground black pepper
    Deep-fried Onions, to serve

1 Separate the grains of the cooked rice with a fork. Cover and set aside. Beat the eggs with the water and seasoning.

2 Heat 15ml/1 tbsp of the oil in a frying pan or wok, pour in about half the egg mixture and cook until set, without stirring. Roll up the omelette, slide it on to a plate, cut into strips and set aside. Make another omelette in the same way.

3 Cut the pork or beef fillet into neat strips. Finely shred one of the chillies and set aside.

4 Put the shrimp paste into a food processor, add the remaining chilli, garlic and onion. Process to a paste.

5 Heat the remaining oil in a wok. Fry the paste, without browning, until it gives off a spicy aroma.

6 Add the strips of pork or beef and toss the meat over the heat, to seal in the juices. Cook the meat in the wok for about 2 minutes, stirring constantly.

7 Add the prawns, cook for 2 minutes, then add the chicken, rice, and soy sauce, with salt and pepper to taste, stirring constantly. Serve in individual bowls, garnished with omelette strips, shredded chilli and Deep-fried Onions.

Energy 463Kcal/1929kJ; Protein 27.3g; Carbohydrate 49.4g, of which sugars 2.1g; Fat 17.1g, of which saturates 2.7g; Cholesterol 151mg; Calcium 49mg; Fibre 0.5g; Sodium 288mg.

POPIAH

THIS IS THE STRAITS CHINESE OR NONYA VERSION OF THE SPRING ROLL. DO NOT BE PUT OFF BY THE NUMBER OF INGREDIENTS; IT TAKES A LITTLE TIME TO GET EVERYTHING TOGETHER BUT ONCE IT IS ALL ON THE TABLE THE COOK CAN RELAX AS GUESTS ASSEMBLE THEIR OWN ROLLS.

MAKES ABOUT TWENTY PANCAKES

INGREDIENTS
  40g/1½oz/⅓ cup cornflour
    (cornstarch)
  215g/7½oz/generous 1¾ cups
    plain (all-purpose) flour
  salt
  450ml/¾ pint/scant 2 cups water
  6 eggs, beaten
  lard (white cooking fat), for frying
For the cooked filling
  30ml/2 tbsp vegetable oil
  1 onion, finely chopped
  2 garlic cloves, crushed
  115g/4oz cooked pork, chopped
  115g/4oz crab meat or peeled cooked
    prawns (shrimp), thawed if frozen
  115g/4oz drained canned bamboo
    shoot, thinly sliced
  1 small yam bean, peeled and grated
    or 12 drained canned water
    chestnuts, finely chopped
  15–30ml/1–2 tbsp yellow
    salted beans
  15ml/1 tbsp light soy sauce
  ground black pepper
For the fresh fillings
  2 hard-boiled eggs, chopped
  2 Chinese sausages, steamed
    and sliced
  115g/4oz packet fried tofu, each
    piece halved
  225g/8oz/4 cups beansprouts
  115g/4oz crab meat or peeled
    cooked prawns
  ½ cucumber, cut into matchsticks
  small bunch of spring onions
    (scallions), finely chopped
  20 lettuce leaves, rinsed and dried
  fresh coriander (cilantro) sprigs, to
    garnish
  selection of sauces, including bottled
    chopped chillies, bottled chopped
    garlic and hoisin sauce, to serve

COOK'S TIP
Yam beans are large tubers with a mild sweet texture similar to water chestnuts.

1 Sift the flours and salt into a bowl. Add the measured water and eggs and mix to a smooth batter.

2 Grease a heavy-based frying pan with lard. Heat the pan, pouring off any excess lard, then pour in just enough batter to cover the base.

3 As soon as it sets, flip and cook the other side. The pancakes should be quite thin. Repeat with the remaining batter to make 20–24 pancakes in all. Pile the cooked pancakes on top of each other, with a layer of greaseproof paper between each to prevent them sticking. Wrap in foil and keep warm in a low oven.

4 Make the cooked filling. Heat the oil in a wok and stir-fry the onion and garlic for 5 minutes until softened but not browned.

5 Add the pork, crab meat or prawns, bamboo shoot and grated yam bean or water chestnuts. Stir-fry the mixture over a medium heat for 2–3 minutes.

6 Add the salted yellow beans and soy sauce to the wok, with pepper to taste. Cover and cook gently for 15–20 minutes, adding a little water if the mixture starts to dry out. Spoon into a serving bowl and allow to cool.

7 Meanwhile, arrange the chopped hard-boiled eggs, sliced Chinese sausages, sliced tofu, beansprouts, crab meat or prawns, cucumber, spring onions and lettuce leaves in piles on a large platter or in separate bowls. Spoon the bottled chopped chillies, bottled chopped garlic and hoisin sauce into small bowls.

8 Each person makes up his or her own popiah by spreading a very small amount of chopped chilli, garlic or hoisin sauce on a pancake, adding a lettuce leaf, a little of the cooked filling and a small selection of the fresh ingredients. The pancake wrapper should not be over-filled.

9 The ends can be tucked in and the pancake rolled up in typical spring roll fashion, then eaten in the hand. They also look attractive simply rolled with the filling showing.

VARIATION
The popiah can be filled and rolled before guests arrive, in which case, garnish with sprigs of coriander. It is more fun though for everyone to fill and roll their own.

Energy 141Kcal/592kJ; Protein 9.2g; Carbohydrate 10.9g, of which sugars 1.3g; Fat 7.1g, of which saturates 1.2g; Cholesterol 89mg; Calcium 162mg; Fibre 0.8g; Sodium 181mg.

FRAGRANT HARBOUR FRIED RICE

THE CHINESE NAME FOR HONG KONG IS FRAGRANT HARBOUR, AND IT IS THE CROSSROADS FOR MANY STYLES OF COOKING. FRIED RICE IS EVER POPULAR AS YET ANOTHER WAY OF USING UP LITTLE BITS OF THIS AND THAT TO MAKE A VERITABLE FEAST. COOK THE RICE THE DAY BEFORE IF POSSIBLE.

SERVES FOUR

INGREDIENTS

225g/8oz/generous 1 cup long
    grain rice
about 90ml/6 tbsp vegetable oil
2 eggs, beaten
4 Chinese dried mushrooms, soaked
    for 30 minutes in warm water to cover
8 shallots or 2 small onions, sliced
115g/4oz peeled cooked prawns
    (shrimp), thawed if frozen
3 garlic cloves, crushed
115g/4oz cooked pork, cut into
    thin strips
115g/4oz Chinese sausage, cooked
    and sliced at an angle
30ml/2 tbsp light soy sauce
115g/4oz/1 cup frozen peas, thawed
2 spring onions (scallions), shredded
1–2 fresh or dried red chillies,
    seeded (optional)
salt and ground black pepper
coriander (cilantro) leaves, to garnish

1 Bring a large pan of lightly salted water to the boil. Add the rice and cook for 12–15 minutes until just tender. Drain and cool quickly. Tip into a bowl and chill. Ideally use the next day.

2 Heat about 15ml/1 tbsp of the oil in a wok over a medium heat, pour in the beaten eggs and allow to set without stirring. Slide the omelette on to a plate, roll it up and with a sharp knife cut into fine strips. Set aside.

3 Drain the mushrooms, cut off and discard the stems and slice the caps finely. Heat a wok, add 15ml/1 tbsp of the remaining oil and, when hot, stir-fry the shallots or onions until crisp and golden brown. Remove with a slotted spoon and set aside.

4 Add the prawns and garlic to the wok, with a little more oil if needed, and fry for 1 minute.

5 Remove the prawns and garlic from the wok and set aside. Add 15ml/1 tbsp more oil to the wok.

6 Stir-fry the shredded pork and the mushrooms for 2 minutes; add the cooked Chinese sausage slices and heat for a further 2 minutes. Lift out from the wok and keep warm.

7 Wipe the wok, reheat with the remaining oil and stir-fry the rice, adding more oil if needed so the grains are coated. Stir in the soy sauce, salt and pepper, plus half the cooked ingredients.

8 Add the peas and half the spring onions and toss over the heat until the peas are cooked.

9 Pile the fried rice on a heated platter and arrange the remaining cooked ingredients on top, with the remaining spring onions. Add the chilli, if using, and the coriander leaves, to garnish.

COOK'S TIP

There are many theories on the best way to cook rice. This method gives excellent results every time: Put 225g/8oz/ generous 1 cup long grain rice in a sieve and rinse thoroughly in cold water. Place in a large bowl, add salt to taste and pour in just under 600ml/1 pint/2½ cups boiling water. Cover with microwave film, leaving a gap, and cook in a 675 watt microwave on full power for 10 minutes. Leave to stand for 5 minutes more. Cool, then stir with a chopstick.

Energy 450Kcal/1872kJ; Protein 14.5g; Carbohydrate 51g, of which sugars 4.4g; Fat 20.9g, of which saturates 3.1g; Cholesterol 113mg; Calcium 48mg; Fibre 1.1g; Sodium 58mg.

CRISPY THAI NOODLE SALAD

RICE NOODLES PUFF UP AND BECOME LIGHT AND CRISPY WHEN DEEP-FRIED AND MAKE A LOVELY BASE FOR THIS TANGY, FRAGRANT SALAD. SERVE AS A SNACK OR LIGHT MEAL, AND ENJOY THE HEADY COMBINATION OF SPICY CHILLIES, FRAGRANT PORK AND PRAWNS, AND CRISPY NOODLES.

SERVES FOUR

INGREDIENTS
sunflower oil, for deep-frying
115g/4oz rice vermicelli
45ml/3 tbsp groundnut (peanut) oil
2 eggs, lightly beaten with 15ml/
    1 tbsp water
30ml/2 tbsp palm sugar
30ml/2 tbsp Thai fish sauce
15ml/1 tbsp rice wine vinegar
30ml/2 tbsp tomato ketchup
1 fresh red chilli, thinly sliced
3 garlic cloves, crushed
5ml/1 tsp finely grated fresh
    root ginger
200g/7oz minced (ground) pork
400g/14oz cooked peeled tiger
    prawns (shrimp)
4 spring onions (scallions),
    finely shredded
60ml/4 tbsp chopped coriander
    (cilantro) leaves

1 Fill a wok one-third full of sunflower oil and heat to 180°C/350°F or until a cube of bread, dropped into the oil, browns in 45 seconds. Working in batches, deep-fry the vermicelli, for 10–20 seconds, or until puffed up. Remove from the wok with a slotted spoon and drain on kitchen paper.

2 Carefully discard the oil and wipe out the wok. Heat 15ml/1 tbsp of the groundnut oil in the wok. Add half the egg mixture and swirl the wok to make a thin omelette. Cook gently for 2–3 minutes, until the egg has just set and then carefully transfer to a board.

3 Repeat with a further 15ml/1 tbsp of groundnut oil and the remaining egg mixture to make a second omelette. Place the second omelette on top of the first and roll up into a cylinder. Using a sharp knife, cut the cylinder crossways to make thin strips, then set the strips aside on a plate.

4 Mix together the palm sugar, fish sauce, rice wine vinegar, tomato ketchup, chilli, garlic and ginger. Stir half this mixture into the pork and mix.

5 Heat the remaining groundnut oil in the wok. When hot, add the pork mixture and stir-fry for 4–5 minutes until cooked through. Add the prawns and stir-fry for 1–2 minutes.

6 Remove the wok from the heat and add the remaining palm sugar mixture, fried vermicelli, spring onions and coriander and toss to combine.

7 Divide the mixture among four warmed plates and top with the shredded omelette. Serve immediately.

Energy 508Kcal/2118kJ; Protein 35.1g; Carbohydrate 33.1g, of which sugars 10.5g; Fat 26.4g, of which saturates 5g; Cholesterol 371mg; Calcium 142mg; Fibre 0.8g; Sodium 405mg.

WARM LAMB AND NOODLE SALAD WITH MINT

THIS THAI-INSPIRED SALAD COMBINES THIN SLICES OF WOK-FRIED LAMB WITH LIGHTLY COOKED FRESH VEGETABLES AND RICE NOODLES, ALL TOSSED TOGETHER WITH A DELICIOUSLY FRAGRANT, AROMATIC, ASIAN-STYLE DRESSING, THEN HEAPED ARTISTICALLY ON INDIVIDUAL PLATES.

SERVES FOUR

INGREDIENTS
30ml/2 tbsp red Thai curry paste
60ml/4 tbsp sunflower oil
750g/1lb 11oz lamb neck fillets,
   thinly sliced
250g/9oz sugar snap peas
500g/1¼lb fresh rice noodles
1 red (bell) pepper, seeded and
   very thinly sliced
1 cucumber, cut into very thin
   slices with a vegetable peeler
6–7 spring onions (scallions),
   sliced diagonally
a large handful of fresh mint leaves
For the dressing
15ml/1 tbsp sunflower oil
juice of 2 limes
1 garlic clove, crushed
15ml/1 tbsp sugar
15ml/1 tbsp Thai fish sauce
30ml/2 tbsp soy sauce

1 In a shallow dish, mix together the red curry paste and half the oil. Add the lamb slices and toss to coat. Cover and leave to marinate in the refrigerator for up to 24 hours.

2 Blanch the sugar snap peas in a wok of lightly salted boiling water for 1–2 minutes. Drain, refresh under cold water, drain again thoroughly and transfer to a large bowl.

3 Put the noodles in a separate bowl and pour over boiling water to cover. Leave to soak for 5–10 minutes, until tender, then drain well and separate into strands with your fingers.

4 Add the noodles to the bowl containing the sugar snap peas, then add the sliced red pepper, cucumber and spring onions. Toss lightly to mix.

5 Heat a wok over a high heat and add the remaining sunflower oil. Stir-fry the lamb, in two batches, for 3–4 minutes, or until cooked through, then add to the bowl of salad ingredients.

6 Place all the dressing ingredients in a screw-top jar, screw on the lid and shake well to combine. Pour the dressing over the warm salad, sprinkle over the fresh mint leaves and toss well to combine. Serve immediately.

Energy 820Kcal/3418kJ; Protein 46g; Carbohydrate 76.4g, of which sugars 9.4g; Fat 36g, of which saturates 11.7g; Cholesterol 143mg; Calcium 55mg; Fibre 4.1g; Sodium 709mg.

COCONUT SPICED LAMB ᴼᴺ POPPADUMS

CRISP, MELT-IN-THE-MOUTH MINI POPPADUMS MAKE A GREAT BASE FOR THESE DIVINE LITTLE BITES.
TOP THEM WITH A DRIZZLE OF YOGURT AND A SPOONFUL OF MANGO CHUTNEY, THEN SERVE
IMMEDIATELY. TO MAKE AN EQUALLY TASTY VARIATION, USE CHICKEN OR PORK IN PLACE OF THE LAMB.

MAKES TWENTY-FIVE

INGREDIENTS
   30ml/2 tbsp sunflower oil
   4 shallots, finely chopped
   30ml/2 tbsp medium curry paste
   300g/11oz minced (ground) lamb
   90ml/6 tbsp tomato purée (paste)
   5ml/1 tsp caster (superfine) sugar
   200ml/7fl oz/scant 1 cup
     coconut cream
   juice of 1 lime
   60ml/4 tbsp chopped fresh
     mint leaves
   vegetable oil, for deep-frying
   salt and ground black pepper
   25 mini poppadums
   natural (plain) yogurt and
     mango chutney, to drizzle
   1 red chilli cut into slivers and mint
     leaves, to garnish

1 Heat the oil in a wok over a medium heat and stir-fry the shallots for 4–5 minutes, then add the curry paste. Stir-fry for 1 minute and then add the lamb. Stir-fry over a high heat for a further 4–5 minutes, then stir in the tomato purée, sugar and coconut cream.

2 Simmer the lamb for 25–30 minutes, until the liquid has been absorbed. Season and stir in the lime juice and mint. Turn off the heat and keep warm.

3 Fill a separate wok one-third full of oil and heat to 180°C/350°F or until a cube of bread browns in 40 seconds. Deep-fry the poppadums for 30–40 seconds. Drain on kitchen paper.

4 Place the poppadums on a serving platter. Put a spoonful of spiced lamb on each one, then top with a little yogurt and mango chutney. Serve immediately, garnished with slivers of red chilli and mint leaves.

Energy 63Kcal/260kJ; Protein 2.7g; Carbohydrate 2.7g, of which sugars 1.3g; Fat 4.7g, of which saturates 1.4g; Cholesterol 9mg; Calcium 7mg; Fibre 0.3g; Sodium 45mg.

SEAFOOD AND FISH

*Some of the finest recipes for the wok feature seafood and fish,
and no wonder, for steaming, stir-frying and deep-frying are
perfect methods for cooking these ingredients. Whether your
taste is for a hearty fish soup, or for something with a crisp
and crunchy coating, such as Deep-fried Skate Wings with
Wasabi, or the sumptuous Langoustine with Lemon Grass
Risotto, the wok will prove to be the perfect utensil. If your
wok is large enough, you can even steam fish whole, wrapped
in banana leaves to seal in the superb flavours. For smaller
portions of fish, use a bamboo steamer, or a stack, which will
allow you to steam vegetables at the same time.*

CURRIED SEAFOOD WITH COCONUT MILK

THIS QUICK CURRY IS BASED ON A THAI CLASSIC. THE LOVELY GREEN COLOUR COMES FROM THE FINELY CHOPPED CHILLI AND FRESH HERBS ADDED DURING THE LAST FEW MOMENTS OF COOKING.

SERVES FOUR

INGREDIENTS

  225g/8oz small ready-prepared squid
  225g/8oz raw tiger prawns
    (jumbo shrimp)
  400ml/14fl oz/1⅔ cups coconut milk
  2 kaffir lime leaves, finely shredded
  30ml/2 tbsp Thai fish sauce
  450g/1lb firm white fish fillets,
    skinned, boned and cut into chunks
  2 fresh green chillies, seeded and
    finely chopped
  30ml/2 tbsp torn fresh basil or
    coriander (cilantro) leaves
  squeeze of fresh lime juice
  cooked Thai jasmine rice,
    to serve
For the curry paste
  6 spring onions (scallions),
    coarsely chopped
  4 fresh coriander (cilantro) stems,
    coarsely chopped, plus 45ml/3 tbsp
    chopped fresh coriander (cilantro)
  4 kaffir lime leaves, shredded
  8 fresh green chillies, seeded and
    coarsely chopped
  1 lemon grass stalk,
    coarsely chopped
  2.5cm/1in piece fresh root ginger,
    peeled and coarsely chopped
  45ml/3 tbsp chopped fresh basil
  15ml/1 tbsp vegetable oil

1 Make the curry paste. Put all the ingredients, except the oil, in a food processor and process to a paste. Alternatively, pound together in a mortar with a pestle. Stir in the oil.

2 Rinse the squid and pat dry with kitchen paper. Cut the bodies into rings and halve the tentacles, if necessary.

3 Heat a wok until hot, add the prawns and stir-fry, without any oil, for about 4 minutes, until they turn pink.

5 Pour the coconut milk into the wok, then bring to the boil over a medium heat, stirring constantly. Add 30ml/ 2 tbsp of curry paste, the shredded lime leaves and fish sauce and stir well to mix. Reduce the heat to low and simmer gently for about 10 minutes.

6 Add the squid, prawns and chunks of fish and cook for about 2 minutes, until the seafood is tender. Take care not to overcook the squid as it will become tough very quickly.

7 Just before serving, stir in the chillies and basil or coriander. Taste and adjust the flavour with a squeeze of lime juice. Garnish with prawns in their shells, and serve with Thai jasmine rice.

VARIATIONS
• You can use any firm-fleshed white fish for this curry, such as monkfish, cod, haddock or John Dory.
• If you prefer, you could substitute shelled scallops for the squid. Slice them in half horizontally and add them with the prawns (shrimp). As with the squid, be careful not to overcook them.

4 Remove the prawns from the wok and leave to cool slightly, then peel off the shells, saving a few with shells on for the garnish. Make a slit along the back of each one and remove the black vein.

Energy 238Kcal/1005kJ; Protein 40.6g; Carbohydrate 7g, of which sugars 6.2g; Fat 5.5g, of which saturates 0.9g; Cholesterol 288mg; Calcium 145mg; Fibre 1.4g; Sodium 622mg.

STIR-FRIED PRAWNS <u>WITH</u> TAMARIND

THIS DISH PERFECTLY ILLUSTRATES HOW VERSATILE THE WOK IS, IT IS USED FIRST FOR DEEP-FRYING, THEN DRY-FRYING THE CHILLIES, AND THEN STIR-FRYING FOR THIS DELICIOUS DISH. LEAVE A FEW PRAWNS IN THEIR SHELLS FOR VISUAL EFFECT.

SERVES FOUR TO SIX

INGREDIENTS

  15ml/1 tbsp chopped garlic
  30ml/2 tbsp sliced shallots
  vegetable oil for deep-frying
  6 dried red chillies
  30ml/2 tbsp vegetable oil
  30ml/2 tbsp chopped onion
  30ml/2 tbsp palm sugar or light
    muscovado (brown) sugar
  30ml/2 tbsp chicken stock or water
  15ml/1 tbsp Thai fish sauce
  90ml/6 tbsp tamarind juice, made
    by mixing tamarind paste with
    warm water
  450g/1lb prawns (shrimp), peeled
  2 spring onions (scallions), chopped,
    to garnish

1 Deep-fry the chopped garlic and sliced shallots, drain on kitchen paper and set aside. Drain the oil from the wok and wipe clean.

2 Add the dried chillies and dry-fry by pressing them against the surface of the wok or pan with a spatula, turning them occasionally. Do not let them burn. Set them aside to cool slightly.

3 Add the oil to the wok or pan and reheat. Add the chopped onion and cook over a medium heat, stirring occasionally, for 2–3 minutes, until softened and golden brown. Add the sugar, stock or water, fish sauce, dry-fried red chillies and the tamarind juice, stirring until the sugar has dissolved.

4 Bring the mixture to the boil, then lower the heat slightly.

5 Add the prawns, and deep-fried garlic and shallots. Toss over the heat for 3–4 minutes, until the prawns are pink and cooked through. Garnish with the spring onions and serve.

Energy 117Kcal/493kJ; Protein 13.6g; Carbohydrate 6.8g, of which sugars 6.4g; Fat 4.2g, of which saturates 0.5g; Cholesterol 146mg; Calcium 69mg; Fibre 0.3g; Sodium 144mg.

FRAGRANT TIGER PRAWNS WITH DILL

THIS ELEGANT DISH HAS A FRESH, LIGHT FLAVOUR AND IS EQUALLY GOOD SERVED AS A SIMPLE SUPPER OR FOR A DINNER PARTY. THE DELICATE TEXTURE OF FRESH PRAWNS GOES REALLY WELL WITH MILD CUCUMBER AND FRAGRANT DILL, AND ALL YOU NEED IS SOME RICE OR NOODLES TO SERVE.

SERVES FOUR TO SIX

INGREDIENTS
  500g/1¼lb raw tiger prawns
    (jumbo shrimp), heads and shells
    removed but tails left on
  500g/1¼lb cucumber
  30ml/2 tbsp butter
  15ml/1 tbsp olive oil
  15ml/1 tbsp finely chopped garlic
  45ml/3 tbsp chopped fresh dill
  juice of 1 lemon
  salt and ground black pepper
  steamed rice or noodles, to serve

1 Using a small, sharp knife, carefully make a shallow slit along the back of each prawn and use the point of the knife to remove the black vein. Set the prawns aside.

2 Peel the cucumber and slice in half lengthways. Using a small teaspoon, gently scoop out all the seeds and discard. Cut the cucumber into 4 x 1cm/1½ x ½in sticks.

3 Heat a wok over a high heat, then add the butter and oil. When the butter has melted, add the cucumber and garlic and fry over a high heat for 2–3 minutes, stirring continuously.

4 Add the prepared prawns to the wok and continue to stir-fry over a high heat for 3–4 minutes, or until the prawns turn pink and are just cooked through, then remove from the heat.

5 Add the fresh dill and lemon juice to the wok and toss to combine. Season well with salt and ground black pepper and serve immediately with steamed rice or noodles.

Energy 192Kcal/798kJ; Protein 23.2g; Carbohydrate 2.5g, of which sugars 1.9g; Fat 9.8g, of which saturates 4.4g; Cholesterol 260mg; Calcium 123mg; Fibre 0.9g; Sodium 287mg.

CURRIED PRAWNS IN COCONUT MILK

IF YOU USE CANNED COCONUT MILK AND BOUGHT CURRY PASTE, THIS IS ONE OF THE QUICKEST AND EASIEST DISHES THERE IS. SERVED WITH NOODLES, IT MAKES THE PERFECT LIGHT SUPPER FOR A LAZY SUMMER EVENING, OR A QUICK LUNCH RUSTLED UP FROM STORE-CUPBOARD INGREDIENTS.

SERVES FOUR TO SIX

INGREDIENTS

600ml/1 pint/2½ cups coconut milk
30ml/2 tbsp yellow curry paste (see below)
15ml/1 tbsp Thai fish sauce
2.5ml/½ tsp salt
5ml/1 tsp sugar
450g/1lb raw king prawns (jumbo shrimp) peeled, thawed if frozen
225g/8oz cherry tomatoes
½ fresh yellow and orange (bell) pepper, seeded and cut into thin strips, plus chives and juice of ½ lime, to garnish

VARIATION
Use cooked prawns for a quick version of this dish. Add them after the tomatoes and heat through for a minute or two.

1 Put half the coconut milk in a wok or heavy pan and bring to the boil. Add the yellow curry paste, stir until it disperses, then lower the heat and simmer for about 10 minutes.

2 Add the Thai fish sauce, salt, sugar and remaining coconut milk to the sauce. Simmer for 5 minutes more, stirring frequently.

3 Add the prawns and cherry tomatoes. Simmer very gently for about 5 minutes until the prawns are pink and tender.

4 Spoon into a serving dish, sprinkle with lime juice and garnish with the yellow and orange pepper and chives.

COOK'S TIP
To make yellow curry paste, put into a food processor or blender 6–8 fresh yellow chillies, the chopped base of 1 lemon grass stalk, 4 chopped shallots, 4 chopped garlic cloves, 15ml/1 tbsp chopped peeled fresh root ginger, 5ml/1 tsp coriander seeds, 5ml/1 tsp mustard powder, 5ml/1 tsp salt, 2.5ml/½ tsp ground cinnamon, 15ml/1 tbsp brown sugar and 30ml/2 tbsp sunflower oil. Process to a paste, scrape into a glass jar, cover and keep in the refrigerator.

Energy 99Kcal/421kJ; Protein 13.8g; Carbohydrate 6.9g, of which sugars 6.9g; Fat 2g, of which saturates 0.5g; Cholesterol 146mg; Calcium 92mg; Fibre 0.4g; Sodium 375mg.

SAMBAL GORENG WITH PRAWNS

SAMBAL GORENG IS AN IMMENSELY USEFUL AND ADAPTABLE SAUCE. HERE IT IS USED AS THE BASIS FOR A WOK-COOKED DISH WITH PRAWNS AND GREEN PEPPER, BUT YOU COULD ADD FINE STRIPS OF CALF'S LIVER, CHICKEN LIVERS, TOMATOES, GREEN BEANS OR HARD-BOILED EGGS.

SERVES FOUR TO SIX

INGREDIENTS
350g/12oz peeled cooked prawns
   (shrimp)
1 green (bell) pepper, seeded and sliced
60ml/4 tbsp tamarind juice
pinch of sugar
45ml/3 tbsp coconut milk or cream
strips of lime rind and red onion
   slices, to garnish
boiled or steamed rice
For the sambal goreng
2.5cm/1in cube shrimp paste
2 onions, roughly chopped
2 garlic cloves, roughly chopped
2.5cm/1in piece fresh galangal,
   peeled and sliced
10ml/2 tsp chilli sambal or 2 fresh
   red chillies, seeded and sliced
1.5ml/¼ tsp salt
30ml/2 tbsp vegetable oil
45ml/3 tbsp tomato purée (paste)
600ml/1 pint/2½ cups vegetable
   stock or water

2 Heat the oil in a wok or frying pan and fry the paste for 1–2 minutes, without browning, until the mixture gives off a rich aroma. Stir in the tomato purée and the stock or water and cook for 10 minutes. Ladle half the sauce into a bowl and leave to cool. The leftover sauce can be used in another recipe (see Cook's Tip).

3 Add the prawns and green pepper to the remaining sauce. Cook over a medium heat for 3–4 minutes, then stir in the tamarind juice, sugar and coconut milk or cream. Spoon the prawns into warmed serving bowls and garnish with strips of lime rind and sliced red onion. Serve at once with boiled or steamed rice.

1 Make the sambal goreng. Grind the shrimp paste with the onions and garlic using a mortar and pestle. Alternatively, put in a food processor and process to a paste. Add the galangal, chilli sambal or sliced chillies and salt. Process or pound to a fine paste.

COOK'S TIP
Store the remaining sauce in a sealed jar in the refrigerator for up to 3 days or freeze it in a tub for up to 3 months.

Energy 108Kcal/452kJ; Protein 11.8g; Carbohydrate 5.9g, of which sugars 5.1g; Fat 4.3g, of which saturates 0.5g; Cholesterol 118mg; Calcium 72mg; Fibre 1.2g; Sodium 175mg.

GOAN PRAWN CURRY <u>WITH</u> MANGO

THIS SWEET, SPICY, HOT-AND-SOUR CURRY COMES FROM THE SHORES OF WESTERN INDIA. IT IS SIMPLE TO MAKE, AND THE ADDITION OF MANGO AND TAMARIND PRODUCES A VERY FULL, RICH FLAVOUR. IF YOU HAVE TIME, MAKE THE SAUCE THE DAY BEFORE TO GIVE THE FLAVOURS TIME TO DEVELOP.

SERVES FOUR

INGREDIENTS
    5ml/1 tsp hot chilli powder
    15ml/1 tbsp paprika
    2.5ml/1/2 tsp ground turmeric
    4 garlic cloves, crushed
    10ml/2 tsp finely grated ginger
    30ml/2 tbsp ground coriander
    10ml/2 tsp ground cumin
    15ml/1 tbsp jaggery or palm sugar
    1 green mango
    400g/14oz can coconut milk
    10ml/2 tsp salt
    15ml/1 tbsp tamarind paste
    1kg/2 1/4lb large prawns (shrimp)
        chopped coriander (cilantro),
        to garnish
    steamed white rice, chopped tomato,
        cucumber and onion salad, to serve

VARIATION
Peel the prawns before cooking if you like, but be careful not to overcook.

1 Wash, stone and slice the mango and set aside. In a large bowl, combine the chilli powder, paprika, turmeric, garlic, ginger, ground coriander, ground cumin and jaggery or palm sugar. Add 400ml/14fl oz/1 2/3 cups cold water to the bowl and stir to combine.

2 Pour the spice mixture into a wok and place over a high heat and bring the mixture to the boil. Cover the wok with a lid, reduce the heat to low and simmer gently for 8–10 minutes.

3 Add the mango, coconut milk, salt and tamarind paste to the wok and stir to combine. Bring to a simmer and then add the prawns.

4 Cover the wok and cook gently for 10–12 minutes, or until the prawns have turned pink and are cooked.

5 Serve the curry garnished with chopped coriander, accompanied by steamed white rice and a tomato, cucumber and onion salad.

Energy 151Kcal/648kJ; Protein 22.1g; Carbohydrate 14.1g, of which sugars 14g; Fat 1.1g, of which saturates 0.5g; Cholesterol 263mg; Calcium 143mg; Fibre 1g; Sodium 2102mg.

HERB- AND CHILLI-SEARED SCALLOPS

TENDER, SUCCULENT SCALLOPS TASTE SIMPLY DIVINE WHEN MARINATED IN FRESH CHILLI, FRAGRANT MINT AND AROMATIC BASIL, THEN QUICKLY SEARED IN A PIPING HOT WOK. IF YOU CAN'T FIND KING SCALLOPS FOR THIS RECIPE, USE TWICE THE QUANTITY OF SMALLER QUEEN SCALLOPS.

SERVES FOUR

INGREDIENTS
20–24 king scallops, cleaned
120ml/4fl oz/½ cup olive oil
finely grated rind and juice
 of 1 lemon
30ml/2 tbsp finely chopped mixed
 fresh mint and basil
1 fresh red chilli, seeded and finely
 chopped
salt and ground black pepper
500g/1¼lb pak choi (bok choy)

1 Place the scallops in a shallow, non-metallic bowl in a single layer. In a clean bowl, mix together half the oil, the lemon rind and juice, chopped herbs and chilli and spoon over the scallops. Season well with salt and black pepper, cover and set aside.

2 Using a sharp knife, cut each pak choi lengthways into four pieces.

VARIATION
If you can't find pak choi (bok choy) use Chinese broccoli, purple sprouting broccoli or Swiss chard instead.

3 Heat a wok over a high heat. When hot, drain the scallops (reserving the marinade) and add to the wok. Cook for 1 minute on each side, or until cooked to your liking.

4 Pour the marinade over the scallops and remove the wok from the heat. Transfer the scallops and juices to a platter and keep warm. Wipe out the wok with a piece of kitchen paper.

5 Place the wok over a high heat. When all traces of moisture have evaporated, add the remaining oil. When the oil is hot add the pak choi and stir-fry over a high heat for 2–3 minutes, until the leaves wilt.

6 Divide the greens among four warmed serving plates, then top with the reserved scallops and their juices and serve immediately.

Energy 410Kcal/1714kJ; Protein 44.5g; Carbohydrate 8.3g, of which sugars 2.1g; Fat 22.3g, of which saturates 3.5g; Cholesterol 82mg; Calcium 286mg; Fibre 3.2g; Sodium 494mg.

SPICED SCALLOPS AND SUGAR SNAP PEAS ON CRISPY NOODLE CAKES

TENDER, JUICY SCALLOPS AND SUGAR SNAP PEAS COOKED IN SPICES AND SERVED ON A BED OF FRIED NOODLES IS A WINNING COMBINATION. IT'S SIMPLE AND STYLISH AND MAKES A GREAT DISH FOR SPECIAL-OCCASION ENTERTAINING.

SERVES FOUR

INGREDIENTS
  45ml/3 tbsp oyster sauce
  10ml/2 tsp soy sauce
  5ml/1 tsp sesame oil
  5ml/1 tsp golden caster
    (superfine) sugar
  30ml/2 tbsp sunflower oil
  2 fresh red chillies, finely sliced
  4 garlic cloves, finely chopped
  10ml/2 tsp finely chopped fresh
    root ginger
  250g/9oz sugar snap peas, trimmed
  500g/1¼lb king scallops, cleaned,
    roes discarded and sliced in half
  3 spring onions (scallions),
    finely shredded
For the noodle cakes
  250g/9oz fresh thin egg noodles
  10ml/2 tsp sesame oil
  120ml/4fl oz/½ cup sunflower oil

1 Cook the noodles in a wok of boiling water for 1 minute, or until tender. Drain well and transfer to a bowl with the sesame oil and 15ml/1 tbsp of the sunflower oil. Spread the noodles out on a large baking sheet and leave to dry in a warm place for 1 hour.

VARIATION
Use king prawns (jumbo shrimp) instead of scallops, if you like.

2 To cook the noodles, heat 15ml/ 1 tbsp of the oil in a non-stick wok over a high heat. Divide the noodle mixture into four portions and add one portion to the wok. Using a spatula, flatten it out and shape it into a cake.

3 Reduce the heat slightly and cook the cake for about 5 minutes on each side, or until crisp and golden. Drain on kitchen paper and keep warm while you make the remaining three noodle cakes in the same way.

4 Mix together the oyster sauce, soy sauce, sesame oil and sugar in a small bowl, stirring until the sugar has dissolved completely.

5 Heat a wok over medium heat and add the sunflower oil. When hot add the chillies, garlic and ginger, and stir-fry for 30 seconds. Add the sugar snap peas and stir-fry for 1–2 minutes.

6 Add the scallops and spring onions to the wok and stir fry over high heat for 1 minute. Stir in the oyster sauce mixture and cook for a further 1 minute until warmed through.

7 To serve, place a noodle cake on each of four warmed plates and top each one with the scallop mixture. Serve immediately.

Energy 689Kcal/2888kJ; Protein 41.4g; Carbohydrate 59.9g, of which sugars 6.2g; Fat 33.3g, of which saturates 5.4g; Cholesterol 78mg; Calcium 73mg; Fibre 5g; Sodium 700mg.

STEAMED SCALLOPS WITH GINGER

IT HELPS TO HAVE TWO WOKS WHEN MAKING THIS DISH. IF YOU ARE NOT DOUBLY BLESSED, BORROW AN EXTRA ONE FROM A FRIEND, OR USE A LARGE, HEAVY PAN WITH A TRIVET FOR STEAMING THE SECOND PLATE OF SCALLOPS. TAKE CARE NOT TO OVERCOOK THE TENDER SEAFOOD.

SERVES FOUR

INGREDIENTS
  24 king scallops in their
    shells, cleaned
  15ml/1 tbsp very finely shredded
    fresh root ginger
  5ml/1 tsp very finely chopped garlic
  1 large fresh red chilli, seeded and
    very finely chopped
  15ml/1 tbsp light soy sauce
  15ml/1 tbsp Chinese
    rice wine
  a few drops of sesame oil
  2–3 spring onions (scallions), very
    finely shredded
  15ml/1 tbsp very finely chopped
    fresh chives
  noodles or rice, to serve

1 Remove the scallops from their shells, then remove the membrane and hard white muscle from each one. Arrange the scallops on two plates. Rinse the shells, dry and set aside.

2 Fill two woks with 5cm/2in water and place a trivet in the base of each one. Bring to the boil.

3 Meanwhile, mix together the ginger, garlic, chilli, soy sauce, rice wine, sesame oil, spring onions and chives.

COOK'S TIP
Use the freshest scallops you can find. If you ask your fishmonger to shuck them, remember to ask for the shells.

4 Spoon the flavourings over the scallops. Lower a plate into each of the woks. Turn the heat to low, cover and steam for 10–12 minutes.

5 Divide the scallops among four, or eight, of the reserved shells and serve immediately with noodles or rice.

Energy 167Kcal/708kJ; Protein 29.8g; Carbohydrate 7g, of which sugars 2.6g; Fat 2g, of which saturates 0.6g; Cholesterol 59mg; Calcium 53mg; Fibre 0.8g; Sodium 496mg.

LANGOUSTINE ᵂⁱᵀᴴ LEMON GRASS RISOTTO

THE WOK IS WONDERFUL FOR MAKING RISOTTO. FOR THIS VERSION, THE TRADITIONAL ITALIAN RISOTTO IS GIVEN A SUBTLE ASIAN TWIST WITH THE ADDITION OF FRAGRANT LEMON GRASS, ASIAN FISH SAUCE AND CHINESE CHIVES: THE PERFECT ACCOMPANIMENT TO SIMPLY STEAMED LANGOUSTINES.

SERVES FOUR

INGREDIENTS
  8 fresh langoustines
  30ml/2 tbsp olive oil
  15ml/1 tbsp butter
  1 onion, finely chopped
  1 carrot, finely diced
  1 celery stick, finely diced
  30ml/2 tbsp very finely chopped
    lemon grass
  300g/11oz/1¹/₂ cups arborio or other
    risotto rice
  200ml/7fl oz/scant 1 cup
    dry white wine
  1.5 litres/2¹/₂ pints/6¹/₄ cups boiling
    vegetable stock
  50ml/2fl oz/¹/₄ cup Thai fish sauce
  30ml/2 tbsp finely chopped
    Chinese chives
  salt and ground black pepper

1 Place the langoustines in a baking parchment-lined bamboo steamer, cover and place over a wok of simmering water. Steam for 6–8 minutes, remove from the heat and keep warm.

2 Heat the oil and butter in a wok and add the vegetables. Cook over a high heat for 2–3 minutes. Add the lemon grass and rice and stir-fry for 2 minutes.

3 Add the wine to the wok, reduce the heat and slowly stir until the wine is absorbed. Add about two thirds of the stock and cook gently, stirring until absorbed. Continue adding the stock, stirring until absorbed before adding more. When the rice is tender, stir in the fish sauce and Chinese chives, check the seasoning and serve immediately, topped with langoustines.

Energy 467Kcal/1949kJ; Protein 23.8g; Carbohydrate 64.2g, of which sugars 3.4g; Fat 8.9g, of which saturates 2.3g; Cholesterol 201mg; Calcium 114mg; Fibre 0.9g; Sodium 218mg.

STIR-FRIED SQUID <u>WITH</u> GINGER

THERE'S AN ANCIENT BELIEF THAT A WELL-LOVED WOK HOLDS THE MEMORY OF ALL THE DISHES THAT HAVE EVER BEEN COOKED IN IT. GIVE YOURS SOMETHING TO THINK ABOUT BY INTRODUCING IT TO THIS CLASSIC COMBINATION OF BABY SQUID IN SOY SAUCE, GINGER AND LEMON JUICE.

SERVES TWO

INGREDIENTS

    4 ready-prepared baby squid, total
      weight about 250g/9oz
    15ml/1 tbsp vegetable oil
    2 garlic cloves, finely chopped
    30ml/2 tbsp soy sauce
    2.5cm/1in piece fresh root ginger,
      peeled and finely chopped
    juice of ½ lemon
    5ml/1 tsp granulated sugar
    2 spring onions (scallions), chopped

VARIATIONS
This dish is often prepared with fresh galangal rather than ginger and works well with most kinds of seafood, including prawns (shrimp) and scallops.

1 Rinse the squid well and pat dry with kitchen paper. Cut the bodies into rings and halve the tentacles, if necessary.

2 Heat the oil in a wok or frying pan and cook the garlic until golden brown, but do not let it burn. Add the squid and stir-fry for 30 seconds over a high heat.

3 Add the soy sauce, ginger, lemon juice, sugar and spring onions. Stir-fry for a further 30 seconds, then serve.

COOK'S TIP
Squid has an undeserved reputation for being rubbery in texture. This is always a result of overcooking it.

Energy 165Kcal/694kJ; Protein 19.7g; Carbohydrate 4.8g, of which sugars 3.2g; Fat 7.6g, of which saturates 1.2g; Cholesterol 281mg; Calcium 20mg; Fibre 0g; Sodium 1206mg.

STEAMED MUSSELS IN COCONUT MILK

MUSSELS STEAMED IN COCONUT MILK AND FRESH AROMATIC HERBS AND SPICES MAKE AN IDEAL DISH FOR INFORMAL ENTERTAINING. IT IS QUICK AND EASY TO MAKE IN A WOK, AND IS GREAT FOR A RELAXED DINNER WITH FRIENDS. SERVE WITH PLENTY OF CRUSTY BREAD.

SERVES FOUR

INGREDIENTS

15ml/1 tbsp sunflower oil
6 garlic cloves, roughly chopped
15ml/1 tbsp finely chopped
  fresh root ginger
2 large fresh red chillies, seeded
  and finely sliced
6 spring onions (scallions),
  finely chopped
400ml/14fl oz/1⅔ cups coconut milk
45ml/3 tbsp light soy sauce
2 limes
5ml/1 tsp caster (superfine) sugar
1.6kg/3½lb mussels, scrubbed
  and beards removed
a large handful of chopped
  coriander (cilantro)
salt and ground black pepper

1 Heat the wok over a high heat and then add the oil. Stir in the garlic, ginger, chillies and spring onions and stir-fry for 30 seconds. Pour in the coconut milk, then add the soy sauce.

2 Grate the zest of the limes into the coconut milk mixture and add the sugar. Stir to mix and bring to the boil.

3 Add the cleaned mussels. Return to the boil, cover and cook briskly for 5–6 minutes, or until all the mussels have opened. Discard any mussels that remain closed.

4 Remove the wok from the heat and stir the chopped coriander into the mussel mixture.

5 Season the mussels well with salt and pepper. Ladle into warmed bowls and serve immediately.

COOK'S TIP

For an informal supper with friends, take the wok straight to the table rather than serving in individual bowls. A wok makes a great serving dish, and there's something utterly irresistible about eating the mussels straight from it.

Energy 165Kcal/702kJ; Protein 21.9g; Carbohydrate 7.7g, of which sugars 7.6g; Fat 5.6g, of which saturates 1g; Cholesterol 48mg; Calcium 276mg; Fibre 0.3g; Sodium 1165mg.

LAKSA LEMAK

THIS SPICY SOUP MAKES A MARVELLOUS PARTY DISH, AND IS SUBSTANTIAL ENOUGH FOR AN ENTIRE MAIN COURSE. GUESTS SPOON NOODLES INTO WIDE SOUP BOWLS, ADD ACCOMPANIMENTS OF THEIR CHOICE, TOP UP WITH SOUP AND THEN TAKE A FEW PRAWN CRACKERS TO NIBBLE.

SERVES SIX

INGREDIENTS

675g/1¹/₂lb small clams
50g/2oz ikan bilis (dried anchovies)
2 × 400ml/14fl oz cans coconut milk
900ml/1¹/₂ pints/3³/₄ cups water
115g/4oz shallots, finely chopped
4 garlic cloves, chopped
6 macadamia nuts or blanched
    almonds, chopped
3 lemon grass stalks, root trimmed
90ml/6 tbsp sunflower oil
1cm/¹/₂in cube shrimp paste
25g/1oz/¹/₄ cup mild curry powder
a few curry leaves
2–3 aubergines (eggplant), trimmed
675g/1¹/₂lb raw peeled prawns
    (shrimp)
10ml/2 tsp sugar
1 head Chinese leaves (Chinese
    cabbage), thinly sliced
115g/4oz/2 cups beansprouts, rinsed
2 spring onions (scallions), finely
    chopped
50g/2oz crispy fried onions
115g/4oz fried tofu
675g/1¹/₂lb mixed noodles
prawn (shrimp) crackers, to serve

1 Scrub the clams and then put in a large pan with 1cm/¹/₂in water. Bring to the boil, cover and steam for 3–4 minutes until all the the clams have opened. Drain.

2 Put the ikan bilis (dried anchovies) in a pan and add the water. Bring to the boil and simmer for 20 minutes.

3 Make up the coconut milk to 1.2 litres/2 pints/5 cups with water.

4 Meanwhile, put the shallots, garlic and nuts into a mortar. Cut off the lower 5cm/2in of two of the lemon grass stalks, chop finely and add to the mortar. Pound the mixture to a paste.

5 Heat the oil in a wok, add the shallot paste and fry until the mixture gives off a rich aroma. Bruise the remaining lemon grass stalk and add to the pan. Toss over the heat to release its flavour.

6 Mix the shrimp paste and curry powder to a paste with a little of the coconut milk, add to the wok and toss the mixture over the heat for 1 minute, stirring all the time, and keeping the heat low. Stir in the remaining coconut milk. Add the curry leaves and leave the mixture to simmer while you prepare the accompaniments.

7 Strain the ikan bilis, retaining the stock. Discard the ikan bilis and return the stock to the pan, bring to the boil, then add the whole aubergines. Cook for about 10 minutes or until the flesh is tender and the skins can be removed with ease.

COOK'S TIP
Dried shrimp or prawn paste, also called blachan, is sold in small blocks and is available from Asian supermarkets.

8 Lift the aubergines out of the pan of stock, peel, discard the skin, and cut the flesh into thick strips. Arrange the aubergines on a serving platter.

9 Sprinkle the prawns with sugar, add to the stock pan and cook for 2–4 minutes until they turn pink. Remove and place next to the aubergines. Gradually stir the remaining ikan bilis stock into the pan of soup and bring to the boil.

10 Place the clams, Chinese leaves, beansprouts, spring onions and crispy fried onions on the platter.

11 Rinse the fried tofu in boiling water, cool slightly and squeeze to remove excess oil. Cut each piece in half and add to the soup. Lower the heat to a very gentle simmer.

12 Cook the noodles according to the instructions, drain and pile in a dish. Remove the curry leaves and lemon grass from the soup.

13 Place the noodles, soup and the platter of seafood and vegetables on the table, along with a bowl of prawn crackers. Guests can then help themselves to what they want.

VARIATION
You could substitute mussels for clams, if you like. Scrub them thoroughly, removing any beards, and cook them in lightly salted water until they open. As when preparing the clams, discard any mussels that remain closed.

Energy 814Kcal/3432kJ; Protein 51.2g; Carbohydrate 101.8g, of which sugars 16.6g; Fat 25.2g, of which saturates 2.2g; Cholesterol 258mg; Calcium 558mg; Fibre 7.7g; Sodium 1302mg.

THAI FRIED NOODLES

THIS TASTY DISH IS OFTEN SERVED FOR BREAKFAST IN THAILAND, SO IF YOU FANCY AN EARLY MORNING WORKOUT WITH A WOK, GIVE IT A TRY. IT ALSO MAKES A GREAT SUPPER.

SERVES FOUR TO SIX

INGREDIENTS

16 raw tiger prawns (jumbo shrimp)
350g/12oz rice noodles
45ml/3 tbsp vegetable oil
15ml/1 tbsp chopped garlic
2 eggs, lightly beaten
15ml/1 tbsp dried
   shrimp, rinsed
30ml/2 tbsp pickled
   mooli (daikon)
50g/2oz fried tofu, cut into
   small slivers
2.5ml/½ tsp dried chilli flakes
1 large bunch garlic chives,
   about 115g/4oz, cut into
   5cm/2in lengths
225g/8oz/4 cups beansprouts
50g/2oz/½ cup roasted peanuts,
   coarsely ground
5ml/1 tsp granulated sugar
15ml/1 tbsp dark soy sauce
30ml/2 tbsp Thai fish sauce
30ml/2 tbsp tamarind juice, made
   by mixing tamarind paste with
   warm water
fresh coriander (cilantro) leaves and
   lime wedges to garnish

1 Peel the prawns, leaving the tails intact. Carefully cut along the back of each prawn and remove the dark vein.

2 Place the rice noodles in a large bowl, add warm water to cover and leave to soak for 20–30 minutes, then drain thoroughly and set aside.

3 Heat 15ml/1 tbsp of the oil in a wok. Stir-fry the garlic until golden. Stir in the prawns and cook for 1–2 minutes, until pink. Remove and set aside.

4 Heat 15ml/1 tbsp of the remaining oil in the wok. Add the eggs and tilt the wok to make a thin layer. Stir to scramble and break up. Remove from the wok and set aside with the prawns.

5 Heat the remaining oil in the same wok. Add the dried shrimp, pickled mooli, tofu slivers and dried chilli flakes. Stir briefly. Add the noodles and stir-fry for about 5 minutes.

6 Add the garlic chives, half the beansprouts and half the peanuts. Add the granulated sugar, then season with soy sauce, fish sauce and tamarind juice. Mix well and cook until the noodles are heated through.

7 Return the prawn and egg mixture to the wok and mix with the noodles. Serve topped with the remaining beansprouts and peanuts, and garnished with the coriander leaves and lime wedges.

COOK'S TIP
There are numerous species of prawns (shrimp) and they range in colour from black to white, although most turn pink when cooked. Genuine Indo-Pacific tiger prawns, of which there are several types, have a fine flavour and a good texture. They grow up to 28cm/11in in length. However, not all large, warm-water varieties are so succulent, and even farmed prawns tend to be quite expensive.

Energy 372Kcal/1553kJ; Protein 14.2g; Carbohydrate 51.1g, of which sugars 2.3g; Fat 11.6g, of which saturates 2g; Cholesterol 128mg; Calcium 57mg; Fibre 1.1g; Sodium 274mg.

FRIED JASMINE RICE <u>WITH</u> PRAWNS

STRIPS OF OMELETTE ARE USED TO GARNISH THIS RICE DISH. USE YOUR WOK FOR FRYING THE OMELETTE — THE SLOPING SIDES MAKE IT EASY TO SPREAD THE BEATEN EGG THINLY AND THEN TO SLIDE IT OUT, READY FOR ROLLING AND SLICING.

SERVES FOUR TO SIX

INGREDIENTS
    45ml/3 tbsp vegetable oil
    1 egg, beaten
    1 onion, chopped
    15ml/1 tbsp chopped garlic
    15ml/1 tbsp shrimp paste
    1kg/2¼lb/4 cups cooked jasmine rice
    350g/12oz cooked shelled prawns
      (shrimp)
    50g/2oz thawed frozen peas
    oyster sauce, to taste
    2 spring onions (scallions), chopped
    15–20 Thai basil leaves, roughly
      snipped, plus an extra sprig,
      to garnish

1 Heat 15ml/1 tbsp of the oil in a wok or frying pan. Add the beaten egg and swirl it around to set like a thin pancake.

2 Cook the pancake (on one side only) over a gentle heat until golden. Slide the pancake on to a board, roll up and cut into thin strips. Set aside.

3 Heat the remaining oil in the wok or pan, add the onion and garlic and stir-fry for 2–3 minutes. Stir in the shrimp paste and mix well until thoroughly combined.

4 Add the rice, prawns and peas and toss and stir together, until everything is heated through.

5 Season with oyster sauce to taste, taking great care as the shrimp paste is salty. Mix in the spring onions and basil leaves. Transfer to a serving dish and top with the strips of egg pancake. Serve, garnished with a sprig of basil.

Energy 357Kcal/1508kJ; Protein 17.6g; Carbohydrate 54.6g, of which sugars 1.7g; Fat 9.2g, of which saturates 1.5g; Cholesterol 154mg; Calcium 111mg; Fibre 1g; Sodium 198mg.

CRAB AND TOFU STIR-FRY

FOR A LIGHT MEAL SUITABLE FOR SERVING AT ANY TIME, THIS SPEEDY STIR-FRY IS THE IDEAL CHOICE. AS YOU NEED ONLY A LITTLE CRAB MEAT — AND YOU COULD USE THE CANNED VARIETY — THIS IS A VERY ECONOMICAL DISH. THE TOFU BOOSTS THE PROTEIN CONTENT.

SERVES TWO

INGREDIENTS

250g/9oz silken tofu
60ml/4 tbsp vegetable oil
2 garlic cloves, finely chopped
115g/4oz white crab meat
130g/4½oz/generous 1 cup baby
  corn, halved lengthways
2 spring onions (scallions), chopped
1 fresh red chilli, seeded and
  finely chopped
30ml/2 tbsp soy sauce
15ml/1 tbsp Thai fish sauce
5ml/1 tsp palm sugar or light
  muscovado (brown) sugar
juice of 1 lime
small bunch fresh coriander
  (cilantro), chopped, to garnish

1 Using a sharp knife, cut the silken tofu into 1cm/½in cubes.

2 Heat the oil in a wok or large, heavy frying pan. Add the tofu cubes and stir-fry until golden all over, taking care not to break them up. Remove the tofu with a slotted spoon and set aside.

3 Add the garlic to the wok or pan and stir-fry until golden. Add the crab meat, tofu, corn, spring onions, chilli, soy sauce, fish sauce and sugar. Cook, stirring constantly, until the vegetables are just tender. Stir in the lime juice, transfer to warmed bowls, sprinkle with the coriander and serve immediately.

Energy 365Kcal/1514kJ; Protein 23.1g; Carbohydrate 5.8g, of which sugars 4.8g; Fat 27.9g, of which saturates 3.3g; Cholesterol 41mg; Calcium 719mg; Fibre 1.2g; Sodium 2131mg.

SOTONG SAMBAL

SQUID IS READILY AVAILABLE THESE DAYS, AND IT NOW COMES CLEANED, WHICH IS A DEFINITE BONUS.
WASH THOROUGHLY INSIDE THE POCKET TO MAKE SURE THAT ALL THE QUILL HAS BEEN REMOVED.

SERVES TWO

INGREDIENTS

   8 small squid, each about 10cm/4in
     long, total weight about 350g/12oz
   lime juice (optional)
   salt
   boiled rice, to serve
For the stuffing
   175g/6oz white fish fillets, such as
     sole or plaice, skinned
   2.5cm/1in piece fresh root ginger,
     peeled and finely sliced
   2 spring onions (scallions), finely
     chopped
   50g/2oz peeled cooked prawns
     (shrimp), roughly chopped
For the sambal sauce
   4 macadamia nuts or
     blanched almonds
   1cm/$\frac{1}{2}$in piece fresh galangal,
     peeled, or 5ml/1 tsp drained
     bottled galangal
   2 lemon grass stalks, root trimmed
   1cm/$\frac{1}{2}$in cube shrimp paste
   4 fresh red chillies, or to taste,
     seeded and roughly chopped
   175g/6oz small onions, roughly
     chopped
   60–90ml/4–6 tbsp vegetable oil
   400ml/14fl oz can coconut milk

1 Clean the squid, leaving them whole.
Set aside with the tentacles.

2 To make the stuffing, put the fish,
ginger and spring onions in a mortar.
Add a little salt and pound to a paste.
Use a food processor to grind the
mixture, if you like, but don't retain a
little texture and don't overprocess.

3 Transfer the fish mixture to a bowl
and stir in the prawns.

4 Divide the filling among the squid,
using a spoon or a forcing bag fitted
with a plain tube to fill them. Tuck the
tentacles into the stuffing and secure
the top of each squid with a cocktail
stick, to stop the filling escaping.

5 Make the sauce. Put the macadamia
nuts or almonds and galangal in a food
processor. Cut off the lower 5cm/2in
from the lemon grass stalks, chop them
roughly and add them to the processor
with the shrimp paste, chillies and
onions. Process to a paste.

6 Heat the oil in a wok and fry the
mixture to bring out the full flavours.
Bruise the remaining lemon grass and
add it to the wok with the coconut milk.
Stir constantly until the sauce comes to
the boil, then lower the heat and
simmer the sauce for 5 minutes.

7 Arrange the squid in the sauce, and
cook for 15–20 minutes. Taste and
season with salt and lime juice, if liked.
Serve with boiled rice.

DEEP-FRIED PLAICE

IN THIS DISH, CALLED KAREI KARA-AGÉ, *THE FLESH OF THE FISH AND ALSO THE SKELETON IS DEEP-FRIED TO SUCH CRISPNESS THAT YOU CAN EAT THE BONES, TAILS AND HEADS, IF YOU LIKE.*

SERVES FOUR

INGREDIENTS
    4 small plaice or flounder, about
        500–675g/1¼–1½lb total weight,
        gutted, not trimmed
    60ml/4 tbsp cornflour (cornstarch)
    vegetable oil, for deep-frying
    salt
For the condiment
    130g/4½oz mooli (daikon), peeled
    4 dried chillies, seeded
    1 bunch of chives, finely chopped
        (to make 50ml/2fl oz/¼ cup)
For the sauce
    20ml/4 tsp rice vinegar
    20ml/4 tsp shoyu

1 Wash the fish under running water and put on a chopping board. Use a very sharp knife to make deep cuts around the gills and across the tail. Cut through the skin from the head down to the tail along the centre of the fish. Slide the knife under the cut near the head and gently cut the fillet from the bone. Fold the fillet with your hand as you cut as if peeling the fillet from the bone. Keep the knife horizontal to the fish.

2 Repeat for the other half, then turn the fish over and do the same to get four fillets from each fish. Place in a dish and sprinkle with a little salt on both sides. Keep the bony skeletons.

3 Pierce the mooli with a skewer or a chopstick in four places to make holes, then insert the chillies. After 15 minutes grate finely.

4 Squeeze out the moisture by hand. Scoop a quarter of the grated mooli and chilli into an egg cup, then press with your fingers. Turn out the cup on to a plate. Make three more mounds.

5 Mix the rice vinegar and shoyu and put in a bowl.

6 Cut the fish fillets into four slices crossways and put into a plastic bag with the cornflour. Shake gently to coat. Heat the oil in a wok or pan to 175°C/ 347°F. Deep-fry the fillets, two to three at a time, until light golden brown.

7 Raise the temperature to 180°C/ 350°F. Dust the skeletons with cornflour and slide into the oil.

8 Cook until golden, drain on a wire rack for 5 minutes, then fry again until very crisp. Drain and sprinkle with salt.

9 Arrange the skeletons and fried fish on the plates. Put the mooli and chives to one side on each plate. Have small plates for the sauce. To eat, mix the condiment with the sauce and dip the fillets and bones into the sauce.

Energy 331Kcal/1378kJ; Protein 19.7g; Carbohydrate 16.2g, of which sugars 1.2g; Fat 21.2g, of which saturates 2.6g; Cholesterol 0mg; Calcium 120mg; Fibre 1.2g; Sodium 640mg.

SWEET AND SOUR FISH

WHEN FISH SUCH AS RED MULLET OR SNAPPER IS DEEP-FRIED IN OIL THE SKIN BECOMES CRISP, WHILE THE FLESH INSIDE REMAINS MOIST AND JUICY. THE SWEET AND SOUR SAUCE IN THIS DISH, WITH ITS COLOURFUL CHERRY TOMATOES, PERFECTLY COMPLEMENTS THE FISH.

SERVES FOUR TO SIX

INGREDIENTS
    1 large or 2 medium fish, such as
      snapper or mullet, cleaned with
      heads removed
    20ml/4 tsp cornflour (cornstarch)
    120ml/4fl oz/½ cup vegetable oil
    15ml/1 tbsp chopped garlic
    15ml/1 tbsp chopped fresh ginger
    30ml/2 tbsp chopped shallots
    225g/8oz cherry tomatoes
    30ml/2 tbsp red wine vinegar
    30ml/2 tbsp granulated sugar
    30ml/2 tbsp tomato ketchup
    15ml/1 tbsp Thai fish sauce
    45ml/3 tbsp water
    salt and ground black pepper
    coriander (cilantro) leaves and
      shredded spring onions
      (scallions), to garnish

1 Rinse and dry the fish. Score the skin diagonally on both sides, then coat the fish lightly all over with 15ml/1 tbsp of the cornflour. Shake off any excess.

2 Heat the oil in a wok or large frying pan. Add the fish and cook over a medium heat for 6–7 minutes. Turn the fish over and cook for 6–7 minutes more, until it is crisp and brown.

3 Remove the fish with a metal spatula or fish slice and place on a large platter. Pour off all but 30ml/2 tbsp of the oil from the wok or pan and reheat. Add the garlic, ginger and shallots and cook over a medium heat, stirring occasionally, for 3–4 minutes, until golden.

4 Add the cherry tomatoes and cook until they burst open. Stir in the vinegar, sugar, tomato ketchup and fish sauce. Lower the heat and simmer gently for 1–2 minutes, then taste and adjust the seasoning, adding more vinegar, sugar and/or fish sauce, if necessary.

5 In a cup, mix the remaining 5ml/1 tsp cornflour to a paste with the water. Stir into the sauce. Heat, stirring, until it thickens. Pour the sauce over the fish, garnish with coriander leaves and shredded spring onions and serve.

Energy 245Kcal/1023kJ; Protein 16.2g; Carbohydrate 14.8g, of which sugars 10.6g; Fat 13.8g, of which saturates 1.6g; Cholesterol 38mg; Calcium 27mg; Fibre 1.1g; Sodium 138mg.

STEAMED FISH WITH CHILLI SAUCE

A LARGE WOK IS IDEAL FOR STEAMING FISH. BY LEAVING THE FISH WHOLE AND ON THE BONE, MAXIMUM FLAVOUR IS RETAINED AND THE FLESH REMAINS BEAUTIFULLY MOIST. THE BANANA LEAF IS BOTH AUTHENTIC AND ATTRACTIVE, BUT YOU CAN USE BAKING PARCHMENT INSTEAD.

SERVES FOUR

INGREDIENTS

1 large or 2 medium firm fish such as sea bass or grouper, scaled and cleaned
30ml/2 tbsp rice wine
3 fresh red chillies, seeded and thinly sliced
2 garlic cloves, finely chopped
2cm/¾in piece fresh root ginger, peeled and finely shredded
2 lemon grass stalks, crushed and finely chopped
2 spring onions (scallions), chopped
30ml/2 tbsp Thai fish sauce
juice of 1 lime
1 fresh banana leaf
For the chilli sauce
10 fresh red chillies, seeded and chopped
4 garlic cloves, chopped
60ml/4 tbsp Thai fish sauce
15ml/1 tbsp granulated sugar
75ml/5 tbsp fresh lime juice

1 Thoroughly rinse the fish under cold running water. Pat it dry with kitchen paper. With a sharp knife, slash the skin of the fish a few times on both sides.

2 Mix together the rice wine, chillies, garlic, shredded ginger, lemon grass and spring onions in a non-metallic bowl. Add the fish sauce and lime juice and mix to a paste. Place the fish on the banana leaf and spread the spice paste evenly over it, rubbing it in well where the skin has been slashed.

3 Put a rack or a small upturned plate in the base of a wok. Pour in boiling water to a depth of 5cm/2in. Lift the banana leaf, together with the fish, and place it on the rack or plate. Cover with a lid and steam for 10–15 minutes, or until the fish is cooked.

4 Meanwhile, make the sauce. Place all the ingredients in a food processor and process until smooth. If the mixture seems to be too thick, add a little cold water. Scrape into a serving bowl.

5 Serve the fish hot, on the banana leaf if you like, with the sweet chilli sauce to spoon over the top.

Energy 228Kcal/960kJ; Protein 35.2g; Carbohydrate 12g, of which sugars 10.1g; Fat 4.7g, of which saturates 0.7g; Cholesterol 140mg; Calcium 254mg; Fibre 1.6g; Sodium 392mg.

FRAGRANT RED SNAPPER IN BANANA LEAVES

SHINY, DARK GREEN BANANA LEAVES MAKE A REALLY GOOD WRAPPING FOR FISH THAT IS STEAMED IN THE WOK. HERE, WHOLE SNAPPERS ARE INFUSED WITH A DELIGHTFUL MIX OF COCONUT CREAM, MINT, CORIANDER, KAFFIR LIME LEAVES, LEMON GRASS AND CHILLI TO MAKE AN IMPRESSIVE MAIN COURSE.

3 Place the coconut cream, chopped herbs, lime juice, spring onions, lime leaves and chillies in a bowl and stir well. Season with salt and pepper.

4 Lay each banana leaf out flat on a work surface and place a fish and a split lemon grass stalk in the centre of each of them. Spread the herb mixture over each fish.

5 Wrap the banana leaf around each one to form four neat parcels. Secure each parcel tightly with a bamboo skewer or a cocktail stick (toothpick).

6 Place the parcels in a single layer in one or two tiers of a large bamboo steamer and place over a wok of simmering water. Cover tightly and steam for 15–20 minutes, or until the fish is cooked through.

7 Remove the fish from the steamer and serve immediately, still in their banana-leaf wrappings, with steamed rice and steamed Asian greens.

COOK'S TIP
When you spread the spicy coconut cream mixture over the fish, work the mixture into the cuts that you have made. This allows the flavours to penetrate the flesh and gives the finished dish a fabulous flavour. If you have time, leave the fish to stand for about half an hour before steaming. Swap the steamer baskets over halfway through cooking, so each gets similar exposure to maximum heat.

SERVES FOUR

INGREDIENTS
   4 small red snapper, grouper, tilapia
   or red bream, gutted and cleaned
   4 large squares of banana leaf
   (approximately 30cm/12in square)
   50ml/2fl oz/¼ cup coconut cream
   90ml/6 tbsp chopped coriander
   (cilantro)
   90ml/6 tbsp chopped mint
   juice of 3 limes
   3 spring onions (scallions),
   finely sliced
   4 kaffir lime leaves, finely shredded
   2 red chillies, seeded and finely
   sliced
   4 lemon grass stalks, split lengthways
   salt and ground black pepper
   steamed rice and steamed Asian
   greens, to serve

1 Using a small sharp knife, score the fish diagonally on each side. Half fill a wok with water and bring to the boil.

2 Dip each square of banana leaf into the boiling water in the wok for 15–20 seconds so they become pliable. Lift out carefully, rinse under cold water and dry with kitchen paper.

Energy 185Kcal/781kJ; Protein 39.4g; Carbohydrate 0.9g, of which sugars 0.8g; Fat 2.7g, of which saturates 0.6g; Cholesterol 74mg; Calcium 87mg; Fibre 0.1g; Sodium 168mg.

STEAMED FISH SKEWERS <u>ON</u> RICE NOODLES

FRESH TROUT IS PERFECT FOR SUMMER ENTERTAINING. IN THIS RECIPE, SUCCULENT FILLETS ARE MARINATED IN A TANGY CITRUS SPICE BLEND, THEN SKEWERED AND STEAMED IN THE WOK BEFORE SERVING ON A BED OF FRAGRANT HERB NOODLES, FLAVOURED WITH CHILLI AND SPRING ONIONS.

SERVES FOUR

INGREDIENTS

4 trout fillets, skinned
2.5ml/½ tsp turmeric
15ml/1 tbsp mild curry paste
juice of 2 lemons
15ml/1 tbsp sunflower oil
salt and ground black pepper
45ml/3 tbsp chilli-roasted peanuts,
  roughly chopped
chopped fresh mint, to garnish
For the noodles
300g/11oz rice noodles
15ml/1 tbsp sunflower oil
1 red chilli, seeded
  and finely sliced
4 spring onions (scallions),
  cut into slivers
60ml/4 tbsp roughly chopped
  fresh mint
60ml/4 tbsp roughly chopped
  fresh sweet basil

1 Trim each fillet and place in a large bowl. Mix together the turmeric, curry paste, lemon juice and oil and pour over the fish. Season with salt and black pepper and toss to mix well.

2 Place the rice noodles in a bowl and pour over enough boiling water to cover. Leave to soak for 3–4 minutes and then drain. Refresh in cold water, drain and set aside.

3 Thread 2 bamboo skewers through each trout fillet and arrange in two tiers of a bamboo steamer lined with baking parchment.

4 Cover the steamer and place over a wok of simmering water (making sure the water doesn't touch the steamer). Steam the fish skewers for 5–6 minutes, or until the fish is just cooked through.

5 Meanwhile, in a clean wok heat the oil. Add the chilli, spring onions and drained noodles and stir-fry for about 2 minutes and then stir in the chopped herbs. Season with salt and ground black pepper and divide among four bowls or plates.

6 Top each bowl of noodles with a steamed fish skewer and scatter over the chilli-roasted peanuts. Garnish with chopped mint and serve immediately.

VARIATION
You can grill (broil) these fillets instead of steaming, if you prefer. If you do use the grill (broiler), you need to soak the bamboo skewers in cold water for at least 30 minutes before threading them through the trout fillets. This will prevent them burning during cooking.

Energy 555Kcal/2317kJ; Protein 36g; Carbohydrate 62.8g, of which sugars 1g; Fat 16.6g, of which saturates 1.6g; Cholesterol 0mg; Calcium 52mg; Fibre 1.3g; Sodium 97mg.

MACKEREL WITH MUSHROOMS AND BLACK BEANS

EARTHY-TASTING SHIITAKE MUSHROOMS, ZESTY FRESH GINGER AND PUNGENT SALTED BLACK BEANS ARE THE PERFECT PARTNERS FOR ROBUSTLY FLAVOURED MACKEREL FILLETS. THE STRIKING COMBINATION OF FLAVOURS ALL COME TOGETHER BEAUTIFULLY.

SERVES FOUR

INGREDIENTS

   8 x 115g/4oz mackerel fillets
   20 dried shiitake mushrooms
   15ml/1 tbsp finely julienned fresh
     root ginger
   3 star anise
   45ml/3 tbsp dark soy sauce
   15ml/1 tbsp Chinese rice wine
   15ml/1 tbsp salted black beans
   6 spring onions (scallions), finely
     shredded
   30ml/2 tbsp sunflower oil
   5ml/1 tsp sesame oil
   4 garlic cloves, very thinly sliced
   sliced cucumber and steamed
     basmati rice, to serve

1 Divide the mackerel fillets between two lightly oiled heatproof plates, with the skin-side up. Using a small, sharp knife, make 3–4 diagonal slits in each one, then set aside.

2 Place the dried shiitake mushrooms in a large bowl and pour over enough boiling water to cover. Leave to soak for 20–25 minutes. Drain, reserving the soaking liquid, discard the stems and slice the caps thinly.

3 Place a trivet or a steamer rack in a large wok and pour in 5cm/2in of the mushroom liquid (top up with water if necessary). Add half the ginger and the star anise.

COOK'S TIP

If the mackerel has been cleaned but you need to fillet it, this is very easy to do. Just open the fish up like a book, lay it on a board with the skin side uppermost, and press down firmly with your fingers all along the backbone. Turn the fish over and the backbone will come away easily. Remove any stray bones with tweezers and cut off the tail.

4 Push the remaining ginger strips into the slits in the fish and scatter over the sliced mushrooms. Bring the liquid in the wok to a boil and lower one of the prepared plates on to the trivet.

5 Cover the wok, reduce the heat and steam for 10–12 minutes, or until the mackerel is cooked. Remove the plate and repeat with the second plate of fish, adding liquid to the wok if necessary.

6 Transfer the steamed fish to a serving platter and keep warm. Ladle 105ml/ 7 tbsp of the steaming liquid into a clean wok with the soy sauce, wine and black beans, place over a gentle heat and bring to a simmer. Spoon over the fish and sprinkle over the spring onions.

7 Wipe out the wok with a piece of kitchen paper and place over a medium heat. Add the oils and garlic and stir-fry for a few minutes until lightly golden. Pour over the fish and serve with sliced cucumber and steamed basmati rice.

Energy 573Kcal/2378kJ; Protein 43.9g; Carbohydrate 3.2g, of which sugars 1.1g; Fat 42.7g, of which saturates 8.2g; Cholesterol 122mg; Calcium 37mg; Fibre 1.2g; Sodium 678mg.

DEEP-FRIED SKATE WINGS WITH WASABI

WHOLE SKATE WINGS DIPPED IN A TEMPURA BATTER AND DEEP-FRIED UNTIL CRISP AND GOLDEN LOOK STUNNING AND TASTE WONDERFUL. THE CREAMY, ZESTY MAYONNAISE FLAVOURED WITH SOY SAUCE, FIERY WASABI PASTE AND SPRING ONIONS MAKES A GREAT ACCOMPANIMENT.

SERVES FOUR

INGREDIENTS
    4 x 250g/9oz skate wings
    65g/2½oz/9 tbsp cornflour
      (cornstarch)
    65g/2½oz/9 tbsp plain
      (all-purpose) flour
    5ml/1 tsp salt
    5ml/1 tsp Chinese five-spice powder
    15ml/1 tbsp sesame seeds
    200ml/7fl oz/scant 1 cup ice-cold
      soda water
    sunflower oil, for frying
For the mayonnaise
    200ml/7fl oz/scant 1 cup mayonnaise
    15ml/1 tbsp light soy sauce
    finely grated rind and juice of 1 lime
    5ml/1 tsp wasabi
    15ml/1 tbsp finely chopped spring
      onion (scallion)

1 Using kitchen scissors, trim away the frill from the edges of the skate wings and discard. Set aside.

2 In a large mixing bowl combine the cornflour, plain flour, salt, five-spice powder and sesame seeds. Gradually pour in the soda water and stir to mix. (It will be quite lumpy.)

3 Fill a large wok one-third full of sunflower oil and heat to 190°C/375°F or until a cube of bread, dropped into the oil, browns in 40 seconds.

4 One at a time, dip the skate wings in the batter, then lower them carefully into the wok and deep-fry for 4–5 minutes, until the skate is fully cooked and crispy. Drain on kitchen paper. Set aside and keep warm.

5 Meanwhile, mix together all the mayonnaise ingredients and divide among four small bowls. Serve immediately with the skate wings.

COOK'S TIP
Look for packets of tempura batter mix at health food shops and Asian markets. It doesn't take long to make your own batter, but sometimes seconds count.

Energy 705Kcal/2921kJ; Protein 31.9g; Carbohydrate 11.7g, of which sugars 1.2g; Fat 59.3g, of which saturates 11g; Cholesterol 38mg; Calcium 112mg; Fibre 0.5g; Sodium 792mg.

FISH MOOLIE

THIS IS A VERY POPULAR SOUTH-EAST ASIAN FISH CURRY IN A COCONUT SAUCE, WHICH IS TRULY DELICIOUS. CHOOSE A FIRM-TEXTURED FISH SO THAT THE PIECES STAY INTACT DURING THE BRIEF COOKING PROCESS. HALIBUT AND COD WORK EQUALLY WELL.

SERVES FOUR

INGREDIENTS
  500g/1¼lb monkfish or other firm-
    textured fish fillets, skinned and cut
    into 2.5cm/1in cubes
  2.5ml/½ tsp salt
  50g/2oz/⅔ cup desiccated (dry,
    unsweetened, shredded) coconut
  6 shallots or small onions, chopped
  6 blanched almonds
  2–3 garlic cloves, roughly chopped
  2.5cm/1in piece fresh root ginger,
    peeled and sliced
  2 lemon grass stalks, trimmed
  10ml/2 tsp ground turmeric
  45ml/3 tbsp vegetable oil
  2 × 400ml/14fl oz cans coconut milk
  1–3 fresh chillies, seeded and sliced
  salt and ground black pepper
  fresh chives, to garnish
  boiled rice, to serve

1 Spread out the pieces of fish in a shallow dish and sprinkle them with the salt. Dry-fry the coconut in a wok or large frying pan over medium heat, stirring constantly until it is crisp. Put in a food processor, process to an oily paste and transfer to a bowl.

2 Add the shallots or onions, almonds, garlic and ginger to the food processor. Chop the lower 5cm/2in of the lemon grass stalks and add to the processor. Process the mixture to a paste. Add the turmeric and process briefly to mix. Bruise the remaining lemon grass and set the stalks aside.

3 Heat the oil in a wok. Add the onion mixture and cook for a few minutes without browning. Stir in the coconut milk and bring to the boil, stirring constantly to prevent curdling.

4 Add the fish, most of the sliced chilli and the bruised lemon grass stalks. Cook for 3–4 minutes. Stir in the coconut paste and cook for a further 2–3 minutes only. Do not overcook the fish. Taste and adjust the seasoning.

5 Remove the lemon grass. Transfer to a hot serving dish and sprinkle with the remaining chilli. Garnish with chives and serve with boiled rice.

Energy 319Kcal/1335kJ; Protein 22.4g; Carbohydrate 16.7g, of which sugars 14.9g; Fat 18.6g, of which saturates 8.3g; Cholesterol 18mg; Calcium 96mg; Fibre 3g; Sodium 249mg.

SPICED HALIBUT AND TOMATO CURRY AND GINGER

THE CHUNKY CUBES OF WHITE FISH CONTRAST VISUALLY WITH THE RICH RED SPICY TOMATO SAUCE AND TASTE JUST AS GOOD AS THEY LOOK. HALIBUT IS USED HERE, BUT YOU CAN USE ANY TYPE OF FIRM WHITE FISH FOR THIS RECIPE.

SERVES FOUR

INGREDIENTS

1 lemon
60ml/4 tbsp rice wine vinegar
30ml/2 tbsp cumin seeds
5ml/1 tsp ground turmeric
5ml/1 tsp chilli powder
5ml/1 tsp salt
750g/1lb 11oz thick halibut
  fillets, skinned and cubed
60ml/4 tbsp sunflower oil
1 onion, finely chopped
3 garlic cloves, finely grated
30ml/2 tbsp finely grated
  fresh root ginger
10ml/2 tsp black mustard seeds
2 x 400g/14oz cans
  chopped tomatoes
5ml/1 tsp sugar
chopped coriander (cilantro)
  and sliced fresh green chilli,
  to garnish
natural (plain) yogurt,
  to drizzle (optional)
basmati rice, pickles and
  poppadums, to serve

1 Squeeze the lemon and pour 60ml/4tbsp of the juice into a shallow glass bowl. Add the vinegar, cumin, turmeric, chilli powder and salt.

2 Add the cubed fish to the bowl and coat evenly. Cover the bowl with clear film (plastic wrap) and refrigerate for 25–30 minutes.

3 Meanwhile, heat a wok over a high heat and add the oil. When hot, add the onion, garlic, ginger and mustard seeds. Reduce the heat to low and cook very gently for about 10 minutes, stirring occasionally.

4 Add the tomatoes and sugar to the wok, bring to the boil, reduce the heat, cover and cook gently for 15–20 minutes, stirring occasionally.

5 Add the fish and its marinade to the wok, stir gently to mix, then cover and simmer gently for 15–20 minutes, or until the fish is cooked through and flakes easily with a fork.

6 Ladle the curry into shallow bowls, garnish with fresh coriander and green chillies, and drizzle over some natural yogurt if you like. Serve with basmati rice, pickles and poppadums.

COOK'S TIP
Halibut is quite a dense fish, so will take about 15 minutes to cook, especially if the cubes are thick. It is important not to overcook the fish, so if you choose a different type, or buy fillets that are relatively thin, check after 5 minutes. As soon as the flesh becomes opaque and the fish flakes easily when prodded with a fork or the tip of a knife, it is ready.

Energy 335Kcal/1409kJ; Protein 41.9g; Carbohydrate 8.4g, of which sugars 8.1g; Fat 15.2g, of which saturates 2.1g; Cholesterol 66mg; Calcium 73mg; Fibre 2.2g; Sodium 622mg.

VEGETARIAN MAIN DISHES

The recipes in this section are exciting and innovative with-out being overly intricate. Aromatic Okra and Coconut Stir-fry, for instance, tastes spectacular, is easy to cook at home, and only takes about 10 minutes. Other unusual offerings are Sweet Pumpkin and Peanut Curry, Thai Noodles with Chinese Chives, and Jewelled Vegetable Rice with Crispy Fried Eggs. A few recipes in this chapter contain Thai fish sauce, so if you or your guests do not eat fish, as well as meat, you will need to substitute the fish sauce with the same amount of mushroom ketchup.

DEEP-FRIED BEAN CURD ROLLS STUFFED WITH SPICED VEGETABLES

BEAN CURD SHEETS ARE MADE FROM BOILED SOYA MILK; THE SKIN THAT FORMS ON THE TOP IS LIFTED OFF AND DRIED IN SHEETS. THEY ARE AVAILABLE IN ASIAN SUPERMARKETS AND NEED TO BE DUNKED BRIEFLY IN WATER BEFORE THEY CAN BE USED.

SERVES FOUR

INGREDIENTS

30ml/2 tbsp groundnut (peanut) oil
50g/2oz fresh enokitake mushrooms,
  finely chopped
1 garlic clove, crushed
5ml/1 tsp grated fresh root ginger
4 spring onions (scallions),
  finely shredded
1 small carrot, cut into thin
  matchsticks
115g/4oz bamboo shoots,
  cut into thin matchsticks
15ml/1 tbsp light soy sauce
5ml/1 tsp chilli sauce
5ml/1 tsp sugar
15ml/1 tbsp cornflour (cornstarch)
8 bean curd sheets (approximately
  18 x 23cm/7 x 9in each)
sunflower oil, for deep-frying
crisp salad leaves, to serve

1 Heat the groundnut oil in a wok over a high heat and add the chopped mushrooms, garlic, ginger, spring onions, carrot and bamboo shoots. Stir-fry for 2–3 minutes and add the soy sauce, chilli sauce and sugar and toss to mix thoroughly.

2 Remove the vegetables from the heat and place in a sieve to drain the juices. Set aside to cool.

3 In a small bowl, mix the cornflour with 60ml/4 tbsp of cold water to form a smooth paste. Soak the bean curd sheets in a bowl of warm water for 10–15 seconds and then lay them out on a clean work surface and pat dry with kitchen paper.

4 Brush the edges of one of the bean curd sheets with the cornflour paste and place 30–45ml/2–3 tbsp of the vegetable mixture at one end of the sheet. Fold the edges over towards the centre and roll up tightly to form a neat roll. Repeat with the remaining bean curd sheets and filling.

5 Place the filled rolls on a baking parchment-lined baking sheet or tray, cover and chill for 3–4 hours.

6 To cook, fill a wok one-third full with sunflower oil and heat to 180°C/350°F or until a cube of bread, dropped into the oil, browns in 45 seconds.

7 Working in batches, deep-fry the rolls for 2–3 minutes, or until they are crisp and golden. Drain on kitchen paper and serve immediately with crisp salad leaves.

Energy 288Kcal/1190kJ; Protein 9.5g; Carbohydrate 3.2g, of which sugars 2.2g; Fat 26.5g, of which saturates 3.2g; Cholesterol 0mg; Calcium 524mg; Fibre 1g; Sodium 10mg.

SWEET PUMPKIN AND PEANUT CURRY

A HEARTY, SOOTHING CURRY PERFECT FOR AUTUMN OR WINTER EVENINGS. ITS CHEERFUL COLOUR ALONE WILL RAISE THE SPIRITS — AND THE COMBINATION OF PUMPKIN AND PEANUTS TASTES GREAT.

SERVES FOUR

INGREDIENTS

30ml/2 tbsp vegetable oil
4 garlic cloves, crushed
4 shallots, finely chopped
30ml/2 tbsp yellow curry paste
600ml/1 pint/2½ cups
  vegetable stock
2 kaffir lime leaves, torn
15ml/1 tbsp chopped fresh galangal
450g/1lb pumpkin, peeled, seeded
  and diced
225g/8oz sweet potatoes, diced
90g/3½ oz/scant 1 cup unsalted,
  roasted peanuts, chopped
300ml/½ pint/1¼ cups coconut milk
90g/3½ oz/1½ cups chestnut
  mushrooms, sliced
30ml/2 tbsp soy sauce
50g/2oz/⅓ cup pumpkin
  seeds, toasted, and fresh green
  chilli flowers, to garnish

1 Heat the oil in a wok. Add the garlic and shallots and cook over a medium heat, stirring occasionally, for 10 minutes, until softened and golden. Do not let them burn.

2 Add the yellow curry paste and stir-fry over medium heat for 30 seconds, until fragrant, then add the stock, lime leaves, galangal, pumpkin and sweet potatoes. Bring to the boil, stirring frequently, then reduce the heat to low and simmer gently for 15 minutes.

3 Add the peanuts, coconut milk and mushrooms. Stir in the soy sauce and simmer for 5 minutes more. Spoon into warmed individual serving bowls, garnish with the pumpkin seeds and chillies and serve.

COOK'S TIP
The well-drained vegetables from any of these curries would make a very tasty filling for a pastry or pie. This may not be a Thai tradition, but it is a good example of fusion food.

Energy 285Kcal/1189kJ; Protein 8.5g; Carbohydrate 24.8g, of which sugars 12.8g; Fat 17.5g, of which saturates 3g; Cholesterol 0mg; Calcium 94mg; Fibre 4.9g; Sodium 535mg.

TOFU AND GREEN BEAN RED CURRY

RED CURRY PASTE IS ONE OF THE AUTHENTIC FLAVOURINGS OF THAI COOKING, AND WORKS JUST AS WELL IN VEGETARIAN DISHES AS IT DOES IN MEAT-BASED RECIPES.

SERVES FOUR TO SIX

INGREDIENTS
600ml/1 pint/2½ cups coconut milk
15ml/1 tbsp Thai red curry paste
45ml/3 tbsp Thai fish sauce or
  mushroom ketchup
10ml/2 tsp palm sugar or light
  muscovado (brown) sugar
225g/8oz/3¼ cups button
  (white) mushrooms
115g/4oz/scant 1 cup green
  beans, trimmed
175g/6oz firm tofu, rinsed, drained
  and cut in 2cm/¾in cubes
4 kaffir lime leaves, torn
2 fresh red chillies, sliced
fresh coriander (cilantro) leaves,
  to garnish

1 Pour about one-third of the coconut milk into a wok. Cook until it starts to separate and an oily sheen appears on the surface.

2 Add the red curry paste, fish sauce or mushroom ketchup and sugar to the wok. Mix thoroughly, then add the mushrooms. Stir and cook for 1 minute.

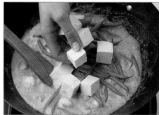

3 Stir in the remaining coconut milk. Bring back to the boil, then add the green beans and tofu cubes. Simmer gently for 4–5 minutes more.

4 Stir in the kaffir lime leaves and sliced red chillies. Spoon the curry into a serving dish, garnish with the coriander leaves and serve immediately.

Energy 79Kcal/333kJ; Protein 3.9g; Carbohydrate 8.2g, of which sugars 7.8g; Fat 3.6g, of which saturates 0.6g; Cholesterol 0mg; Calcium 189mg; Fibre 0.8g; Sodium 647mg.

THAI YELLOW VEGETABLE CURRY

THIS HOT AND SPICY CURRY MADE WITH COCONUT MILK HAS A CREAMY RICHNESS THAT CONTRASTS
WONDERFULLY WITH THE HEAT OF CHILLI AND THE BITE OF LIGHTLY COOKED VEGETABLES.

SERVES FOUR

INGREDIENTS
  30ml/2 tbsp sunflower oil
  200ml/7fl oz/scant 1 cup
    coconut cream
  300ml/½ pint/1¼ cups coconut milk
  150ml/¼ pint/⅔ cup vegetable
    stock
  200g/7oz snake beans, cut into
    2cm/¾in lengths
  200g/7oz baby corn
  4 baby courgettes (zucchini), sliced
  1 small aubergine (eggplant), cubed
    or sliced
  10ml/2 tsp palm sugar
  fresh coriander (cilantro) leaves,
    to garnish
  noodles or rice, to serve
For the curry paste
  10ml/2 tsp hot chilli powder
  10ml/2 tsp ground coriander
  10ml/2 tsp ground cumin
  5ml/1 tsp ground turmeric
  15ml/1 tbsp chopped fresh
    galangal
  10ml/2 tsp finely grated garlic
  30ml/2 tbsp finely chopped
    lemon grass
  4 red Asian shallots, finely
    chopped
  5ml/1 tsp finely chopped lime rind

1 Make the curry paste. Place the spices, galangal, garlic, lemon grass, shallots and lime rind in a small food processor and blend with 30–45ml/2–3 tbsp of cold water to make a smooth paste. Add a little more water if the paste seems too dry.

2 Heat a large wok over a medium heat and add the sunflower oil. When hot add 30–45ml/2–3 tbsp of the curry paste and stir-fry for 1–2 minutes. Add the coconut cream and cook gently for 8–10 minutes, or until the mixture starts to separate.

3 Add the coconut milk, stock and vegetables and cook gently for 8–10 minutes, until the vegetables are just tender. Stir in the palm sugar, garnish with coriander leaves and serve with noodles or rice.

COOK'S TIP
To make your own curry paste you will need a good food processor or blender, preferably one with an attachment for processing smaller quantities. Alternatively, you can use a large mortar and pestle, but be warned – it will be hard work. Store any remaining curry paste in a screw-top jar in the refrigerator for up to a week.

Energy 126Kcal/528kJ; Protein 4.7g; Carbohydrate 12.7g, of which sugars 11.9g; Fat 6.7g, of which saturates 1.1g; Cholesterol 5mg; Calcium 90mg; Fibre 2.5g; Sodium 752mg.

CORN AND CASHEW NUT CURRY

A SUBSTANTIAL CURRY, DUE TO THE POTATOES AND CORN, THIS COMBINES ALL THE ESSENTIAL FLAVOURS OF SOUTHERN THAILAND. IT IS DELICIOUSLY AROMATIC, BUT THE FLAVOUR IS FAIRLY MILD.

SERVES FOUR

INGREDIENTS
30ml/2 tbsp vegetable oil
4 shallots, chopped
90g/3½oz/scant 1 cup cashew nuts
5ml/1 tsp Thai red curry paste
400g/14oz potatoes, peeled and cut into chunks
1 lemon grass stalk, finely chopped
200g/7oz can chopped tomatoes
600ml/1 pint/2½ cups boiling water
200g/7oz/generous 1 cup drained canned whole kernel corn
4 celery sticks, sliced
2 kaffir lime leaves, rolled into cylinders and thinly sliced
15ml/1 tbsp tomato ketchup
15ml/1 tbsp light soy sauce
5ml/1 tsp palm sugar or light muscovado (brown) sugar
4 spring onions (scallions), thinly sliced
small bunch fresh basil, chopped

COOK'S TIP
Rolling the lime leaves into cylinders before slicing with a sharp knife produces very fine strips – a technique known as cutting *en chiffonnade*. Remove the central rib from the leaves before cutting them.

1 Heat the oil in a wok. Add the shallots and stir-fry over a medium heat for 2–3 minutes, until softened. Add the cashew nuts and stir-fry for a few minutes until they are golden.

2 Stir in the red curry paste. Stir-fry for 1 minute, then add the potatoes, lemon grass, tomatoes and boiling water.

3 Bring back to the boil, then reduce the heat to low, cover and simmer gently for 15–20 minutes, or until the potatoes are tender.

4 Stir the corn, celery, lime leaves, ketchup, soy sauce, sugar and spring onions into the pan or wok. Simmer for a further 5 minutes, until heated through, then spoon into warmed serving bowls. Sprinkle with the sliced spring onions and basil and serve.

Energy 401Kcal/1681kJ; Protein 9.9g; Carbohydrate 51.7g, of which sugars 16.3g; Fat 18.6g, of which saturates 3.2g; Cholesterol 0mg; Calcium 41mg; Fibre 3.9g; Sodium 698mg.

AROMATIC OKRA <u>AND</u> COCONUT STIR-FRY

STIR-FRIED OKRA SPICED WITH MUSTARD, CUMIN AND RED CHILLIES AND SPRINKLED WITH FRESHLY GRATED COCONUT MAKES A GREAT QUICK SUPPER. IT IS THE PERFECT WAY TO ENJOY THESE SUCCULENT PODS, WITH THE SWEETNESS OF THE COCONUT COMPLEMENTING THE WARM SPICES.

SERVES FOUR

INGREDIENTS
  600g/1lb 6oz okra
  60ml/4 tbsp sunflower oil
  1 onion, finely chopped
  15ml/1 tbsp mustard seeds
  15ml/1 tbsp cumin seeds
  2–3 dried red chillies
  10–12 curry leaves
  2.5ml/½ tsp ground turmeric
  90g/3½ oz freshly grated coconut
  salt and ground black pepper
  poppadums, rice or naan, to serve

1 With a sharp knife, cut each of the okra diagonally into 1cm/½ in lengths. Set aside. Heat the wok and add the sunflower oil.

2 When the oil is hot add the chopped onion and stir-fry over a medium heat for about 5 minutes until softened.

3 Add the mustard seeds, cumin seeds, red chillies and curry leaves to the onions and stir-fry over a high heat for about 2 minutes.

4 Add the okra and turmeric to the wok and continue to stir-fry over a high heat for 3–4 minutes.

5 Remove the wok from the heat, sprinkle over the coconut and season well with salt and ground black pepper. Serve immediately with poppadums, steamed rice or naan bread.

COOK'S TIP
Fresh okra is widely available from most supermarkets and Asian stores. Choose fresh, firm, green specimens and avoid any that are limp or turning brown.

Energy 211Kcal/873kJ; Protein 5g; Carbohydrate 6.3g, of which sugars 5.2g; Fat 18.7g, of which saturates 7.1g; Cholesterol 0mg; Calcium 246mg; Fibre 7.6g; Sodium 15mg.

STIR-FRIED SEEDS AND VEGETABLES

THE CONTRAST BETWEEN THE CRUNCHY SEEDS AND VEGETABLES AND THE RICH, SAVOURY SAUCE IS WHAT MAKES THIS DISH SO DELICIOUS. SUPER-SPEEDY WHEN TOSSED TOGETHER IN THE WOK, IT CAN BE SERVED ON ITS OWN, OR WITH RICE OR NOODLES.

SERVES FOUR

INGREDIENTS

- 30ml/2 tbsp vegetable oil
- 30ml/2 tbsp sesame seeds
- 30ml/2 tbsp sunflower seeds
- 30ml/2 tbsp pumpkin seeds
- 2 garlic cloves, finely chopped
- 2.5cm/1in piece fresh root ginger, peeled and finely chopped
- 2 large carrots, cut into batons
- 2 large courgettes (zucchini), cut into batons
- 90g/3½oz/1½ cups oyster mushrooms, broken in pieces
- 150g/5oz watercress or spinach leaves, coarsely chopped
- small bunch fresh mint or coriander (cilantro), leaves and stems chopped
- 60ml/4 tbsp black bean sauce
- 30ml/2 tbsp light soy sauce
- 15ml/1 tbsp palm sugar or light muscovado (brown) sugar
- 30ml/2 tbsp rice vinegar

1 Heat the oil in a wok. Add the seeds. Toss over a medium heat for 1 minute, then add the garlic and ginger and continue to stir-fry until the ginger is aromatic and the garlic is golden. Do not let the spices or garlic burn or they will taste bitter.

2 Add the carrot and courgette batons and the mushroom pieces to the wok and stir-fry over a medium heat for a further 5 minutes, or until all the vegetables are crisp-tender and are golden at the edges.

3 Add the watercress or spinach with the fresh herbs. Toss over the heat for 1 minute, then stir in the black bean sauce, soy sauce, sugar and vinegar. Stir-fry for 1–2 minutes, until combined and hot. Serve immediately.

COOK'S TIP
Oyster mushrooms have acquired their name because of their texture, rather than flavour, which is quite superb. They are delicate, so it is usually better to tear them into pieces along the lines of the gills, rather than slice them with a knife.

Energy 205Kcal/849kJ; Protein 6.9g; Carbohydrate 9.7g, of which sugars 7.7g; Fat 15.6g, of which saturates 2g; Cholesterol 0mg; Calcium 159mg; Fibre 3.4g; Sodium 294mg.

STUFFED SWEET PEPPERS

THIS IS AN UNUSUAL RECIPE IN THAT THE STUFFED PEPPERS ARE STEAMED RATHER THAN BAKED, BUT THE RESULT IS LIGHT AND TENDER. THE FILLING OF LIGHTLY CURRIED MUSHROOMS LOOKS ATTRACTIVE AND TASTES WONDERFUL. CREAMY YOGURT WOULD MAKE A GOOD ACCOMPANIMENT.

SERVES FOUR

INGREDIENTS

3 garlic cloves, finely chopped
2 coriander (cilantro) roots,
    finely chopped
400g/14oz/3 cups
    mushrooms, quartered
5ml/1 tsp Thai red curry paste
1 egg, lightly beaten
15ml/1 tbsp Thai fish sauce or
    mushroom ketchup
15ml/1 tbsp light soy sauce
2.5ml/½ tsp granulated sugar
3 kaffir lime leaves, finely chopped
4 yellow (bell) peppers, halved
    lengthways and seeded

1 In a mortar or spice grinder pound or grind the garlic with the coriander roots. Scrape into a bowl.

2 Put the mushrooms in a food processor and pulse briefly until they are finely chopped. Add to the garlic mixture, then stir in the curry paste, egg, sauces, sugar and lime leaves.

3 Place the pepper halves in a single layer in a steamer basket. Spoon the mixture loosely into the pepper halves. Do not pack the mixture down tightly or the filling will dry out too much. Bring the water in the wok to the boil, then lower the heat to a simmer. Steam the peppers for 15 minutes, or until the flesh is tender. Serve hot.

Energy 103Kcal/429kJ; Protein 6.1g; Carbohydrate 14.4g, of which sugars 12g; Fat 2.7g, of which saturates 0.7g; Cholesterol 48mg; Calcium 30mg; Fibre 4.4g; Sodium 297mg.

STIR-FRIED CRISPY TOFU

THE ASPARAGUS GROWN IN THE PART OF ASIA WHERE THIS RECIPE ORIGINATED TENDS TO HAVE SLENDER STALKS. LOOK FOR IT IN THAI MARKETS OR SUBSTITUTE THE THIN ASPARAGUS POPULARLY KNOWN AS SPRUE. IF YOU USE THICKER ASPARAGUS, YOU MAY NEED TO COOK IT FOR LONGER.

SERVES TWO

INGREDIENTS
250g/9oz fried tofu cubes
30ml/2 tbsp groundnut (peanut) oil
15ml/1 tbsp Thai green curry paste
30ml/2 tbsp light soy sauce
2 kaffir lime leaves, rolled into
  cylinders and thinly sliced
30ml/2 tbsp granulated sugar
150ml/¼ pint/⅔ cup vegetable stock
250g/9oz Asian asparagus, trimmed
  and sliced into 5cm/2in lengths
30ml/2 tbsp roasted peanuts,
  finely chopped

VARIATION
Substitute slim carrot sticks or broccoli florets for the asparagus.

1 Preheat the grill (broiler) to medium. Place the tofu cubes in a grill pan and grill (broil) for 2–3 minutes, then turn them over and continue to cook until they are crisp and golden brown all over. Watch them carefully; they must not be allowed to burn.

2 Heat the oil in a wok or heavy frying pan. Add the green curry paste and cook over a medium heat, stirring constantly, for 1–2 minutes, until it gives off its aroma.

3 Stir the soy sauce, lime leaves, sugar and vegetable stock into the wok or pan and mix well. Bring to the boil, then reduce the heat to low so that the mixture is just simmering.

4 Add the asparagus and simmer gently for 5 minutes. Meanwhile, chop each piece of tofu into four, then add to the pan with the peanuts.

5 Toss to coat all the ingredients in the sauce, then spoon into a warmed dish and serve immediately.

Energy 287Kcal/1195kJ; Protein 14.3g; Carbohydrate 20.3g, of which sugars 19.5g; Fat 17g, of which saturates 2.1g; Cholesterol 0mg; Calcium 682mg; Fibre 2.2g; Sodium 1075mg.

MARINATED TOFU AND BROCCOLI WITH CRISPY FRIED SHALLOTS

THIS MELTINGLY TENDER TOFU FLAVOURED WITH A FRAGRANT BLEND OF SPICES AND SERVED WITH TENDER YOUNG STEMS OF BROCCOLI MAKES A PERFECT LIGHT SUPPER OR LUNCH. YOU CAN BUY THE CRISPY FRIED SHALLOTS FROM ASIAN SUPERMARKETS, BUT THEY ARE VERY EASY TO MAKE YOURSELF.

SERVES FOUR

INGREDIENTS

500g/1¼lb block of firm tofu, drained
45ml/3 tbsp kecap manis
30ml/2 tbsp sweet chilli sauce
45ml/3 tbsp soy sauce
5ml/1 tsp sesame oil
5ml/1 tsp finely grated fresh root ginger
400g/14oz tenderstem broccoli, halved lengthways
45ml/3 tbsp roughly chopped coriander (cilantro)
30ml/2 tbsp toasted sesame seeds
30ml/2 tbsp crispy fried shallots
steamed white rice or noodles, to serve
For the crispy fried shallots
10 Thai shallots, sliced into paper thin rings and separated
oil for deep-frying

1 Make the crispy shallots. Add the shallot rings to a wok one-third full of hot oil, then lower the heat and stir constantly until crisp. Spread on kitchen paper to drain.

2 Cut the tofu into 4 triangular pieces: slice the block in half widthways, then diagonally. Place in a heatproof dish.

3 In a small bowl, combine the kecap manis, chilli sauce, soy sauce, sesame oil and ginger, then pour over the tofu. Leave the tofu to marinate for at least 30 minutes, turning occasionally.

4 Place the broccoli on a heatproof plate and place on a trivet or steamer rack in the wok. Cover and steam for 4–5 minutes, until just tender. Remove and keep warm.

5 Place the dish of tofu on the trivet or steamer rack in the wok, cover and steam for 4–5 minutes. Divide the broccoli among four warmed serving plates and top each one with a triangle of tofu.

6 Spoon the remaining juices over the tofu and broccoli, then sprinkle over the coriander, sesame seeds and crispy shallots. Serve immediately with steamed white rice or noodles.

Energy 202Kcal/840kJ; Protein 16.5g; Carbohydrate 6.9g, of which sugars 5.6g; Fat 12.1g, of which saturates 1.7g; Cholesterol 0mg; Calcium 750mg; Fibre 3.5g; Sodium 938mg.

NOODLES AND VEGETABLES IN COCONUT SAUCE

WHEN EVERYDAY VEGETABLES ARE LIVENED UP WITH THAI SPICES AND FLAVOURS, THE RESULT IS A DELECTABLE DISH THAT EVERYONE WILL ENJOY. NOODLES ADD BULK AND A WELCOME CONTRAST IN TEXTURE, AND THE RED CURRY AND COCONUT SAUCE MARRIES EVERYTHING TOGETHER PERFECTLY.

SERVES FOUR TO SIX

INGREDIENTS
30ml/2 tbsp sunflower oil
1 lemon grass stalk, finely chopped
15ml/1 tbsp Thai red curry paste
1 onion, thickly sliced
3 courgettes (zucchini), thickly sliced
115g/4oz Savoy cabbage,
 thickly sliced
2 carrots, thickly sliced
150g/5oz broccoli, stem thickly
 sliced and head separated
 into florets
2 × 400ml/14fl oz cans coconut milk
475ml/16fl oz/2 cups vegetable stock
150g/5oz dried egg noodles
30ml/2 tbsp soy sauce
60ml/4 tbsp chopped fresh
 coriander (cilantro)
For the garnish
2 lemon grass stalks
1 bunch fresh coriander (cilantro)
8–10 small fresh red chillies

1 Heat the oil in a wok. Add the lemon grass and red curry paste and stir-fry for 2–3 seconds. Add the onion and cook over medium heat, stirring occasionally, until the onion has softened but not browned.

2 Add the courgettes, cabbage, carrots and slices of broccoli stem. Using two spoons, toss the vegetables with the onion mixture. Reduce the heat to low and cook gently, stirring occasionally, for a further 5 minutes.

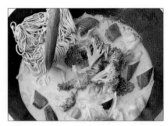

3 Increase the heat to medium, stir in the coconut milk and vegetable stock and bring to the boil. Add the broccoli florets and the noodles, lower the heat and simmer gently for 20 minutes.

4 Meanwhile, make the garnish. Split the lemon grass stalks lengthways through the root. Gather the coriander into a small bouquet and lay it on a platter, following the curve of the rim.

5 Tuck the lemon grass halves into the coriander bouquet and add the chillies to resemble flowers.

6 Stir the soy sauce and chopped coriander into the noodle mixture. Spoon on to the platter, taking care not to disturb the herb bouquet, and serve immediately.

Energy 192Kcal/808kJ; Protein 5.6g; Carbohydrate 29.4g, of which sugars 11.5g; Fat 6.6g, of which saturates 1.4g; Cholesterol 8mg; Calcium 83mg; Fibre 2.4g; Sodium 554mg.

THAI NOODLES <u>WITH</u> CHINESE CHIVES

THIS RECIPE REQUIRES A LITTLE TIME FOR PREPARATION, BUT THE COOKING TIME IS VERY FAST. EVERYTHING IS COOKED IN A HOT WOK AND SHOULD BE EATEN IMMEDIATELY. THIS IS A FILLING AND TASTY VEGETARIAN DISH, IDEAL FOR A WEEKEND LUNCH.

SERVES FOUR

INGREDIENTS
350g/12oz dried rice noodles
1cm/½in piece fresh root ginger,
  peeled and grated
30ml/2 tbsp light soy sauce
45ml/3 tbsp vegetable oil
225g/8oz Quorn (mycoprotein), cut
  into small cubes
2 garlic cloves, crushed
1 large onion, cut into thin wedges
115g/4oz fried tofu, thinly sliced
1 fresh green chilli, seeded and
  thinly sliced
175g/6oz/3 cups beansprouts
2 large bunches garlic chives, total
  weight about 115g/4oz, cut into
  5cm/2in lengths
50g/2oz/½ cup roasted
  peanuts, ground
30ml/2 tbsp dark soy sauce
30ml/2 tbsp chopped fresh coriander
  (cilantro), and 1 lemon, cut into
  wedges, to garnish

1 Place the noodles in a bowl, cover with warm water and leave to soak for 30 minutes. Drain and set aside.

2 Mix the ginger, light soy sauce and 15ml/1 tbsp of the oil in a bowl. Add the Quorn, then set aside for 10 minutes. Drain, reserving the marinade.

3 Heat 15ml/1 tbsp of the remaining oil in a wok and cook the garlic for a few seconds. Add the Quorn and stir-fry for 3–4 minutes. Using a slotted spoon, transfer to a plate and set aside.

4 Heat the remaining oil in the wok and stir-fry the onion for 3–4 minutes, until softened and tinged with brown. Add the tofu and chilli, stir-fry briefly and then add the noodles. Stir-fry over a medium heat for 4–5 minutes.

5 Stir in the beansprouts, garlic chives and most of the ground peanuts, reserving a little for the garnish. Stir well, then add the Quorn, the dark soy sauce and the reserved marinade.

6 When hot, spoon on to serving plates and garnish with the remaining ground peanuts, the coriander and lemon.

Energy 584Kcal/2435kJ; Protein 19.7g; Carbohydrate 82.9g, of which sugars 7.5g; Fat 18.2g, of which saturates 2.6g; Cholesterol 0mg; Calcium 242mg; Fibre 5.8g; Sodium 984mg.

MEE KROB

THE NAME OF THIS DISH MEANS "DEEP-FRIED NOODLES" AND IT IS VERY POPULAR IN THAILAND. THE TASTE IS A STUNNING COMBINATION OF SWEET AND HOT, SALTY AND SOUR, WHILE THE TEXTURE CONTRIVES TO BE BOTH CRISP AND CHEWY. TO SOME WESTERN PALATES, IT MAY SEEM RATHER UNUSUAL, BUT THIS DELICIOUS DISH IS WELL WORTH MAKING.

SERVES TWO

INGREDIENTS
vegetable oil, for deep-frying
130g/4½oz rice vermicelli noodles
For the sauce
  30ml/2 tbsp vegetable oil
  130g/4½oz fried tofu, cut into
    thin strips
  2 garlic cloves, finely chopped
  2 small shallots, finely chopped
  15ml/1 tbsp light soy sauce
  30ml/2 tbsp palm sugar or light
    muscovado (brown) sugar
  60ml/4 tbsp vegetable stock
  juice of 1 lime
  2.5ml/½ tsp dried chilli flakes
For the garnish
  15ml/1 tbsp vegetable oil
  1 egg, lightly beaten with
    15ml/1 tbsp cold water
  25g/1oz/⅓ cup beansprouts
  1 spring onion (scallion),
    thinly shredded
  1 fresh red chilli, seeded and
    finely chopped
  1 whole head pickled garlic, sliced
    across the bulb so each slice looks
    like a flower

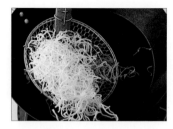

1 Heat the oil for deep-frying in a wok or large pan to 190°C/375°F or until a cube of bread, added to the oil, browns in about 40 seconds. Add the noodles and deep-fry until golden and crisp. Drain on kitchen paper and set aside.

2 Make the sauce. Heat the oil in a wok, add the fried tofu and cook over a medium heat until crisp. Using a slotted spoon, transfer it to a plate.

3 Add the garlic and shallots to the wok and cook until golden brown. Stir in the soy sauce, sugar, stock, lime juice and chilli flakes. Cook, stirring, until the mixture begins to caramelize.

4 Add the reserved tofu and stir until it has soaked up some of the liquid. Remove the wok from the heat and set aside.

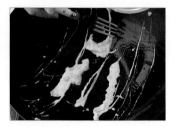

5 Prepare the egg garnish. Heat the oil in a wok or frying pan. Pour in the egg in a thin stream to form trails. As soon as it sets, lift it out with a fish slice or metal spatula and place on a plate.

6 Crumble the noodles into the tofu sauce, mix well, then spoon into warmed serving bowls. Sprinkle with the beansprouts, spring onion, fried egg strips, chilli and pickled garlic "flowers" and serve immediately.

COOK'S TIP
Successful deep-frying depends, to a large extent, on the type of oil used and the temperature to which it is heated. A bland-tasting oil, such as sunflower, will not alter the flavour of the food. All fats have a "smoke point" – the temperature at which they begin to decompose. Most vegetable oils have a high smoke point, with groundnut (peanut) oil the highest of all and so also the safest.

Energy 497Kcal/2075kJ; Protein 10.2g; Carbohydrate 70.2g, of which sugars 18.3g; Fat 19.95g, of which saturates 2.8g; Cholesterol 104.5mg; Calcium 51mg; Fibre .7g; Sodium 583.5mg.

SWEET AND HOT VEGETABLE NOODLES

THIS NOODLE DISH HAS THE COLOUR OF FIRE, BUT ONLY THE MILDEST SUGGESTION OF HEAT. GINGER AND PLUM SAUCE GIVE IT ITS FRUITY FLAVOUR, WHILE LIME JUICE AND TAMARIND PASTE ADD A DELICIOUS TANG TO THE AROMATIC STIR-FRIED VEGETABLES AND CHOPPED CORIANDER.

SERVES FOUR

INGREDIENTS

130g/4½oz dried rice noodles
30ml/2 tbsp groundnut (peanut) oil
2.5cm/1in piece fresh root ginger,
    sliced into thin batons
1 garlic clove, crushed
130g/4½oz drained canned bamboo
    shoots, sliced into thin batons
2 medium carrots, sliced into batons
130g/4½oz/1½ cups beansprouts
1 small white cabbage, shredded
10ml/2 tsp tamarind paste
30ml/2 tbsp soy sauce
30ml/2 tbsp plum sauce
10ml/2 tsp sesame oil
15ml/1 tbsp palm sugar or light
    muscovado (brown) sugar
juice of ½ lime
90g/3½oz mooli (daikon), sliced into
    thin batons
small bunch fresh coriander
    (cilantro), chopped
60ml/4 tbsp sesame seeds, toasted

1 Cook the noodles in a large pan of boiling water, following the instructions on the packet. Meanwhile, heat the oil in a wok or large frying pan and stir-fry the ginger and garlic for 2–3 minutes over a medium heat, until golden. Drain the noodles and set them aside.

2 Add the bamboo shoots to the wok, increase the heat to high and stir-fry for 5 minutes. Add the carrots, beansprouts and cabbage and stir-fry for a further 5 minutes, until they are beginning to char on the edges.

3 Stir in the tamarind paste, soy and plum sauces, sesame oil, sugar and lime juice. Add the mooli and coriander, toss to mix, then spoon into a warmed bowl, sprinkle with toasted sesame seeds and serve immediately.

COOK'S TIP
Use a large, sharp knife for shredding cabbage. Remove any tough outer leaves, if necessary, then cut the cabbage into quarters. Cut off and discard the hard core from each quarter, place flat side down, then shred the cabbage thinly.

Energy 321Kcal/1333kJ; Protein 7.1g; Carbohydrate 37.8g, of which sugars 9.8g; Fat 15.4g, of which saturates 2.1g; Cholesterol 0mg; Calcium 142mg; Fibre 4.3g; Sodium 413mg.

VEGETABLE NOODLES WITH BEAN SAUCE

YELLOW BEAN SAUCE ADDS A DISTINCTIVE CHINESE FLAVOUR TO THIS WONDERFULLY SIMPLE DISH OF SPICY VEGETABLES AND NOODLES. THE SAUCE IS MADE FROM FERMENTED YELLOW BEANS AND HAS A MARVELLOUS TEXTURE AND SPICY, AROMATIC FLAVOUR, IF USED IN THE RIGHT PROPORTION.

SERVES FOUR

INGREDIENTS
   150g/5oz thin egg noodles
   200g/7oz baby leeks, sliced
   lengthways
   200g/7oz baby courgettes (zucchini),
   halved lengthways
   200g/7oz sugarsnap
   peas, trimmed
   200g/7oz peas
   15ml/1 tbsp sunflower oil
   5 garlic cloves, sliced
   45ml/3 tbsp yellow bean sauce
   45ml/3 tbsp sweet chilli sauce
   30ml/2 tbsp sweet soy sauce
   roasted cashew nuts, to garnish

1 Cook the noodles according to the packet instructions, drain and set aside.

2 Line a large bamboo steamer with perforated baking parchment and place the leeks, courgettes and both types of peas in it.

3 Cover the steamer and suspend it over a wok of simmering water. Steam the vegetables for about 5 minutes, then remove and set aside.

4 Pour the water from the wok and wipe dry with kitchen paper. Pour the sunflower oil into the wok and place over a medium heat. Add the sliced garlic and stir-fry for 1–2 minutes.

5 In a separate bowl, mix together the yellow bean, sweet chilli and soy sauces, then pour into the wok. Stir to mix with the garlic, then add the steamed vegetables and the noodles and toss together to combine.

6 Cook the vegetables and noodles for 2–3 minutes, stirring frequently, until heated through.

7 To serve, divide the noodles among four warmed serving bowls and scatter over the cashew nuts to garnish.

Energy 296Kcal/1241kJ; Protein 14.2g; Carbohydrate 44.9g, of which sugars 7.4g; Fat 7.8g, of which saturates 1.6g; Cholesterol 11mg; Calcium 61mg; Fibre 8.2g; Sodium 209mg.

CANTONESE FRIED NOODLES

CHOW MEIN IS HUGELY POPULAR WITH THE THRIFTY CHINESE, WHO BELIEVE IN TURNING LEFTOVERS INTO TASTY DISHES. FOR THIS DELICIOUS DISH, BOILED NOODLES ARE FRIED TO FORM A CRISPY CRUST, WHICH IS TOPPED WITH A SAVOURY SAUCE CONTAINING WHATEVER TASTES GOOD AND NEEDS EATING UP.

SERVES TWO TO THREE

INGREDIENTS

 225g/8oz can bamboo shoots, drained
 1 leek, trimmed
 150g/5oz Chinese leaves (Chinese
  cabbage)
 25g/1oz Chinese dried mushrooms,
  soaked for 30 minutes in 120ml/
  4fl oz/^{1}/$_2$ cup warm water
 450g/1lb cooked egg noodles
  (225g/8oz dried), drained well
 90ml/6 tbsp vegetable oil
 30ml/2 tbsp dark soy sauce
 15ml/1 tbsp cornflour (cornstarch)
 15ml/1 tbsp rice wine or sherry
 5ml/1 tsp sesame oil
 5ml/1 tsp sugar
 salt and ground black pepper

1 Slice the bamboo shoots and leek into matchsticks. Cut the Chinese leaves into 2.5cm/1in diamond-shaped pieces and sprinkle with salt.

2 Drain the mushrooms, reserving 90ml/6 tbsp of the soaking water. Cut off and discard the stems, then slice the caps finely. Pat the noodles dry with kitchen paper. Divide into three piles.

3 Heat a third of the oil in a large wok or frying pan and sauté one pile of noodles. After turning it over once, press the noodles evenly against the bottom of the pan with a wooden spatula until they form a flat, even cake. Cook over medium heat for about 4 minutes or until the noodles at the bottom have become crisp.

4 Turn the noodle cake over with a spatula or fish slice or invert on to a large plate and slide back into the wok. Cook for 3 minutes more, then slide on to a heated plate. Keep warm. Repeat with the other two piles of noodles.

5 Heat 30ml/2 tbsp of the remaining oil in the wok. Add the strips of leek, and stir-fry for 10–15 seconds. Sprinkle over half of the the soy sauce and then add the bamboo shoots and the mushrooms, with salt and pepper to taste. Toss over the heat for 1 minute, then transfer this mixture to a plate and set aside.

6 Heat the remaining oil in the wok and sauté the Chinese leaves for 1 minute. Return the vegetable mixture to the wok and sauté with the leaves for 30 seconds, stirring constantly.

7 Mix the cornflour with the reserved mushroom water. Stir into the wok along with the rice wine or sherry, sesame oil, sugar and remaining soy sauce. Cook for 15 seconds to thicken. Divide the noodles among 2–3 serving dishes and pile the vegetables on top.

Energy 481Kcal/2006kJ; Protein 24.4g; Carbohydrate 28.9g, of which sugars 7.8g; Fat 30.5g, of which saturates 5.7g; Cholesterol 53mg; Calcium 67mg; Fibre 4.4g; Sodium 791mg.

SICHUAN NOODLES WITH SESAME SAUCE

NOODLES AND ASIAN VEGETABLES SEEM MADE FOR EACH OTHER, AND WHEN THE MARRIAGE TAKES PLACE IN A WOK, WITH A FINE SAUCE TO GUARANTEE HARMONY, THE RESULTS ARE INEVITABLY EXCELLENT. ROASTED NUTS ADD TEXTURE WHILE BOOSTING THE NUTRITIONAL VALUE OF THIS DISH.

SERVES THREE TO FOUR

INGREDIENTS

450g/1lb fresh or 225g/8oz dried
  egg noodles
1/2 cucumber, sliced lengthways,
  seeded and diced
4–6 spring onions (scallions)
a bunch of radishes, about 115g/4oz
225g/8oz mooli (daikon), peeled
115g/4oz/2 cups beansprouts,
  rinsed then left in iced water
  and drained
60ml/4 tbsp groundnut (peanut) oil
  or sunflower oil
2 garlic cloves, crushed
45ml/3 tbsp toasted sesame paste
15ml/1 tbsp sesame oil
15ml/1 tbsp light soy sauce
5–10ml/1–2 tsp chilli sauce, to taste
15ml/1 tbsp rice vinegar
120ml/4fl oz/1/2 cup chicken stock
  or water
5ml/1 tsp sugar, or to taste
salt and ground black pepper
roasted peanuts or cashew nuts,
  to garnish

1 If using fresh noodles, cook them in boiling water for 1 minute then drain well. Rinse the noodles in fresh water and drain again. Cook dried noodles according to the instructions on the packet, draining and rinsing them as for fresh noodles.

2 Sprinkle the cucumber with salt, leave for 15 minutes, rinse well, then drain and pat dry on kitchen paper. Place in a large salad bowl.

3 Cut the spring onions into fine shreds. Cut the radishes in half and slice finely. Coarsely grate the mooli using a mandolin or a food processor. Add all the vegetables to the cucumber and toss gently.

4 Heat half the oil in a wok or frying pan and stir-fry the noodles for about 1 minute. Using a slotted spoon, transfer the noodles to a large serving bowl and keep warm. Add the remaining oil to the wok. When it is hot, fry the garlic to flavour the oil.

COOK'S TIP
When warming through the sauce, it is important not to heat it too much or too quickly to avoid it over-thickening.

5 Remove from the heat and stir in the sesame paste, with the sesame oil, soy and chilli sauces, vinegar and stock or water. Add a little sugar and season to taste. Warm through over a gentle heat. Pour the sauce over the noodles and toss well. Garnish with the nuts and serve with the vegetables.

Energy 440Kcal/1838kJ; Protein 11g; Carbohydrate 44.6g, of which sugars 4.6g; Fat 25.4g, of which saturates 4.1g; Cholesterol 17mg; Calcium 128mg; Fibre 4.2g; Sodium 384mg.

INDIAN MEE GORENG

*THIS IS A TRULY INTERNATIONAL DISH, COMBINING INDIAN, CHINESE AND WESTERN INGREDIENTS.
IT IS A DELICIOUS TREAT FOR LUNCH OR SUPPER AND IN SINGAPORE AND MALAYSIA CAN BE BOUGHT
IN MANY STREETS FROM ONE OF THE MANY FOODSELLERS' STALLS.*

2 If using fried tofu, cut each cube in half, refresh it in a pan of boiling water, then drain well. Heat 30ml/2 tbsp of the oil in a large frying pan. If using plain tofu, cut into cubes and fry until brown, then lift it out with a slotted spoon and set aside.

3 Beat the eggs with the water. Add to the oil in the frying pan and cook without stirring until set. Flip over, cook the other side, then slide it out of the pan, roll up and slice thinly.

4 Heat the remaining oil in a wok and fry the onion and garlic for 2–3 minutes. Add the drained noodles, soy sauce, ketchup and chilli sauce. Toss well over medium heat for 2 minutes.

SERVES FOUR TO SIX

INGREDIENTS
450g/1lb fresh yellow egg noodles
60–90ml/4–6 tbsp vegetable oil
115g/4oz fried tofu or 150g/5oz
  firm tofu
2 eggs
30ml/2 tbsp water
1 onion, sliced
1 garlic clove, crushed
15ml/1 tbsp light soy sauce
30–45ml/2–3 tbsp tomato ketchup
15ml/1 tbsp chilli sauce (or to taste)
1 large cooked potato, diced
4 spring onions (scallions), cut in
  half and shredded
1–2 fresh green chillies

1 Bring a large pan of water to the boil, add the fresh egg noodles and cook for just 2 minutes. Drain the noodles and immediately rinse them under cold water to halt cooking. Drain again and set aside, spreading them out on a large platter to dry.

5 Add the diced potato to the wok. Seed and finely slice the green chilli Reserve a few shredded spring onions for the garnish and stir the rest into the noodles with the chilli and tofu.

6 When hot, stir in the omelette. Serve on a hot platter garnished with the remaining spring onion.

Energy 478Kcal/2010kJ; Protein 16.8g; Carbohydrate 64.2g, of which sugars 5.1g; Fat 18.9g, of which saturates 3.2g; Cholesterol 86mg; Calcium 323mg; Fibre 2.9g; Sodium 466mg.

SWEET AND SOUR VEGETABLES WITH TOFU

BIG, BOLD AND BEAUTIFUL, THIS IS A HEARTY STIR-FRY THAT WILL SATISFY THE HUNGRIEST GUESTS. STIR-FRIES ARE ALWAYS A GOOD CHOICE WHEN ENTERTAINING, BECAUSE YOU CAN PREPARE THE INGREDIENTS AHEAD OF TIME AND THEN COOK THEM INCREDIBLY QUICKLY IN THE WOK.

SERVES FOUR

INGREDIENTS
4 shallots
3 garlic cloves
30ml/2 tbsp groundnut (peanut) oil
250g/9oz Chinese leaves (Chinese cabbage), shredded
8 baby corn cobs, sliced on the diagonal
2 red (bell) peppers, seeded and thinly sliced
200g/7oz/1¾ cups mangetouts (snow peas), trimmed and sliced
250g/9oz tofu, rinsed, drained and cut in 1cm/½ in cubes
60ml/4 tbsp vegetable stock
30ml/2 tbsp light soy sauce
15ml/1 tbsp granulated sugar
30ml/2 tbsp rice vinegar
2.5ml/½ tsp dried chilli flakes
small bunch coriander (cilantro), chopped

1 Slice the shallots thinly using a sharp knife. Finely chop the garlic.

2 Heat the oil in a wok or large frying pan and cook the shallots and garlic for 2–3 minutes over a medium heat, until golden. Do not let the garlic burn or it will taste bitter.

3 Add the shredded cabbage, toss over the heat for 30 seconds, then add the corn cobs and repeat the process.

4 Add the red peppers, mangetouts and tofu in the same way, each time adding a single ingredient and tossing it over the heat for about 30 seconds before adding the next ingredient.

5 Pour in the stock and soy sauce. Mix together the sugar and vinegar in a small bowl, stirring until the sugar has dissolved, then add to the wok or pan. Sprinkle over the chilli flakes and coriander, toss to mix well and serve.

Energy 180Kcal/751kJ; Protein 9.1g; Carbohydrate 17g, of which sugars 15.6g; Fat 8.7g, of which saturates 1.1g; Cholesterol 0mg; Calcium 386mg; Fibre 4.1g; Sodium 575mg.

JEWELLED VEGETABLE RICE
WITH CRISPY FRIED EGGS

INSPIRED BY THE TRADITIONAL INDONESIAN DISH NASI GORENG,
THIS VIBRANT, COLOURFUL STIR-FRY MAKES A TASTY LIGHT MEAL.
ALTERNATIVELY, SERVE IT AS AN ACCOMPANIMENT TO SIMPLY
GRILLED MEAT OR FISH. TO MAKE AN EXTRA-HEALTHY OPTION, USE
BROWN BASMATI RICE IN PLACE OF THE WHITE RICE.

SERVES FOUR

INGREDIENTS
   2 fresh corn on the cob
   60ml/4 tbsp sunflower oil
   2 garlic cloves, finely chopped
   4 red Asian shallots, thinly sliced
   1 small fresh red chilli, finely sliced
   90g/3½oz carrots, cut into
      thin matchsticks
   90g/3½oz fine green beans,
      cut into 2cm/¾in lengths
   1 red (bell) pepper, seeded and
      cut into 1cm/½in dice
   90g/3½oz baby button
      (white) mushrooms
   500g/1¼lb cooked long grain rice,
      completely cooled
   45ml/3 tbsp light soy sauce
   10ml/2 tsp green Thai curry paste
   4 eggs
   crisp green salad leaves and
      lime wedges, to serve

1 First shuck the corn cobs. Remove all the papery leaves, and the silky threads, then with a sharp knife cut at the base of the kernels right down the length of the cob.

2 Heat 30ml/2 tbsp of the sunflower oil in a wok over a high heat. When hot, add the garlic, shallots and chilli. Stir-fry for about 2 minutes.

3 Add the carrots, green beans, corn, red pepper and mushrooms to the wok and stir-fry for 3–4 minutes. Add the cooked, cooled rice and stir-fry for a further 4–5 minutes.

4 Mix together the light soy sauce and curry paste and add to the wok. Toss to mix well and stir-fry for 2–3 minutes until piping hot.

5 Meanwhile, fry the eggs one at a time in a clean wok. Make sure that the oil is sizzling hot before you pour the egg in, as this will give the white a lovely crispy edge. When the egg is cooked, remove it from the wok and keep warm until the others are fried.

6 Ladle the rice into four bowls or plates and top each portion with a crispy fried egg. Serve with crisp green salad leaves and wedges of lime to squeeze over.

COOK'S TIP
When making this dish, it is better to use cold cooked rice rather than hot, freshly cooked rice. Hot boiled rice tends to clump together when stir-frying, whereas the grains of cooled rice will remain separate.

Energy 392Kcal/1648kJ; Protein 13.6g; Carbohydrate 51.4g, of which sugars 8.2g; Fat 16.1g, of which saturates 3.6g; Cholesterol 261mg; Calcium 79mg; Fibre 2.1g; Sodium 968mg.

SAVOURY FRIED RICE

THE TITLE MAKES THIS SOUND LIKE RATHER AN ORDINARY DISH, BUT IT IS NOTHING OF THE KIND. CHILLI, NUTS AND TOASTED COCONUT GIVE THE MIXTURE OF RICE AND BEANS AND WILTED GREENS PLENTY OF FLAVOUR, AND THE EGG THAT IS STIRRED IN PROVIDES THE PROTEIN CONTENT.

SERVES TWO

INGREDIENTS

30ml/2 tbsp vegetable oil
2 garlic cloves, finely chopped
1 small fresh red chilli, seeded and
  finely chopped
50g/2oz/½ cup cashew nuts, toasted
50g/2oz/⅔ cup desiccated
  (dry unsweetened shredded)
  coconut, toasted
2.5ml/½ tsp palm sugar or light
  muscovado (brown) sugar
30ml/2 tbsp light soy sauce
15ml/1 tbsp rice vinegar
1 egg
115g/4oz/1 cup green beans, sliced
½ spring cabbage or 115g/4oz spring
  greens (collards) or pak choi (bok
  choy), shredded
90g/3½oz jasmine rice, cooked
lime wedges, to serve

1 Heat the oil in a wok or large, heavy frying pan. Add the garlic and cook over a medium to high heat until golden. Do not let it burn or it will taste bitter.

2 Add the red chilli, cashew nuts and toasted coconut to the wok or pan and stir-fry briefly, taking care to prevent the coconut from scorching. Stir in the sugar, soy sauce and rice vinegar. Toss over the heat for 1–2 minutes.

3 Push the stir-fry to one side of the wok or pan and break the egg into the empty side. When the egg is almost set, stir it into the garlic and chilli mixture with a wooden spatula or spoon.

4 Add the green beans, greens and cooked rice. Stir over the heat until the greens have just wilted, then spoon into a dish to serve. Offer the lime wedges separately, for squeezing over the rice.

Energy 570Kcal/2366kJ; Protein 16.1g; Carbohydrate 30.5g, of which sugars 8.7g; Fat 43.6g, of which saturates 18.2g; Cholesterol 95mg; Calcium 187mg; Fibre 8.5g; Sodium 1196mg.

RICE CONGEE

ORIGINATING IN CHINA, THIS DISH HAS NOW SPREAD THROUGHOUT THE WHOLE OF SOUTH-EAST ASIA AND IS LOVED FOR ITS COMFORTING BLANDNESS. IT IS INVARIABLY TEAMED WITH A FEW STRONGLY FLAVOURED ACCOMPANIMENTS TO PROVIDE CONTRASTING TASTES AND TEXTURES.

SERVES TWO

INGREDIENTS
900ml/1½ pints/3¾ cups
  vegetable stock
200g/7oz cooked rice
15ml/1 tbsp Thai fish sauce, or
  mushroom ketchup
2 heads pickled garlic,
  finely chopped (see Cook's Tip)
1 celery stick, finely diced
salt and ground black pepper
To garnish
30ml/2 tbsp groundnut (peanut) oil
4 garlic cloves, thinly sliced
4 small red shallots, finely sliced

1 Make the garnishes by heating the groundnut oil in a wok and cooking the garlic and shallots over a low heat until brown. Drain on kitchen paper and reserve for the soup.

2 Pour the stock into a large pan. Bring to the boil and add the rice.

3 Stir in the sauce and pickled garlic and simmer for 10 minutes to let the flavours develop. Stir in the celery.

4 Serve the rice congee in individual warmed bowls. Sprinkle the prepared garlic and shallots on top and season with plenty of ground pepper.

COOK'S TIP
Pickled garlic has a distinctive flavour and is available from Asian food stores.

Energy 509Kcal/2126kJ; Protein 27.3g; Carbohydrate 37.2g, of which sugars 0.8g; Fat 29g, of which saturates 6.3g; Cholesterol 74mg; Calcium 39mg; Fibre 1.8g; Sodium 86mg.

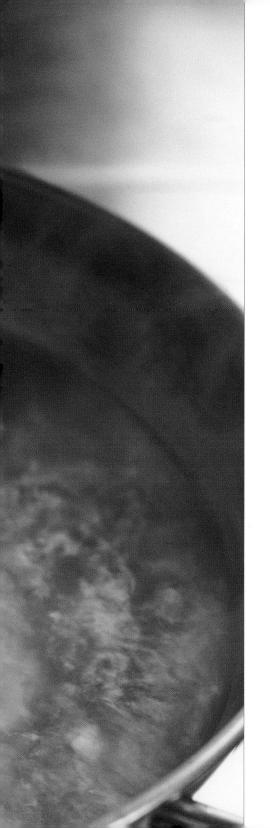

VEGETABLES AND SIDE DISHES

Although it is perfectly possible to cook an entire meal in a wok — and many of the recipes in this book let you do just that — it can also be a very useful utensil for making side dishes. A vegetable stir-fry may not be the first dish that comes to mind for serving with the Sunday roast, but why not? The crisp, clean flavours would be an ideal contrast to more classic accompaniments, and the colours would look lovely on the plate. A wok is great for making a warm salad, too, whether you simply use it for dry-roasting rice, as in Bamboo Shoot Salad, or let it take a leading role in a dish such as Spicy Chickpeas with Spinach.

BAMBOO SHOOT SALAD

GRAINS OF GLUTINOUS RICE THAT HAVE BEEN DRY-ROASTED IN THE WOK, THEN GROUND TO FINE CRUMBS, MAKE AN INTERESTING ADDITION TO THIS COLOURFUL AND UNUSUAL SALAD. THE CRUNCH THEY PROVIDE MAKES A GOOD CONTRAST TO THE SILKY SMOOTHNESS OF THE BAMBOO SHOOTS.

SERVES FOUR

INGREDIENTS

400g/14oz canned bamboo shoots, in large pieces
25g/1oz/about 3 tbsp Thai sticky rice, cooked
30ml/2 tbsp chopped shallots
15ml/1 tbsp chopped garlic
45ml/3 tbsp chopped spring onions (scallions)
30ml/2 tbsp Thai fish sauce
30ml/2 tbsp fresh lime juice
5ml/1 tsp granulated sugar
2.5ml/½ tsp dried chilli flakes
20–25 small fresh mint leaves
15ml/1 tbsp toasted sesame seeds

1 Rinse the bamboo shoots under cold running water, then drain them and pat them thoroughly dry with kitchen paper and set them aside.

2 Dry-roast the rice in a wok until it is golden brown. Leave to cool slightly, then grind to find crumbs in a mortar.

3 Transfer the rice to a bowl and add the shallots, garlic, spring onions, fish sauce, lime juice, sugar, chilli flakes and half the mint leaves. Mix well.

4 Add the bamboo shoots to the bowl and toss to mix. Serve sprinkled with the toasted sesame seeds and mint.

Energy 85Kcal/357kJ; Protein 4.2g; Carbohydrate 11.3g, of which sugars 4.1g; Fat 2.7g, of which saturates 0.4g; Cholesterol 0mg; Calcium 51mg; Fibre 2g; Sodium 6mg.

NOODLE, TOFU AND SPROUTED BEAN SALAD

BEAN THREAD NOODLES LOOK LIKE SPUN GLASS ON THIS STUNNING SALAD, WHICH OWES ITS GOODNESS TO FRESH BEANSPROUTS, DICED TOMATO AND CUCUMBER IN A SWEET-SOUR DRESSING. THE SALAD TAKES ONLY MINUTES TO TOSS TOGETHER.

SERVES FOUR

INGREDIENTS
- 25g/1oz bean thread noodles
- 500g/1¼lb mixed sprouted beans and pulses (aduki, chickpea, mung, red lentil)
- 4 spring onions (scallions), finely shredded
- 115g/4oz firm tofu, diced
- 1 ripe plum tomato, seeded and diced
- ½ cucumber, peeled, seeded and diced
- 60ml/4 tbsp chopped fresh coriander (cilantro)
- 45ml/3 tbsp chopped fresh mint
- 60ml/4 tbsp rice vinegar
- 10ml/2 tsp caster (superfine) sugar
- 10ml/2 tsp sesame oil
- 5ml/1 tsp chilli oil
- salt and ground black pepper

1 Place the bean thread noodles in a bowl and pour over enough boiling water to cover. Leave to soak for 12–15 minutes.

2 Drain the noodles and then refresh them under cold, running water and drain again. Using a pair of scissors, cut the noodles into roughly 7.5cm/3in lengths and transfer to a bowl.

3 Fill a wok one-third full of boiling water and place over high heat. Add the sprouted beans and pulses and blanch for 1 minute. Drain, transfer to the noodle bowl and add the spring onions, tofu, tomato, cucumber and herbs.

4 Combine the rice vinegar, sugar, sesame oil and chilli oil and toss into the noodle mixture. Transfer to a serving dish and chill for 30 minutes before serving.

COOK'S TIP
If you leave the salad to stand for half an hour to an hour, the flavours will improve as they develop and fuse together.

Energy 113Kcal/475kJ; Protein 6.8g; Carbohydrate 14.1g, of which sugars 6.6g; Fat 3.5g, of which saturates 0.5g; Cholesterol 0mg; Calcium 184mg; Fibre 2.4g; Sodium 11mg.

FRAGRANT MUSHROOMS IN LETTUCE LEAVES

THIS QUICK AND EASY VEGETABLE DISH IS SERVED ON LETTUCE LEAF "SAUCERS" SO CAN BE EATEN WITH THE FINGERS — A GREAT TREAT FOR CHILDREN AND FUN FOR ADULTS TOO.

SERVES TWO

INGREDIENTS

30ml/2 tbsp vegetable oil
2 garlic cloves, finely chopped
2 baby cos or romaine lettuces,
  or 2 Little Gem (Bibb) lettuces
1 lemon grass stalk, finely chopped
2 kaffir lime leaves, rolled in
  cylinders and thinly sliced
200g/7oz/3 cups oyster or chestnut
  mushrooms, sliced
1 small fresh red chilli, seeded
  and finely chopped
juice of ½ lemon
30ml/2 tbsp light soy sauce
5ml/1 tsp palm sugar or light
  muscovado (brown) sugar
small bunch fresh mint leaves

1 Heat the oil in a wok or frying pan. Add the garlic and cook over a medium heat, stirring occasionally, until golden. Do not let it burn or it will taste bitter.

2 Meanwhile, separate the individual lettuce leaves. Wash and dry them, then set them aside in a bowl.

3 Increase the heat under the wok or pan and add the lemon grass, lime leaves and sliced mushrooms. Stir-fry for about 2 minutes.

4 Add the chilli, lemon juice, soy sauce and sugar to the wok or pan. Toss the mixture over the heat to combine the ingredients together, then stir-fry for a further 2 minutes.

5 Arrange the lettuce on a plate. Spoon a small amount of mushroom mixture on to each leaf and top with a mint leaf.

Energy 154Kcal/641kJ; Protein 3.9g; Carbohydrate 7.1g, of which sugars 6.8g; Fat 12.5g, of which saturates 1.6g; Cholesterol 0mg; Calcium 66mg; Fibre 2.9g; Sodium 1079mg.

CABBAGE SALAD

THIS IS A SIMPLE AND DELICIOUS WAY OF SERVING A SOMEWHAT MUNDANE VEGETABLE. THE WOK COMES IN HANDY FOR STIR-FRYING THE AROMATIC VEGETABLES THAT FLAVOUR THE CABBAGE.

SERVES FOUR TO SIX

INGREDIENTS
   30ml/2 tbsp vegetable oil
   2 large fresh red chillies, seeded and
     cut into thin strips
   6 garlic cloves, thinly sliced
   6 shallots, thinly sliced
   1 small cabbage, shredded
   30ml/2 tbsp coarsely chopped
     roasted peanuts, to garnish
For the dressing
   30ml/2 tbsp Thai fish sauce
   grated rind of 1 lime
   30ml/2 tbsp fresh lime juice
   120ml/4fl oz/½ cup coconut milk

VARIATION
Other vegetables, such as cauliflower, broccoli and Chinese leaves (Chinese cabbage), can be cooked in this way.

1 Make the dressing by mixing the fish sauce, lime rind and juice and coconut milk in a bowl. Whisk until thoroughly combined, then set aside.

2 Heat the oil in a wok. Stir-fry the chillies, garlic and shallots over a medium heat for 3–4 minutes, until the shallots are brown and crisp. Remove with a slotted spoon and set aside.

3 Bring a large pan of lightly salted water to the boil. Add the cabbage and blanch for 2–3 minutes. Tip it into a colander, drain well and put into a bowl.

4 Whisk the dressing again, add it to the warm cabbage and toss to mix. Transfer the salad to a serving dish. Sprinkle with the fried shallot mixture and the peanuts. Serve immediately.

Energy 96Kcal/400kJ; Protein 2.7g; Carbohydrate 7.7g, of which sugars 6.6g; Fat 6.2g, of which saturates 0.9g; Cholesterol 0mg; Calcium 50mg; Fibre 2.2g; Sodium 147mg.

LIGHT AND CRISPY SEVEN-SPICE AUBERGINES

THAI SEVEN SPICE POWDER IS A COMMERCIAL BLEND OF SPICES, INCLUDING CORIANDER, CUMIN, CINNAMON, STAR ANISE, CHILLI, CLOVES AND LEMON PEEL. IT GIVES THESE AUBERGINES A LOVELY WARM FLAVOUR THAT GOES VERY WELL WITH THE LIGHT, CURRY BATTER.

SERVES FOUR

INGREDIENTS
2 egg whites
90ml/6 tbsp cornflour (cornstarch)
5ml/1 tsp salt
15ml/1 tbsp Thai or Chinese seven-
   spice powder
15ml/1 tbsp mild chilli powder
500g/1¼lb aubergines (eggplant),
   thinly sliced
sunflower oil, for deep-frying
fresh mint leaves, to garnish
steamed rice or noodles and hot
   chilli sauce, to serve

1 Whisk the egg whites in a large bowl until light and foamy, but not dry.

2 Combine the cornflour, salt, seven-spice powder and chilli powder and spread evenly on to a large plate.

3 Fill a wok one-third full of oil and heat to 180°C/350°F (or until a cube of bread, dropped into the oil, browns in 40 seconds).

4 Dip the aubergine slices in the egg white and then into the spiced flour mixture to coat. Deep-fry in batches for 3–4 minutes, or until crisp and golden. Drain on kitchen paper and keep warm.

5 Serve the aubergine garnished with mint leaves and with hot chilli sauce on the side for dipping.

Energy 203Kcal/850kJ; Protein 2.7g; Carbohydrate 23.5g, of which sugars 2.5g; Fat 11.7g, of which saturates 1.4g; Cholesterol 0mg; Calcium 17mg; Fibre 2.5g; Sodium 45mg.

ASIAN-STYLE COURGETTE FRITTERS

THIS IS A TWIST ON JAPANESE TEMPURA, USING INDIAN SPICES AND GRAM FLOUR IN THE BATTER.
ALSO KNOWN AS BESAN, GRAM FLOUR IS MORE COMMONLY USED IN INDIAN COOKING AND GIVES A
WONDERFULLY CRISP TEXTURE, WHILE THE COURGETTE BATON INSIDE BECOMES MELTINGLY TENDER.

SERVES FOUR

INGREDIENTS

  90g/3½oz/¾ cup gram flour
  5ml/1 tsp baking powder
  2.5ml/½ tsp ground turmeric
  10ml/2 tsp ground coriander
  5ml/1 tsp ground cumin
  5ml/1 tsp chilli powder
  250ml/8fl oz/1 cup beer
  600g/1lb 6oz courgettes (zucchini),
    cut into batons
  sunflower oil, for deep-frying
  salt
  steamed basmati rice, natural (plain)
    yogurt and pickles, to serve

1 Sift the gram flour, baking powder, turmeric, coriander, cumin and chilli powder into a large bowl. Stir lightly to mix through.

2 Season the mixture with salt and then gradually add the beer, mixing gently as you pour it in, to make a thick batter – be careful not to overmix.

3 Fill a large wok, one-third full with sunflower oil and heat to 180°C/350°F or until a cube of bread, dropped into the oil, browns in 45 seconds.

4 Working in batches, dip the courgette batons in the spiced batter and then deep-fry for 1–2 minutes, or until crisp and golden. Lift out of the wok using a slotted spoon. Drain on kitchen paper and keep warm. Serve the courgettes immediately with steamed basmati rice, yogurt and pickles.

Energy 241Kcal/999kJ; Protein 7.3g; Carbohydrate 15.3g, of which sugars 4.6g; Fat 15.6g, of which saturates 1.9g; Cholesterol 0mg; Calcium 83mg; Fibre 3.8g; Sodium 15mg.

FRIED VEGETABLES WITH CHILLI SAUCE

A WOK MAKES THE IDEAL PAN FOR FRYING SLICES OF AUBERGINE, BUTTERNUT SQUASH AND COURGETTE BECAUSE THEY BECOME BEAUTIFULLY TENDER AND SUCCULENT. THE BEATEN EGG IN THIS RECIPE GIVES A SATISFYINGLY SUBSTANTIAL BATTER.

SERVES FOUR

INGREDIENTS
    3 large (US extra large) eggs
    1 aubergine (eggplant), halved
        lengthways and cut into long,
        thin slices
    ½ small butternut squash,
        peeled, seeded and cut into
        long, thin slices
    2 courgettes (zucchini),
        trimmed and cut into long,
        thin slices
    105ml/7 tbsp vegetable or
        sunflower oil
    salt and ground black pepper
    sweet chilli sauce, to serve

1 Beat the eggs in a large bowl. Season the egg mixture with salt and pepper. Add the slices of aubergine, butternut squash and courgette. Toss the vegetables slices until they are coated all over in the egg.

2 Have a warmed dish ready lined with kitchen paper. Heat the oil in a wok. When it is hot, add the vegetables, one strip at a time, making sure that each strip has plenty of egg clinging to it.

3 Do not cook more than eight strips of vegetable at a time or the oil will cool down too much.

4 As each strip turns golden and is cooked, lift it out, using a wire basket or slotted spoon, and transfer to the plate. Keep hot while cooking the remaining vegetables. Serve with the sweet chilli sauce as a dip.

Energy 281Kcal/1162kJ; Protein 8.8g; Carbohydrate 5.7g, of which sugars 4.8g; Fat 25.1g, of which saturates 3.9g; Cholesterol 171mg; Calcium 92mg; Fibre 3.2g; Sodium 65mg.

INDIAN-STYLE SPICED RED LENTIL DHAL

A KARAHI IS THE INDIAN EQUIVALENT OF THE WOK. HERE IT IS USED TO GREAT EFFECT TO MAKE WHAT CAN ONLY BE DESCRIBED AS CLASSIC COMFORT FOOD. THERE'S NOTHING LIKE A BOWL OF DHAL SPICED WITH MUSTARD SEEDS, CUMIN AND CORIANDER TO CLEAR AWAY THE BLUES.

SERVES FOUR

INGREDIENTS

30ml/2 tbsp sunflower oil
1 fresh green chilli, halved
2 red onions, halved
 and thinly sliced
10ml/2 tsp crushed garlic
10ml/2 tsp finely grated fresh
 root ginger
10ml/2 tsp black mustard seeds
15ml/1 tbsp cumin seeds
10ml/2 tsp crushed coriander seeds
10 curry leaves
250g/9oz/generous 1 cup red lentils
2.5ml/½ tsp ground turmeric
2 plum tomatoes
salt
coriander (cilantro) leaves and crispy
 fried onion, to garnish (optional)
yogurt, poppadums and griddled
 flatbread or naans, to serve

1 Heat a karahi or wok and add the sunflower oil. When it is hot add the green chilli and onions, stir to combine, lower the heat and cook gently for 10–12 minutes, until softened.

2 Increase the heat slightly and add the garlic, ginger, mustard seeds, cumin seeds, coriander seeds and curry leaves and stir-fry for 2–3 minutes.

3 Rinse the lentils in cold water, drain, then add to the wok with 700ml/1 pint 2fl oz/scant 3 cups cold water. Stir in the turmeric and season with salt. Bring to the boil.

4 Chop the tomatoes and add to the wok. Reduce the heat and cook gently for 25–30 minutes, stirring occasionally.

5 Check the seasoning, then garnish with coriander leaves and crispy fried onion, if liked, and serve with yogurt, poppadums and flatbread or naans.

VARIATION
If you prefer, you can use yellow split peas in place of the lentils. Like red lentils, these only need to be rinsed, not soaked, before cooking.

Energy 284Kcal/1198kJ; Protein 16.1g; Carbohydrate 42.7g, of which sugars 7.3g; Fat 6.6g, of which saturates 0.8g; Cholesterol 0mg; Calcium 54mg; Fibre 4.6g; Sodium 29mg.

THAI ASPARAGUS

IF YOU'VE NEVER HAD ASPARAGUS COOKED IN THE WOK, DO YOURSELF A FAVOUR AND TRY THIS DELICIOUS RECIPE. THE ZINGY FLAVOURS OF GALANGAL AND CHILLI, COUPLED WITH THE SWEET AND SPICY SAUCE TRANSFORM WHAT CAN BE A SUBTLE TASTE INTO SOMETHING OF A SENSATION.

SERVES FOUR

INGREDIENTS

    350g/12oz asparagus stalks
    30ml/2 tbsp vegetable oil
    1 garlic clove, crushed
    15ml/1 tbsp sesame seeds, toasted
    2.5cm/1in piece fresh galangal,
      finely shredded
    1 fresh red chilli, seeded and
      finely chopped
    15ml/1 tbsp Thai fish sauce
    15ml/1 tbsp light soy sauce
    45ml/3 tbsp water
    5ml/1 tsp palm sugar or light
      muscovado (brown) sugar

VARIATIONS
Try this with broccoli or pak choi (bok choy). The sauce also works very well with green beans.

1 Snap the asparagus stalks. They will break naturally at the junction between the woody base and the more tender portion of the stalk. Discard the woody parts of the stems.

2 Heat a wok and add the oil. Stir-fry the garlic, sesame seeds and galangal for 3–4 seconds, until the garlic is just beginning to turn golden.

3 Add the asparagus stalks and chilli, toss to mix, then add the fish sauce, soy sauce, water and sugar.

4 Using two spoons, toss over the heat for a further 2 minutes, or until the asparagus just begins to soften and the liquid is reduced by half. Serve the asparagus immediately, with the sauce spooned over it.

Energy 99Kcal/410kJ; Protein 3.4g; Carbohydrate 3.1g, of which sugars 3g; Fat 8.2g, of which saturates 1.1g; Cholesterol 0mg; Calcium 50mg; Fibre 1.8g; Sodium 269mg.

BABY ASPARAGUS WITH CRISPY NOODLES

TENDER ASPARAGUS SPEARS TOSSED WITH SESAME SEEDS AND SERVED ON A BED OF CRISPY, DEEP-FRIED NOODLES MAKES A LOVELY DISH FOR CASUAL ENTERTAINING. THE LIGHTLY COOKED ASPARAGUS RETAINS ALL ITS FRESH FLAVOUR AND BITE AND CONTRASTS WONDERFULLY WITH THE NOODLES.

SERVES FOUR

INGREDIENTS
    15ml/1 tbsp sunflower oil
    350g/12oz thin asparagus spears
    5ml/1 tsp salt
    5ml/1 tsp ground black pepper
    5ml/1 tsp golden caster
      (superfine) sugar
    30ml/2 tbsp Chinese cooking wine
    45ml/3 tbsp light soy sauce
    60ml/4 tbsp oyster sauce
    10ml/2 tsp sesame oil
    60ml/4 tbsp toasted
      sesame seeds
For the noodles
    50g/2oz dried bean thread noodles
      or thin rice noodles
    sunflower oil, for deep-frying

3 Heat a clean wok over a high heat and add the sunflower oil. Add the asparagus and stir-fry for 3 minutes.

4 Add the salt, pepper, sugar, wine and both sauces to the wok and stir-fry for 2–3 minutes. Add the sesame oil, toss to combine and remove from the heat.

5 To serve, divide the crispy noodles between 4 warmed plates or bowls and top with the asparagus and juices. Scatter over the toasted sesame seeds and serve immediately.

VARIATION
Try this with baby leeks. Toss them in the sauce until just tender.

1 First make the crispy noodles. Fill a wok one-third full of oil and heat to 180°C/350°F or until a cube of bread, dropped into the oil, browns in 45 seconds. Add a small bunch of noodles to the oil; they will crisp and puff up in seconds.

2 Using a slotted spoon, remove from the wok and drain on kitchen paper. Set aside. Cook the remaining noodles in the same way.

COOK'S TIP
Bean thread noodles, also sold as cellophane or transparent noodles, an be difficult to track down outside big cities, so buy a few packets when you get the chance, as they make excellent store-cupboard standbys.

Energy 210Kcal/872kJ; Protein 3.8g; Carbohydrate 18.2g, of which sugars 7.7g; Fat 13g, of which saturates 1.6g; Cholesterol 0mg; Calcium 30mg; Fibre 1.6g; Sodium 1540mg.

HERB AND CHILLI AUBERGINES

PLUMP AND JUICY AUBERGINES ARE DELICIOUS STEAMED IN THE WOK UNTIL TENDER AND THEN TOSSED IN A FRAGRANT MINTY DRESSING WITH CORIANDER AND CRUNCHY PEANUTS AND WATER CHESTNUTS. THE COMBINATION OF TEXTURES AND FLAVOURS IS ABSOLUTELY SENSATIONAL.

SERVES FOUR

INGREDIENTS

500g/1¼lb firm, baby aubergines
  (eggplants)
30ml/2 tbsp sunflower oil
6 garlic cloves, very finely chopped
15ml/1 tbsp very finely chopped
  fresh root ginger
8 spring onions (scallions), cut
  diagonally into 2.5cm/1in lengths
2 fresh red chillies, seeded and
  thinly sliced
45ml/3 tbsp light soy sauce
15ml/1 tbsp Chinese rice wine
15ml/1 tbsp golden caster
  (superfine) sugar or palm sugar
a handful of fresh mint leaves
30–45ml/2–3 tbsp roughly chopped
  fresh coriander (cilantro) leaves
115g/4oz water chestnuts
50g/2oz/½ cup roasted peanuts,
  roughly chopped
steamed egg noodles or rice, to serve

1 Cut the aubergines in half lengthways and place on a heatproof plate.

2 Place a steamer rack in a wok and add 5cm/2in of water. Bring the water to the boil and lower the plate on to the rack and reduce the heat to low.

3 Cover and steam the aubergines for 25–30 minutes, until they are cooked through. (Check the water level regularly, adding more if necessary.) Set the aubergines aside to cool.

4 Place the oil in a clean, dry wok and place over a medium heat. When hot, add the garlic, ginger, spring onions and chillies and stir-fry for 2–3 minutes. Remove from the heat and stir in the soy sauce, rice wine and sugar.

5 Add the mint leaves, chopped coriander, water chestnuts and peanuts to the aubergine and toss. Pour the garlic-ginger mixture evenly over the vegetables, toss gently and serve with steamed egg noodles or rice.

Energy 177Kcal/739kJ; Protein 6.2g; Carbohydrate 12.1g, of which sugars 9g; Fat 12g, of which saturates 1.9g; Cholesterol 0mg; Calcium 46mg; Fibre 4.4g; Sodium 823mg.

STEAMED VEGETABLES WITH CHILLI DIP

AN INEXPENSIVE BAMBOO STEAMER IS A GREAT WOK ACCESSORY, MAKING IT POSSIBLE TO COOK VEGETABLES QUICKLY AND EASILY SO THAT THEY RETAIN MAXIMUM NUTRIENTS AND KEEP THEIR COLOUR. MIX IN FRESH VEGETABLES, ADD A SPICY DIP AND YOU HAVE A HEALTHY AND TASTY DISH.

SERVES FOUR

INGREDIENTS
  1 head broccoli, divided
    into florets
  130g/4½oz/1 cup green
    beans, trimmed
  130g/4½oz asparagus, trimmed
  ½ head cauliflower, divided
    into florets
  8 baby corn cobs
  130g/4½oz mangetouts (snow peas)
    or sugar snap peas
  salt
For the dip
  1 fresh green chilli, seeded
  4 garlic cloves, peeled
  4 shallots, peeled
  2 tomatoes, halved
  5 pea aubergines (eggplants)
  30ml/2 tbsp lemon juice
  30ml/2 tbsp soy sauce
  2.5ml/½ tsp salt
  5ml/1 tsp granulated sugar

COOK'S TIP
Cauliflower varieties with pale green curds have a more delicate flavour than those with white curds. Look out for baby brassicas – miniature cauliflowers and heads of broccoli – for serving whole.

1 Place the broccoli, green beans, asparagus and cauliflower in a bamboo steamer and steam over boiling water in a wok for about 4 minutes, until just tender but still with a "bite". Transfer to a bowl and add the corn cobs and mangetouts or sugar snap peas. Season to taste with a little salt. Toss to mix.

2 Make the dip. Preheat the grill (broiler). Wrap the chilli, garlic cloves, shallots, tomatoes and aubergines in a foil package. Grill (broil) for 10 minutes, until the vegetables have softened, turning the package over once or twice.

3 Unwrap the foil and tip its contents into a mortar or food processor. Add the lemon juice, soy sauce, salt and sugar. Pound with a pestle or process to a fairly liquid paste.

4 Scrape the dip into a serving bowl or four individual bowls. Serve, surrounded by the steamed and raw vegetables.

VARIATIONS
You can use a combination of other vegetables if you like. Use pak choi (bok choy) instead of the cauliflower or substitute raw baby carrots for the corn cobs and mushrooms in place of the mangetouts (snow peas).

Energy 129Kcal/541kJ; Protein 13.3g; Carbohydrate 13.3g, of which sugars 11.3g; Fat 2.8g, of which saturates 0.6g; Cholesterol 0mg; Calcium 138mg; Fibre 8.5g; Sodium 772mg.

STEAMED AUBERGINES WITH SESAME SAUCE

THIS JAPANESE RECIPE REPRESENTS A TYPICAL ZEN TEMPLE COOKING STYLE. FRESH SEASONAL VEGETABLES ARE CHOSEN AND SIMPLY COOKED WITH CARE. THEN A SAUCE MADE OF CAREFULLY BALANCED FLAVOURS IS ADDED. THIS DISH IS ALSO DELICIOUS COLD.

SERVES FOUR

INGREDIENTS
 2 large aubergines (eggplants)
 400ml/14fl oz/1⅔ cups second dashi
  stock made using water and instant
  dashi powder
 25ml/1½ tbsp caster (superfine)
  sugar
 15ml/1 tbsp shoyu
 15ml/1 tbsp sesame seeds, finely
  ground
 15ml/1 tbsp sake
 15ml/1 tbsp cornflour (cornstarch)
 salt
For the accompanying vegetables
 130g/4½oz shimeji mushrooms
 115g/4oz/¾ cup fine green beans
 100ml/3fl oz/scant ½ cup second
  dashi stock, made using water and
  instant dashi powder
 25ml/1½ tbsp caster (superfine)
  sugar
 15ml/1 tbsp sake
 1.5ml/¼ tsp salt
 dash of shoyu

1 Peel the aubergines and cut them in quarters lengthways. Prick all over with a skewer, then plunge into a bowl of salted water for 30 minutes.

2 Drain the aubergine wedges and place them side by side in a bamboo steamer basket. Place the basket on a trivet, on top of a wok containing boiling water. Cover and steam for 20 minutes. Do not let the water touch the bottom of the steamer basket.

3 Mix the dashi stock, sugar, shoyu and 1.5ml/¼ tsp salt together in a large pan. Gently transfer the aubergines to this pan, then cover and cook over a low heat for a further 15 minutes. Take a few tablespoonfuls of stock from the pan and mix with the ground sesame seeds. Add this mixture to the pan.

4 Thoroughly mix the sake with the cornflour, add to the pan with the aubergines and stock and shake the pan gently, but quickly. When the sauce becomes quite thick, remove the pan from the heat.

5 While the aubergines are cooking, prepare and cook the accompanying vegetables. Cut off the hard base part of the mushrooms and separate the large block into smaller chunks with your fingers. Trim the green beans and cut them in half.

6 Mix the stock with the sugar, sake, salt and shoyu in a shallow pan. Add the green beans and mushrooms and cook for 7 minutes until just tender. Serve the aubergines and their sauce in individual bowls with the accompanying vegetables over the top.

Energy 127Kcal/536kJ; Protein 3.3g; Carbohydrate 20.9g, of which sugars 16.8g; Fat 3.1g, of which saturates 0.5g; Cholesterol 0mg; Calcium 60mg; Fibre 4.3g; Sodium 8mg.

SPICY CHICKPEAS WITH SPINACH

THIS RICHLY FLAVOURED DISH MAKES A GREAT ACCOMPANIMENT TO A DRY CURRY, OR WITH A RICE-BASED STIR FRY. IT IS PARTICULARLY GOOD SERVED DRIZZLED WITH A LITTLE PLAIN YOGURT — THE SHARP, CREAMY FLAVOUR COMPLEMENTS THE COMPLEX SPICES PERFECTLY.

SERVES FOUR

INGREDIENTS

200g/7oz dried chickpeas
30ml/2 tbsp sunflower oil
2 onions, halved and thinly sliced
10ml/2 tsp ground coriander
10ml/2 tsp ground cumin
5ml/1 tsp hot chilli powder
2.5ml/½ tsp ground turmeric
15ml/1 tbsp medium curry powder
400g/14oz can chopped tomatoes
5ml/1 tsp caster (superfine) sugar
salt and ground black pepper
30ml/2 tbsp chopped mint leaves
115g/4oz baby leaf spinach
steamed rice or bread, to serve

1 Soak the chickpeas in cold water overnight. Drain, rinse and place in a large pan. Cover with water and bring to the boil. Reduce the heat and simmer for 45 minutes, or until just tender. Drain and set aside.

2 Heat the oil in a wok, add the onions and cook over a low heat for 15 minutes, until lightly golden. Add the ground coriander and cumin, chilli powder, turmeric and curry powder and stir-fry for 1–2 minutes.

COOK'S TIP
You can save time and effort by using canned chickpeas. Tip the contents of two 400g/14oz cans of chickpeas into a colander, rinse gently under cold water and drain before adding to the spicy tomato sauce in the wok. Reheat gently before stirring in the mint.

3 Add the tomatoes, sugar and 105ml/7 tbsp water to the wok and bring to the boil. Cover, reduce the heat and simmer gently for 15 minutes.

4 Add the chickpeas to the wok, season well and cook gently for 8–10 minutes. Stir in the chopped mint.

5 Divide the spinach leaves between shallow bowls, top with the chickpea mixture and serve with some steamed rice or bread.

Energy 267Kcal/1122kJ; Protein 13.3g; Carbohydrate 35.5g, of which sugars 10.2g; Fat 9g, of which saturates 1.1g; Cholesterol 0mg; Calcium 170mg; Fibre 8.2g; Sodium 83mg.

CARROT IN SWEET VINEGAR

FOR THIS JAPANESE SIDE DISH CARROT STRIPS ARE MARINATED IN RICE VINEGAR, SHOYU AND MIRIN. IT IS A GOOD ACCOMPANIMENT FOR RICH DISHES SUCH AS FRIED AUBERGINE WITH MISO SAUCE BELOW.

SERVES FOUR

INGREDIENTS
  2 large carrots, peeled
  5ml/1 tsp salt
  30ml/2 tbsp sesame seeds
For the sweet vinegar marinade
  75ml/5 tbsp rice vinegar
  30ml/2 tbsp shoyu (use the pale
    awakuchi soy sauce if available)
  45ml/3 tbsp mirin

COOK'S TIP
This marinade is called *san bai zu*, and is one of the essential basic sauces in Japanese cooking. Dilute the marinade with 15ml/1 tbsp second dashi stock, then add sesame seeds and a few dashes of sesame oil for a very tasty and healthy salad dressing.

1 Cut the carrots into thin matchsticks, 5cm/2in long. Put the carrots and salt into a mixing bowl, and mix well with your hands. After 25 minutes, rinse the wilted carrot in cold water, then drain.

2 In another bowl, mix together the marinade ingredients. Add the carrots, and leave to marinate for 3 hours.

3 Put a wok on a high heat, add the sesame seeds and toss constantly until the seeds start to pop. Remove from the heat and cool.

4 Chop the sesame seeds with a large, sharp knife on a large chopping board. Place the carrots in a bowl, sprinkle with the sesame seeds and serve cold.

FRIED AUBERGINE WITH MISO SAUCE

THIS WELL-FLAVOURED STIR-FRIED AUBERGINE IS COATED IN A RICH MISO SAUCE. MAKE SURE THE OIL IS SMOKING HOT WHEN ADDING THE AUBERGINE PIECES, SO THEY DO NOT ABSORB TOO MUCH OIL.

SERVES FOUR

INGREDIENTS
  2 large aubergines (eggplants)
  1–2 dried red chillies
  45ml/3 tbsp sake
  45ml/3 tbsp mirin
  45ml/3 tbsp caster (superfine) sugar
  30ml/2 tbsp shoyu
  45ml/3 tbsp red miso (use either the
    dark red aka miso or even darker
    hatcho miso)
  90ml/6 tbsp sesame oil
  salt

VARIATION
Sweet (bell) peppers could also be used for this dish instead of the aubergines (eggplants). Take 1 red, 1 yellow and 2 green peppers. Remove the seeds and chop them into 1cm/½ in strips, then follow the rest of the recipe.

1 Cut the aubergines into bitesize pieces and place in a large colander, sprinkle with some salt and leave for 30 minutes to remove the bitter juices. Squeeze the aubergine pieces by hand. Remove the seeds from the chillies and chop the chillies into thin rings.

2 Mix the sake, mirin, sugar and shoyu in a cup. In a separate bowl, mix the red miso with 45ml/3 tbsp water to make a loose paste.

3 Heat the oil in a wok and add the chilli. When you see pale smoke rising from the oil, add the aubergine, and stir-fry for about 8 minutes, or until the aubergine pieces are tender. Lower the heat to medium.

4 Add the sake mixture to the pan, and stir for 2–3 minutes. If the sauce starts to burn, lower the heat. Add the miso paste to the pan and cook, stirring, for another 2 minutes. Serve hot.

Energy 66Kcal/272kJ; Protein 1.9g; Carbohydrate 4.6g, of which sugars 4.3g; Fat 4.5g, of which saturates 0.7g; Cholesterol 0mg; Calcium 64mg; Fibre 1.8g; Sodium 1039mg.
Energy 94Kcal/397kJ; Protein 1.8g; Carbohydrate 16.8g, of which sugars 16.4g; Fat 1.4g, of which saturates 0.3g; Cholesterol 0mg; Calcium 24mg; Fibre 3g; Sodium 806mg.

PAK CHOI WITH LIME DRESSING

THE LIME DRESSING FOR THIS THAI SPECIALITY IS TRADITIONALLY MADE USING FISH SAUCE, BUT VEGETARIANS COULD USE MUSHROOM SAUCE INSTEAD. THIS IS A WOK DISH THAT PACKS A FIERY PUNCH; USE FEWER CHILLIES IF YOU PREFER, OR REMOVE THE SEEDS BEFORE STIR-FRYING.

SERVES FOUR

INGREDIENTS
30ml/2 tbsp oil
3 fresh red chillies, cut into
  thin strips
4 garlic cloves, thinly sliced
6 spring onions (scallions),
  sliced diagonally
2 pak choi (bok choy), shredded
15ml/1 tbsp crushed peanuts
For the dressing
30ml/2 tbsp fresh lime juice
15–30ml/1–2 tbsp Thai fish sauce
250ml/8fl oz/1 cup coconut milk

1 Make the dressing. Put the lime juice and fish sauce in a bowl and mix well together, then gradually whisk in the coconut milk until combined.

2 Heat the oil in a wok and stir-fry the chillies for 2–3 minutes, until crisp. Transfer to a plate using a slotted spoon. Add the garlic to the wok and stir-fry for 30–60 seconds, until golden brown. Transfer to the plate.

3 Stir-fry the white parts of the spring onions for about 2–3 minutes, then add the green parts and stir-fry for 1 minute more. Transfer to the plate.

4 Bring a large pan of lightly salted water to the boil and add the pak choi. Stir twice, then drain immediately.

5 Place the pak choi in a large bowl, add the dressing and toss to mix. Spoon into a large serving bowl and sprinkle with the crushed peanuts and the stir-fried ingredients. Serve warm or cold.

VARIATION
If you don't like particularly spicy food, substitute red (bell) pepper strips for some or all of the chillies.

Energy 93Kcal/384kJ; Protein 2.9g; Carbohydrate 6.2g, of which sugars 5.7g; Fat 6.4g, of which saturates 0.9g; Cholesterol 0mg; Calcium 157mg; Fibre 2.1g; Sodium 354mg.

HOT AND SPICY YAM

THE YAM OF THE TITLE ISN'T THE VEGETABLE THAT RESEMBLES SWEET POTATO, BUT IS RATHER A NAME GIVEN TO A SPICY SAUCE BASED ON COCONUT MILK AND MUSHROOMS. IT IS EASY TO MAKE IN THE WOK AND TASTES GOOD WITH STEAMED GREENS, BEANSPROUTS, BEANS AND BROCCOLI.

SERVES FOUR

INGREDIENTS

  90g/3½oz Chinese leaves (Chinese
    cabbage); shredded
  90g/3½oz/scant 2 cups beansprouts
  90g/3½oz/scant 1 cup green
    beans, trimmed
  90g/3½oz broccoli, preferably the
    purple sprouting variety, divided
    into florets
  15ml/1 tbsp sesame seeds, toasted
For the yam
  60ml/4 tbsp coconut cream
  5ml/1 tsp Thai red curry paste
  90g/3½oz/1¼ cups oyster
    mushrooms or field
    (portabello) mushrooms, sliced
  60ml/4 tbsp coconut milk
  5ml/1 tsp ground turmeric
  5ml/1 tsp thick tamarind juice, made
    by mixing tamarind paste with
    warm water
  juice of ½ lemon
  60ml/4 tbsp light soy sauce
  5ml/1 tsp palm sugar or light
    muscovado (brown) sugar

1 Steam the shredded Chinese leaves, beansprouts, green beans and broccoli separately or blanch them in boiling water for 1 minute per batch. Drain, place in a serving bowl and leave to cool.

2 Make the yam. Pour the coconut cream into a wok or frying pan and heat gently for 2–3 minutes, until it separates. Stir in the red curry paste. Cook over a low heat for 30 seconds.

3 Increase the heat to high and add the mushrooms to the wok or pan. Cook for a further 2–3 minutes.

4 Pour in the coconut milk and add the ground turmeric, tamarind juice, lemon juice, soy sauce and sugar to the wok or pan. Mix thoroughly.

5 Pour the yam mixture over the prepared vegetables in the serving bowl and toss well so they are all coated with the sauce. Sprinkle with the toasted sesame seeds and serve immediately.

COOK'S TIPS
• There's no need to buy coconut cream especially for this dish. Use a carton or can of coconut milk. Skim the cream off the top and cook 60ml/4 tbsp of it before adding the curry paste. Add the measured coconut milk later, as described in the recipe.
• Oyster mushrooms may have fawn, peacock-blue or yellow caps, depending on the variety.

Energy 66Kcal/277kJ; Protein 3.9g; Carbohydrate 6.6g, of which sugars 5.8g; Fat 2.9g, of which saturates 0.5g; Cholesterol 0mg; Calcium 74mg; Fibre 2.4g; Sodium 752mg.

SICHUAN-SPICED AUBERGINE

*THIS STRAIGHTFORWARD YET VERSATILE VEGETARIAN DISH CAN BE SERVED HOT, WARM OR COLD,
AS THE OCCASION DEMANDS. TOPPED WITH A SPRINKLING OF TOASTED SESAME SEEDS, IT IS EASY
TO PREPARE, COOKS QUICKLY IN THE WOK, AND TASTES ABSOLUTELY DELICIOUS.*

SERVES FOUR TO SIX

INGREDIENTS

2 aubergines (eggplants), total weight
  about 600g/1lb 6oz, cut into large
  chunks
15ml/1 tbsp salt
5ml/1 tsp chilli powder or to taste
75–90ml/5–6 tbsp sunflower oil
15ml/1 tbsp rice wine or
  medium-dry sherry
100ml/3½fl oz/scant ½ cup water
75ml/5 tbsp chilli bean sauce
  (see Cook's Tip)
salt and ground black pepper
a few toasted sesame seeds,
  to garnish

1 Place the aubergine chunks on a
plate, sprinkle them with the salt and
leave to stand for 15–20 minutes. Rinse
well, drain and dry thoroughly on
kitchen paper. Toss the aubergine
cubes in the chilli powder.

2 Heat a wok and add the oil. When the
oil is hot, add the aubergine chunks,
with the rice wine or sherry. Stir
constantly until the aubergine chunks
start to turn a little brown. Stir in the
water, cover the wok and steam for
2–3 minutes. Add the chilli bean sauce
and cook for 2 minutes. Season to
taste, then spoon on to a serving dish,
scatter with sesame seeds and serve.

COOK'S TIP

If you can't get hold of chilli bean sauce,
use 15–30ml/1–2 tbsp chilli paste mixed
with 2 crushed garlic cloves, 15ml/
1 tbsp each of dark soy sauce and rice
vinegar, and 10ml/2 tsp light soy sauce.

KAN SHAO GREEN BEANS

*A PARTICULAR STYLE OF COOKING FROM SICHUAN, KAN SHAO MEANS "DRY-COOKED" — IN OTHER WORDS
USING NO STOCK OR WATER. THE SLIM GREEN BEANS AVAILABLE ALL THE YEAR ROUND FROM SUPERMARKETS
ARE IDEAL FOR USE IN THIS QUICK AND TASTY RECIPE.*

SERVES SIX

INGREDIENTS

175ml/6fl oz/¾ cup sunflower oil
450g/1lb fresh green beans, topped,
  tailed and cut in half
5 × 1cm/2 × ½in piece fresh
  root ginger, peeled and cut
  into matchsticks
5ml/1 tsp sugar
10ml/2 tsp light soy sauce
salt and ground black pepper

VARIATION

This simple recipe works just as well
with other fresh green vegetables, such
as baby asparagus spears and okra.
Vegetables that can be piled on a serving
plate look the most dramatic. The sauce
gives them a lovely sheen.

1 Heat the oil in a wok. When the oil
is very hot and just beginning to smoke,
carefully add the beans and fry them,
stirring constantly, for 1–2 minutes until
they are just tender.

2 Lift out the green beans on to a plate
lined with kitchen paper. Using a ladle,
carefully remove all but 30ml/2 tbsp oil
from the wok.

3 Reheat the remaining oil, add the
ginger and stir-fry for a minute or two to
flavour the oil.

4 Return the green beans to the wok,
stir in the sugar, soy sauce and salt and
pepper, and toss together quickly to
ensure the beans are well coated. Pile
up the glazed beans on a serving plate
and serve at once.

Energy 108Kcal/448kJ; Protein 1.5g; Carbohydrate 3.7g, of which sugars 2.2g; Fat 9.6g, of which saturates 1.2g; Cholesterol 0mg; Calcium 13mg; Fibre 2.5g; Sodium 3mg.
Energy 170Kcal/698kJ; Protein 1.5g; Carbohydrate 3.2g, of which sugars 2.6g; Fat 16.9g, of which saturates 2.1g; Cholesterol 0mg; Calcium 28mg; Fibre 1.7g; Sodium 119mg.

SLOW-COOKED SHIITAKE WITH SHOYU

SHIITAKE COOKED SLOWLY ARE SO RICH AND FILLING, THAT SOME PEOPLE CALL THEM "VEGETARIAN STEAK". MUSHROOMS COOKED IN THIS MANNER WILL KEEP FOR SEVERAL DAYS IN THE REFRIGERATOR, AND CAN BE EATEN AS THEY ARE OR USED TO FLAVOUR OTHER DISHES.

SERVES FOUR

INGREDIENTS
20 dried shiitake mushrooms
45ml/3 tbsp vegetable oil
30ml/2 tbsp shoyu
25ml/1½ tbsp caster (superfine)
   sugar
15ml/1 tbsp toasted sesame oil

VARIATION
To make shiitake rice, cut the slow-cooked shiitake into thin strips. Mix with 600g/1lb 6oz/5¼ cups cooked rice and 15ml/1 tbsp finely chopped chives. Serve in individual rice bowls and sprinkle with toasted sesame seeds.

1 Start soaking the dried shiitake the day before. Put them in a large bowl almost full of water. Cover the shiitake with a plate or lid to stop them floating to the surface of the water. Leave to soak overnight.

2 Measure 120ml/4fl oz/½ cup liquid from the bowl. Drain the shiitake into a sieve. Remove and discard the stalks.

3 Heat the oil in a wok or a large pan. Stir-fry the shiitake over a high heat for 5 minutes, stirring continuously.

4 Reduce the heat to the lowest setting, then add the measured liquid, the shoyu and sugar. Cook until there is almost no moisture left, stirring frequently. Add the sesame oil and remove from the heat.

5 Leave to cool, then slice and arrange the shiitake on a large plate.

Energy 133Kcal/553kJ; Protein 1.2g; Carbohydrate 7.4g, of which sugars 7.2g; Fat 11.2g, of which saturates 1.4g; Cholesterol 0mg; Calcium 8mg; Fibre 0.6g; Sodium 537mg.

NEW POTATOES COOKED IN DASHI STOCK

THIS IS A SIMPLE YET SCRUMPTIOUS JAPANESE DISH, INVOLVING LITTLE MORE THAN NEW SEASON'S POTATOES AND ONION COOKED IN DASHI STOCK. AS THE STOCK EVAPORATES, THE ONION BECOMES MELTINGLY SOFT AND CARAMELIZED, MAKING A WONDERFUL SAUCE THAT COATS THE POTATOES.

SERVES FOUR

INGREDIENTS

15ml/1 tbsp toasted sesame oil
1 small onion, thinly sliced
1kg/2¼lb baby new potatoes,
   unpeeled
200ml/7fl oz/scant 1 cup second
   dashi stock, made using water and
   instant dashi powder
45ml/3 tbsp shoyu

COOK'S TIP
Japanese chefs use toasted sesame oil for its distinctive strong aroma. If the smell is too strong, use a mixture of half sesame and half vegetable oil.

1 Heat the sesame oil in a wok or large pan. Add the onion slices and stir-fry for 30 seconds, then add the potatoes. Stir constantly until all the potatoes are well coated in sesame oil.

2 Pour on the dashi stock and shoyu and reduce the heat to the lowest setting. Cover and cook for 15 minutes, turning the potatoes every 5 minutes so that they are evenly cooked.

3 Uncover the wok or pan for a further 5 minutes to reduce the liquid. If there is already very little liquid remaining, remove the wok or pan from the heat, cover and leave to stand for 5 minutes. Check that the potatoes are cooked, then remove from the heat.

4 Transfer the potatoes and onions to a deep serving bowl. Pour the sauce over the top and serve immediately.

Energy 207Kcal/876kJ; Protein 4.6g; Carbohydrate 41.8g, of which sugars 4.4g; Fat 3.5g, of which saturates 0.7g; Cholesterol 0mg; Calcium 20mg; Fibre 2.7g; Sodium 295mg.

MORNING GLORY WITH FRIED SHALLOTS

OTHER NAMES FOR MORNING GLORY INCLUDE WATER SPINACH, WATER CONVOLVULUS AND SWAMP CABBAGE. IT IS A GREEN LEAFY VEGETABLE WITH LONG JOINTED STEMS AND ARROW-SHAPED LEAVES. THE STEMS REMAIN CRUNCHY WHILE THE LEAVES WILT LIKE SPINACH WHEN COOKED.

SERVES FOUR

INGREDIENTS
   2 bunches morning glory, total weight
     about 250g/9oz, trimmed and
     coarsely chopped into 2.5cm/
     1in lengths
   30ml/2 tbsp vegetable oil
   4 shallots, thinly sliced
   6 large garlic cloves, thinly sliced
   sea salt
   1.5ml/¼ tsp dried chilli flakes

VARIATIONS
Use spinach instead of morning glory, or substitute young spring greens (collards), sprouting broccoli or Swiss chard.

1 Place the morning glory in a steamer and steam over a pan of boiling water for 30 seconds, until just wilted. If necessary, cook it in batches. Place the leaves in a bowl or spread them out on a large serving plate.

2 Heat the oil in a wok and stir-fry the shallots and garlic over a medium to high heat until golden. Spoon the mixture over the morning glory, sprinkle with a little sea salt and the chilli flakes and serve immediately.

Energy 77Kcal/316kJ; Protein 2.4g; Carbohydrate 3.2g, of which sugars 1.9g; Fat 6.1g, of which saturates 0.7g; Cholesterol 0mg; Calcium 111mg; Fibre 1.8g; Sodium 88mg.

STIR-FRIED PINEAPPLE WITH GINGER

THIS DISH MAKES AN INTERESTING ACCOMPANIMENT TO GRILLED MEAT OR STRONGLY FLAVOURED FISH SUCH AS TUNA OR SWORDFISH. IF THE IDEA SEEMS STRANGE, THINK OF IT AS RESEMBLING A FRESH MANGO CHUTNEY, BUT WITH PINEAPPLE AS THE PRINCIPAL INGREDIENT.

SERVES FOUR

INGREDIENTS
- 1 pineapple
- 15ml/1 tbsp vegetable oil
- 2 garlic cloves, finely chopped
- 2 shallots, finely chopped
- 5cm/2in piece fresh root ginger, peeled and finely shredded
- 30ml/2 tbsp light soy sauce
- juice of ½ lime
- 1 large fresh red chilli, seeded and finely shredded

VARIATION
This also tastes excellent if peaches or nectarines are substituted for the diced pineapple. Use three or four, depending on their size.

1 Trim and peel the pineapple. Cut out the core and dice the flesh.

2 Heat the oil in a wok or frying pan. Stir-fry the garlic and shallots over a medium heat for 2–3 minutes, until golden. Do not let the garlic burn or the dish will taste bitter.

3 Add the pineapple. Stir-fry for about 2 minutes, or until the pineapple cubes start to turn golden on the edges.

4 Add the ginger, soy sauce, lime juice and shredded chilli. Toss together until well mixed. Cook over a low heat for a further 2 minutes, then serve.

Energy 115Kcal/490kJ; Protein 1.2g; Carbohydrate 22g, of which sugars 21.6g; Fat 3.2g, of which saturates 0.3g; Cholesterol 0mg; Calcium 41mg; Fibre 2.6g; Sodium 539mg.

SWEET DISHES AND DESSERTS

It may surprise you to discover just how many sweet dishes

can be cooked in the wok, from steamed custards to sweet rice

vermicelli. It is a practical pan for deep-fried treats such as

fritters and crispy wontons, since less oil is needed than for

conventional deep-frying, yet the inverted bowl shape gives

you a good surface area. The wok can also be used for

poaching fruit, such as Vanilla, Honey and Saffron Pears, or

cooking desserts such as Caramelized Pineapple with Lemon

Grass. If you use a wok for poaching fruit, make sure it

has a non-stick surface, or the acidity may react with

the metal and cause discoloration.

STEAMED CUSTARD IN NECTARINES

STEAMING NECTARINES OR PEACHES IN THE WOK BRINGS OUT THEIR NATURAL COLOUR AND SWEETNESS, SO THIS IS A GOOD WAY OF MAKING THE MOST OF FRUIT THAT ISN'T QUITE AS RIPE AS IT COULD BE, OR WHICH NEEDS A FLAVOUR BOOST.

SERVES FOUR TO SIX

INGREDIENTS
  6 nectarines
  1 large (US extra large) egg
  45ml/3 tbsp palm sugar or light
    muscovado (brown) sugar
  30ml/2 tbsp coconut milk

COOK'S TIP
Palm sugar, also known as jaggery, is made from the sap of certain Asian palm trees, such as coconut and palmyrah. It is available from Asian food stores. If you buy it as a cake or large lump, you need to grate it before use. Muscovado sugar makes a good substitute as it has a similar, toffee-like flavour.

1 Cut the nectarines in half. Using a teaspoon, scoop out the stones (pits) and a little of the surrounding flesh.

2 Lightly beat the egg, then add the sugar and the coconut milk. Beat until the sugar has dissolved.

3 Transfer the nectarines to steamer tiers and carefully fill the cavities three-quarters full with the custard mixture. Steam over a pan of simmering water for 5–10 minutes. Remove from the heat and leave to cool completely before transferring to plates and serving.

Energy 213Kcal/897kJ; Protein 12.6g; Carbohydrate 21.6g, of which sugars 21.6g; Fat 9.4g, of which saturates 2.6g; Cholesterol 317mg; Calcium 64mg; Fibre 1.8g; Sodium 124mg.

MANGO WONTONS WITH RASPBERRY SAUCE

*THESE CRISP, GOLDEN PARCELS FILLED WITH MELTINGLY SWEET, HOT MANGO ARE PERFECT FOR A
CASUAL SUPPER OR A SOPHISTICATED DINNER. THE SWEET RASPBERRY SAUCE LOOKS STUNNING
DRIZZLED OVER THE WONTONS AND TASTES EVEN BETTER. SERVE ANY EXTRA SAUCE IN A BOWL.*

SERVES FOUR

INGREDIENTS
  2 firm, ripe mangoes
  24 fresh wonton wrappers
    (approximately 7.5cm/3in square)
  oil, for deep-frying
  icing (confectioners') sugar, to dust
For the sauce
  400g/14oz/3½ cups raspberries
  45ml/3 tbsp icing
    (confectioners') sugar
  a squeeze of lemon juice

1 First make the sauce. Place the
raspberries and icing sugar in a food
processor and blend until smooth.

2 Press the raspberry purée through a
sieve (strainer) to remove the seeds,
then stir a squeeze of lemon juice into
the sauce. Cover and place in the
refrigerator until ready to serve.

3 Peel the mangoes, then carefully slice
the flesh away from one side of the flat
stone (pit). Repeat on the second side,
then trim off any remaining flesh from
around the stone. Cut the mango flesh
into 1cm/½in dice.

COOK'S TIP
To check that a mango is ripe, cup it
gently in your hand and give it a sniff. A
ripe mango will yield to the touch and
smell fragrant. Slightly unripe mangoes
will ripen if placed in a paper bag with a
banana for a day or two.

4 Lay 12 wonton wrappers on a clean
work surface and place 10ml/2 tsp of
the chopped mango in the centre
of each one. Brush the edges with water
and top with the remaining wonton
wrappers. Press the edges to seal.

5 Heat the oil in a wok to 180°C/350°F
or until a cube of bread, dropped into
the oil, browns in 45 seconds. Deep-fry
the wontons, 2–3 at a time, for about
2 minutes, or until crisp and golden.

6 Remove the cooked wontons from the
oil using a slotted spoon and drain on
kitchen paper. Dust with icing sugar
and serve on individual plates drizzled
with the raspberry sauce.

VARIATION
This also tastes good with apricot sauce.
Simply poach ready-to-eat dried apricots
in water or apple juice until soft, then
blitz in a blender.

Energy 314Kcal/1331kJ; Protein 5.5g; Carbohydrate 56.1g, of which sugars 27.3g; Fat 9.2g, of which saturates 1.2g; Cholesterol 0mg; Calcium 93mg; Fibre 5.6g; Sodium 6mg.

CHINESE-STYLE TOFFEE APPLES

THIS CLASSIC DESSERT WILL MAKE A GREAT END TO ANY MEAL. WEDGES OF CRISP APPLE ARE ENCASED IN A LIGHT BATTER, THEN DIPPED IN CRISPY CARAMEL TO MAKE A SWEET, STICKY DESSERT THAT IS GUARANTEED TO GET STUCK IN YOUR TEETH! YOU CAN USE BABY BANANAS IN PLACE OF THE APPLES.

SERVES FOUR

INGREDIENTS
115g/4oz/1 cup plain
  (all-purpose) flour
10ml/2 tsp baking powder
60ml/4 tbsp cornflour (cornstarch)
4 firm apples
sunflower oil, for deep-frying
200g/7oz/1 cup caster
  (superfine) sugar

1 In a large mixing bowl, combine the flour, baking powder, cornflour and 175ml/6fl oz/¾ cup water. Stir to make a smooth batter and set aside.

2 Peel and core the apples, then cut each one into 8 thick wedges.

3 Fill a wok one-third full of sunflower oil and heat to 180°C/350°F or until a cube of bread, dropped into the oil, browns in 45 seconds.

4 Working quickly, in batches, dip the apple wedges in the batter, drain off any excess and deep-fry for 2 minutes, or until golden brown. Remove with a slotted spoon and place on kitchen paper to drain.

5 Reheat the oil to 180°C/350°F and fry the wedges for a second time, again giving them about 2 minutes. Drain well on kitchen paper and set aside.

6 Very carefully, pour off all but 30ml/2 tbsp of the oil from the wok and stir in the sugar. Heat gently until the sugar melts and starts to caramelize. When the mixture is light brown, add a few pieces of apple at a time and toss to coat evenly.

7 Fill a large bowl with ice cubes and chilled water. Plunge the coated apple pieces briefly into the iced water to harden the caramel, then remove with a slotted spoon and serve immediately.

COOK'S TIP
Don't cook the apples in advance or the caramel will soften.

Energy 457Kcal/1940kJ; Protein 3.4g; Carbohydrate 97.3g, of which sugars 61.6g; Fat 8.8g, of which saturates 1.1g; Cholesterol 0mg; Calcium 73mg; Fibre 2.5g; Sodium 14mg.

SWEET AND SPICY RICE FRITTERS

THESE DELICIOUS LITTLE GOLDEN BALLS OF RICE ARE SCENTED WITH SWEET, WARM SPICES AND WILL FILL THE KITCHEN WITH WONDERFUL AROMAS WHILE YOU'RE COOKING. TO ENJOY THEM AT THEIR BEST, SERVE PIPING HOT, AS SOON AS YOU'VE DUSTED THEM WITH SUGAR.

SERVES FOUR

INGREDIENTS
    175g/6oz cooked basmati rice
    2 eggs, lightly beaten
    60ml/4 tbsp caster (superfine) sugar
    a pinch of nutmeg
    2.5ml/½ tsp ground cinnamon
    a pinch of ground cloves
    10ml/2 tsp vanilla extract
    50g/2oz/½ cup plain
      (all-purpose) flour
    10ml/2 tsp baking powder
    a pinch of salt
    25g/1oz desiccated (dry unsweetened
      shredded) coconut
    sunflower oil, for deep-frying
    icing (confectioners') sugar,
      to dust

1 Place the cooked rice, eggs, sugar, nutmeg, cinnamon, cloves and vanilla extract in a large bowl and whisk together to combine.

2 Sift in the flour, baking powder and salt and add the coconut. Mix well until thoroughly combined.

3 Fill a wok one-third full of the oil and heat to 180°C/350°F or until a cube of bread, dropped into the oil, browns in 45 seconds.

4 Very gently, drop tablespoonfuls of the mixture into the oil, one at a time, and fry for 2–3 minutes, or until golden. Carefully remove the fritters from the wok using a slotted spoon and drain well on kitchen paper.

5 Divide the fritters into four portions, or simply pile them up on a single large platter. Dust them with icing sugar and serve immediately.

Energy 316Kcal/1321kJ; Protein 6.6g; Carbohydrate 45.8g, of which sugars 16.3g; Fat 12.4g, of which saturates 4.8g; Cholesterol 95mg; Calcium 46mg; Fibre 1.3g; Sodium 38mg.

COCONUT AND MANDARIN CUSTARDS

THESE SCENTED CUSTARDS WITH A FABULOUS MELT-IN-THE-MOUTH TEXTURE ARE BEST SERVED WARM. HOWEVER, THEY ARE ALSO DELICIOUS SERVED CHILLED, MAKING THEM PERFECT FOR HASSLE-FREE ENTERTAINING. YOU CAN MAKE THE PRALINE A FEW DAYS IN ADVANCE.

SERVES FOUR

INGREDIENTS
    200ml/7fl oz/scant 1 cup
      coconut cream
    200ml/7fl oz/scant 1 cup double
      (heavy) cream
    2.5ml/½ tsp finely ground star anise
    75ml/5 tbsp golden caster
      (superfine) sugar
    15ml/1 tbsp very finely grated
      mandarin or orange rind
    4 egg yolks
For the praline
    175g/6oz/scant 1 cup caster
      (superfine) sugar
    50g/2oz/½ cup roughly chopped
      mixed nuts (cashews, almonds and
      peanuts)

1 Make the praline. Place the sugar in a
non-stick wok with 15–30ml/1–2 tbsp
water. Cook over a medium heat until
the sugar dissolves and turns light gold.

2 Remove the syrup from the heat and
pour on to a baking sheet lined with
baking parchment. Spread out using the
back of a spoon, then sprinkle the
chopped nuts evenly over the top and
leave to harden.

3 Meanwhile place the coconut cream,
double cream, star anise, sugar,
mandarin or orange rind and egg yolks
in a large bowl. Whisk to combine and
pour the mixture into 4 lightly greased
ramekins or small, heatproof bowls.

4 Place the ramekins or cups in a large
steamer, cover and place in a wok and
steam over gently simmering water
for 12–15 minutes, or until the custards
are just set.

5 Carefully lift the custards from the
steamer and leave to cool slightly
for about 10 minutes.

6 To serve, break up the praline into
rough pieces and serve on top of, or
alongside, the custards.

Energy 643Kcal/2688kJ; Protein 6.7g; Carbohydrate 71g, of which sugars 69.3g; Fat 38.9g, of which saturates 19.6g; Cholesterol 270mg; Calcium 100mg; Fibre 0.4g; Sodium 115mg.

ORANGE AND DATE BUTTERMILK PANCAKES

SERVE THESE SWEET, STICKY, GOLDEN PANCAKES FOR BREAKFAST, BRUNCH OR DESSERT. THEY'RE BURSTING WITH THE FLAVOUR OF ZESTY ORANGE AND SWEET JUICY DATES AND ARE UTTERLY MOREISH. MEDJOOL DATES HAVE AN INTENSELY SWEET FLESH AND WILL GIVE THE BEST RESULTS.

SERVES FOUR

INGREDIENTS

150g/5oz/1¼ cups self-raising
  (self-rising) flour
2.5ml/½ tsp baking powder
a pinch of salt
250ml/8fl oz/1 cup buttermilk
3 eggs
15ml/1 tbsp caster
  (superfine) sugar
200g/7oz/1¼ cup Medjool
  dates, stoned
finely grated rind and juice
  from 1 small orange
50g/2oz/¼ cup unsalted (sweet)
  butter, melted
sunflower oil, for greasing
clear honey, to drizzle
natural (plain) yogurt,
  to serve

1 Sift the flour and baking soda into a large bowl with a pinch of salt. Whisk in the buttermilk, eggs, sugar, dates, orange rind and juice and melted butter. Leave to stand for 15 minutes.

2 Brush a wok with a little oil and heat over a medium heat. When hot, pour a small ladleful of the mixture into the wok. Cook for 2–3 minutes until just set.

3 Cook the second side for 35–45 seconds. Transfer to a plate and keep warm while you cook the remaining batter in the same way. (You should make about 16 pancakes in total.)

4 To serve, divide the pancakes among four warmed plates, piling them up in a stack. Drizzle honey over each stack and top with a dollop of yogurt.

Energy 373Kcal/1569kJ; Protein 11.2g; Carbohydrate 51.5g, of which sugars 23g; Fat 15.2g, of which saturates 7.8g; Cholesterol 172mg; Calcium 166mg; Fibre 2.1g; Sodium 161mg.

VANILLA, HONEY AND SAFFRON PEARS

THESE SWEET JUICY PEARS, POACHED IN A HONEY SYRUP INFUSED WITH VANILLA, SAFFRON AND LIME, MAKE A TRULY ELEGANT DESSERT. FOR A LOW-FAT VERSION YOU CAN EAT THEM ON THEIR OWN, BUT FOR A REALLY LUXURIOUS, INDULGENT TREAT, SERVE WITH CREAM OR ICE CREAM.

SERVES FOUR

INGREDIENTS

150g/5oz/¾ cup caster
  (superfine) sugar
105ml/7 tbsp clear honey
5ml/1 tsp finely grated lime rind
a large pinch of saffron
2 vanilla pods (beans)
4 large, firm ripe dessert pears
single (light) cream or ice cream,
  to serve

COOK'S TIP

For the best results use firm varieties of dessert pears, such as comice or conference, that are well ripened.

1 Place the caster sugar and honey in a medium, non-stick wok, then add the lime rind and the saffron. Using a small, sharp knife, split the vanilla pods in half and scrape the seeds into the wok, then add the vanilla pods as well.

2 Pour 500ml/17fl oz/scant 2¼ cups water into the wok and bring the mixture to the boil. Reduce the heat to low and simmer, stirring occasionally, while you prepare the pears.

3 Peel the pears, then add to the wok and gently turn in the syrup to coat evenly. Cover the wok and simmer gently for 12–15 minutes, turning the pears halfway through cooking, until they are just tender.

4 Lift the pears from the syrup using a slotted spoon and transfer to four serving bowls. Set aside.

5 Bring the syrup back to the boil and cook gently for about 10 minutes, or until reduced and thickened. Spoon the syrup over the pears and serve either warm or chilled with single cream or ice cream.

COOK'S TIP

You can try using different flavourings in the syrup. Use 10ml/2 tsp chopped fresh root ginger and 1 or 2 star anise in place of the saffron and vanilla, or 1 cinnamon stick, 3 cloves and 105ml/7tbsp maple syrup in place of the spices and honey. If the syrup seems too sweet for your taste, sharpen it with a little lemon or lime juice.

Energy 283Kcal/1207kJ; Protein 0.8g; Carbohydrate 74.3g, of which sugars 74.3g; Fat 0.2g, of which saturates 0g; Cholesterol 0mg; Calcium 38mg; Fibre 3.3g; Sodium 10mg.

CARAMELIZED PINEAPPLE WITH LEMON GRASS

*THIS STUNNING DESSERT, GARNISHED WITH JEWEL-LIKE POMEGRANATE SEEDS, IS SUPERB FOR
ENTERTAINING. THE TANGY, ZESTY FLAVOURS OF LEMON GRASS AND MINT BRING OUT THE EXQUISITE
SWEETNESS OF THE PINEAPPLE TO CREATE A TRULY LUSCIOUS COMBINATION.*

SERVES FOUR

INGREDIENTS

30ml/2 tbsp very finely chopped
   lemon grass, and 2 lemon grass
   stalks, halved lengthways
350g/12oz/1¾ cups caster
   (superfine) sugar
10ml/2 tsp chopped fresh mint
   leaves
2 small, ripe pineapples, about
   600g/1lb 5oz each
15ml/1 tbsp sunflower oil
60ml/4 tbsp pomegranate seeds
crème fraîche, to serve

1 Place the chopped lemon grass,
250g/9oz of the sugar and the mint
leaves in a non-stick wok. Pour over
150ml/¼ pint/⅔ cup of water and bring
to the boil over medium heat.

2 Reduce the heat under the wok and
simmer the mixture for 10–15 minutes,
until thickened. Strain into a glass bowl,
reserving the halved lemon grass stalks,
then set aside.

3 Using a sharp knife, peel and core
the pineapples and cut into 1cm/½in-
thick slices, then sprinkle the slices
with the remaining sugar.

4 Brush a large non-stick wok with the
oil and place over a medium heat.
Working in batches, cook the sugared
pineapple slices for 2–3 minutes until
they are lightly caramelised, then turn
over and cook the other side for another
2–3 minutes.

5 Transfer the pineapple slices to a
flat serving dish and scatter over the
pomegranate seeds.

6 Pour the lemon grass syrup over
the fruit and garnish with the reserved
stalks. Serve hot or at room temperature
with crème fraîche.

COOK'S TIP
To remove pomegranate seeds, halve
the fruit and hold it over a bowl, cut
side down. Tap all over with a wooden
spoon and the seeds should drop out.

Energy 493Kcal/2101kJ; Protein 1.6g; Carbohydrate 121.7g, of which sugars 121.7g; Fat 3.4g, of which saturates 0.3g; Cholesterol 0mg; Calcium 101mg; Fibre 3.6g; Sodium 11mg.

CARAMELIZED PLUMS WITH COCONUT RICE

RED, JUICY PLUMS ARE QUICKLY SEARED IN A WOK WITH SUGAR TO MAKE A RICH CARAMEL COATING, THEN SERVED WITH STICKY COCONUT-FLAVOURED RICE FOR A SATISFYING DESSERT. THE GLUTINOUS RICE IS AVAILABLE FROM ASIAN STORES, BUT REMEMBER THAT YOU HAVE TO SOAK IT OVERNIGHT.

3 Cover the rice and steam over simmering water for 25–30 minutes, until the rice is tender. (Check the water level and add more if necessary.)

4 Transfer the steamed rice to a wide bowl and set aside for a moment.

5 Combine the coconut cream with the sugar and salt and pour into a clean wok. Heat gently and bring to the boil, then remove from the heat and pour over the rice. Stir to mix well.

6 Using a sharp knife, cut the plums in half and remove their stones (pits). Sprinkle the sugar over the cut sides.

7 Heat a non-stick wok over a medium-high flame. Working in batches, place the plums in the wok, cut side down, and cook for 1–2 minutes, or until the sugar caramelizes. You may need to wipe out the wok with kitchen paper in between batches.

8 Mould the rice into rounds and place on warmed plates, then spoon over the caramelized plums. Alternatively, simply spoon the rice into four warmed bowls and top with the plums. Drizzle any syrup remaining in the wok over and around the fruit.

VARIATION
Try this with greengages. They look very pretty when piled on the discs of sticky rice. Red plums taste good if you add just a touch of balsamic vinegar to the syrup on serving.

SERVES FOUR

INGREDIENTS
 6 or 8 firm, ripe plums
 90g/3½oz/½ cup caster
 (superfine) sugar
For the rice
 115g/4oz sticky glutinous rice
 150ml/¼ pint/⅔ cup coconut cream
 45ml/3 tbsp caster (superfine) sugar
 a pinch of salt

1 First prepare the rice. Rinse it in several changes of water, then leave to soak overnight in a bowl of cold water.

2 Line a large bamboo steamer that will fit in your wok with muslin (cheesecloth). Drain the rice and transfer it to the lined steamer.

Energy 298Kcal/1265kJ; Protein 3.6g; Carbohydrate 71.7g, of which sugars 50.2g; Fat 0.7g, of which saturates 0.1g; Cholesterol 0mg; Calcium 53mg; Fibre 2.4g; Sodium 47mg.

SWEET RICE VERMICELLI

THE COMBINATION OF SWEETENED RICE VERMICELLI, DRIED FRUIT, NUTS AND SPICES MAY SOUND A LITTLE UNUSUAL, BUT IT MAKES A DELICIOUSLY STICKY, MOIST, AROMATIC DESSERT THAT TASTES ABSOLUTELY DIVINE DRIZZLED WITH CREAM OR SERVED WITH BIG SCOOPS OF ICE CREAM.

SERVES FOUR

INGREDIENTS

60g/2½oz/5 tbsp unsalted
  (sweet) butter
60ml/4 tbsp vegetable oil
185g/6½oz thin rice vermicelli,
  broken into 3cm/1¼in lengths
1.5ml/¼ tsp ground allspice
30ml/2 tbsp roasted cashew nuts
15ml/1 tbsp chopped almonds
30ml/2 tbsp sultanas (golden raisins)
50g/2oz/⅓ cup ready-to-eat dried
  apricots, roughly chopped
90g/3½oz/½ cup caster
  (superfine) sugar
175ml/6fl oz/¾ cup warm water
15ml/1 tbsp rose water
pistachio nuts, to garnish
single (light) cream or ice cream,
  to serve (optional)

1 Put the butter and oil in a wok and place over a low heat. When the butter has melted, add the rice vermicelli and stir-fry for 3–4 minutes.

2 Add the allspice, cashew nuts, almonds, sultanas and apricots to the wok and stir-fry for 1–2 minutes.

3 Sprinkle the sugar over the vermicelli mixture, stir to combine, then add the warm water. Cover and bring to the boil.

4 Reduce the heat and simmer very gently for 8–10 minutes until all the liquid has been absorbed and the vermicelli is tender.

5 Stir the rose water into the vermicelli mixture until well mixed, then ladle into individual warmed bowls, scatter over the pistachio nuts and serve with cream or ice cream, if you like.

Energy 589Kcal/2455kJ; Protein 8.6g; Carbohydrate 71.1g, of which sugars 29.4g; Fat 31.1g, of which saturates 10.3g; Cholesterol 32mg; Calcium 64mg; Fibre 0.7g; Sodium 124mg.

LEMON AND GINGER STEAMED PUDDINGS

*THESE DECADENTLY MOIST LITTLE DESSERTS FLAVOURED WITH
LEMON AND GINGER AND SERVED WITH A LUSCIOUS CARDAMOM-
SPICED SYRUP WILL DEFINITELY BECOME A FIRM FAMILY FAVOURITE.*

SERVES FOUR

INGREDIENTS
  150g/5oz/10 tbsp butter
  150g/5oz/¾ cup golden caster
    (superfine) sugar
  10ml/2 tsp ground ginger
  2 eggs
  150g/5oz/1¼ cups self-raising
    (self-rising) flour
  a pinch of salt
  115g/4oz/1 cup finely chopped
    pistachio nuts
  shredded lemon rind, pistachio nuts
    and chopped preserved stem ginger,
    to garnish
For the syrup
  150g/5oz/¾ cup golden caster
    (superfine) sugar
  1.5ml/¼ tsp crushed cardamom
    seeds
  5ml/1 tsp ground ginger
  10ml/2 tsp finely grated lemon rind
    and juice of 2 lemons
  5ml/1 tsp arrowroot powder

1 Make the syrup. Place the sugar, cardamom seeds and ginger in a non-stick wok and pour in 150ml/¼ pint/²⁄₃ cup water. Heat gently until the sugar has dissolved completely, then add the lemon rind and juice. Bring to the boil and cook for 3–4 minutes.

2 Mix the arrowroot with 30ml/2 tbsp cold water and whisk into the syrup. Simmer gently for 2 minutes, or until the syrup has thickened slightly. Transfer to a bowl and set aside.

3 Grease 4 x 200ml/7fl oz/scant 1 cup heatproof bowls and set aside.

4 Whisk together the butter and sugar until pale and fluffy. Add the ginger and beat in the eggs, one at a time. Sift in the flour and salt, add the chopped nuts, and mix thoroughly to combine.

5 Spoon 20ml/4 tsp of the syrup into the base of each greased bowl (reserving the remaining syrup) and swirl to coat the sides. Spoon in the pudding mixture and level the tops. Cover tightly with greaseproof (waxed) paper or foil and secure with string.

6 Place the puddings in a bamboo steamer. Pour about 5cm/2in boiling water into a wok and place the steamer over it. Cover and steam for 1 hour and 15 minutes (replenishing the water when necessary), until the puddings have risen and are firm to the touch.

7 Reheat the remaining syrup, then carefully unmould the puddings on to individual plates and spoon over the syrup. Decorate with the lemon rind, nuts and stem ginger and serve.

Energy 868Kcal/3630kJ; Protein 12.4g; Carbohydrate 98.4g, of which sugars 69.1g; Fat 50g, of which saturates 22.5g; Cholesterol 175mg; Calcium 139mg; Fibre 2.9g; Sodium 420mg.

CALAS

These sweet rice fritters are an American/Creole speciality, sold by "Calas" women on the streets of the French Quarter of New Orleans to residents and office workers, for whom they make a popular and tasty breakfast.

MAKES OVER 40

INGREDIENTS
115g/4oz/generous ½ cup short grain
pudding rice
900ml/1½ pints/3¾ cups mixed
milk and water
30ml/2 tbsp caster (superfine) sugar
50g/2oz/½ cup plain (all purpose)
flour
7.5ml/1½ tsp baking powder
5ml/1 tsp grated lemon rind
2.5ml/½ tsp ground cinnamon
1.5ml/¼ tsp ground ginger
generous pinch of grated nutmeg
2 eggs
sunflower oil, for deep frying
salt
icing sugar, for dusting
cherry or strawberry jam and thick
cream, to serve

1 Put the rice in a saucepan and pour in the milk and water. Add a pinch of salt and bring to the boil. Stir, then cover and simmer over a very gentle heat for 15–20 minutes until the rice is tender.

2 Switch off the heat under the pan, then add the sugar. Stir well, cover and leave until completely cool, by which time the rice should have absorbed all the liquid and become very soft.

VARIATION
For a slightly spicy variation mix the icing sugar with some cinnamon and grated nutmeg before dusting.

3 Put the rice in a food processor or blender and add the flour, baking powder, lemon rind, spices and eggs. Process for about 20–30 seconds so that the mixture is like a thick batter.

4 Heat the oil in a wok to 160°C/325°F. Scoop up a generous teaspoon of batter and, using a second spoon, push into the hot oil. Add four or five more and fry for 3–4 minutes, turning them occasionally, until the calas are golden brown. Drain on kitchen paper and keep warm while cooking in batches.

5 Dust the calas generously with icing sugar and serve warm with fruit jam and thick cream.

Energy 50Kcal/206kJ; Protein 0.9g; Carbohydrate 3.5g, of which sugars 1.3g; Fat 3.6g, of which saturates 0.6g; Cholesterol 10mg; Calcium 16mg; Fibre 0g; Sodium 8mg.

RICH SPICED CARROT AND RAISIN HALWA

THIS IS ANOTHER UNUSUAL DESSERT THAT TASTES ABSOLUTELY DELICIOUS. HALWA IS A CLASSIC INDIAN SWEET, AND THERE ARE MANY VARIATIONS. HERE GRATED CARROTS ARE COOKED IN MILK WITH GHEE, SUGAR, SPICES AND RAISINS UNTIL MELTINGLY TENDER AND SWEET.

SERVES FOUR

INGREDIENTS
300g/11oz carrots
90g/3½oz ghee
250ml/8fl oz/1 cup milk
150g/5oz/¾ cup golden caster (superfine) sugar
5–6 lightly crushed cardamom pods
1 clove
1 cinnamon stick
50g/2oz/scant ½ cup raisins

COOK'S TIP
Ghee is clarified butter and is widely used in Indian cooking. It is an essential ingredient in halwa and is available in cans from Asian stores.

1 Peel and grate the carrots Place a non-stick wok over a low heat and add half the ghee. When the ghee has melted, add the grated carrot and stir-fry for 6–8 minutes, by which time the carrot will have softened and taken on more colour.

2 Pour the milk into the wok and bring to the boil, reduce the heat to low and simmer gently for 10–12 minutes.

3 Stir the remaining ghee into the carrot mixture, then stir in the sugar, crushed cardamom pods, clove, cinnamon stick and raisins.

4 Gently simmer the carrot mixture for 6–7 minutes, stirring occasionally, until thickened and glossy. Serve immediately in small serving bowls.

Energy 439Kcal/1838kJ; Protein 3g; Carbohydrate 56.7g, of which sugars 56.3g; Fat 23.8g, of which saturates 15.6g; Cholesterol 67mg; Calcium 120mg; Fibre 2.1g; Sodium 56mg.

INDEX

NOTES

NOTES

NOTES

NOTES

NOTES

NOTES